Public and
Private Education
in America

Recent Titles in Contemporary Debates

The Affordable Care Act: Examining the Facts
Purva H. Rawal

Climate Change: Examining the Facts
Daniel Bedford and John Cook

Immigration: Examining the Facts
Cari Lee Skogberg Eastman

Marijuana: Examining the Facts
Karen T. Van Gundy and Michael S. Staunton

Muslims in America: Examining the Facts
Craig Considine

Prisons and Punishment in America: Examining the Facts
Michael O'Hear

American Journalism and "Fake News": Examining the Facts
Seth Ashley, Jessica Roberts, and Adam Maksl

Free Speech and Censorship: Examining the Facts
H. L. Pohlman

Poverty and Welfare in America: Examining the Facts
David Wagner

Voting in America: Examining the Facts
H. L. Pohlman

Race Relations in America: Examining the Facts
Nikki Khanna and Noriko Matsumoto

Guns in America: Examining the Facts
Donald J. Campbell

Public and Private Education in America

Examining the Facts

Casey D. Cobb and Gene V Glass

Contemporary Debates

BLOOMSBURY ACADEMIC
NEW YORK • LONDON • OXFORD • NEW DELHI • SYDNEY

BLOOMSBURY ACADEMIC
Bloomsbury Publishing Inc
1385 Broadway, New York, NY 10018, USA
50 Bedford Square, London, WC1B 3DP, UK
29 Earlsfort Terrace, Dublin 2, Ireland

BLOOMSBURY, BLOOMSBURY ACADEMIC and the Diana logo
are trademarks of Bloomsbury Publishing Plc

First published in the United States of America by ABC-CLIO 2021
Paperback edition published by Bloomsbury Academic 2025

Copyright © Bloomsbury Publishing Inc, 2025

COVER PHOTO: (Monkey Business Images/Dreamstime.com)

All rights reserved. No part of this publication may be reproduced or transmitted in any form or by any means, electronic or mechanical, including photocopying, recording, or any information storage or retrieval system, without prior permission in writing from the publishers.

Bloomsbury Publishing Inc does not have any control over, or responsibility for, any third-party websites referred to or in this book. All internet addresses given in this book were correct at the time of going to press. The author and publisher regret any inconvenience caused if addresses have changed or sites have ceased to exist, but can accept no responsibility for any such changes.

Library of Congress Cataloging-in-Publication Data
Names: Cobb, Casey D., author. | Glass, Gene V, 1940– author.
Title: Public and private education in America : examining the facts / Casey D. Cobb and Gene V Glass.
Description: Santa Barbara, California : ABC-CLIO, 2021. | Includes bibliographical references and index.
Identifiers: LCCN 2021006686 (print) | LCCN 2021006687 (ebook) | ISBN 9781440863745 (hardback) | ISBN 9781440863752 (ebook)
Subjects: LCSH: Public schools—United States. | Private schools—United States. | Education and state—United States. | Educational change—United States. | Academic achievement—United States.
Classification: LCC LA217.2 .C62 2021 (print) | LCC LA217.2 (ebook) | DDC 379.73—dc23
LC record available at https://lccn.loc.gov/2021006686
LC ebook record available at https://lccn.loc.gov/2021006687

ISBN: HB: 978-1-4408-6374-5
PB: 979-8-2162-0168-7
ePDF: 978-1-4408-6375-2
eBook: 979-8-2161-3404-6

Series: Contemporary Debates

To find out more about our authors and books visit www.bloomsbury.com and sign up for our newsletters.

Contents

How to Use This Book		ix
Introduction		xi
1	**Private vs. Public Schools**	**1**
	Q1. Do students in private schools outperform students enrolled in public schools?	2
	Q2. Are political conservatives and corporations the biggest supporters of privatization of the American K–12 school system?	7
	Q3. Do private schools accept students with disabilities?	14
	Q4. Are public and private school teachers similar in their educational and socioeconomic backgrounds?	18
2	**School Choice: Competition, Stratification, Homeschooling, and Vouchers**	**21**
	Q5. Do market-based reforms such as school choice increase competition and improve school performance?	22
	Q6. Do school choice programs contribute to the resegregation of American schools?	32
	Q7. Does homeschooling lead to better outcomes for students than traditional public schools?	38
	Q8. Do school vouchers produce better student outcomes?	45

	Q9. Do education tax credits and education savings accounts divert money from public to private schools?	53
3	**School Choice: Charter Schools**	59
	Q10. Do charter schools have significant variations in structure, operations, and performance from school to school?	60
	Q11. Are charter schools actually public schools?	66
	Q12. Are charter schools more innovative than traditional public schools?	79
	Q13. Do charter schools perform better than traditional public schools?	85
	Q14. Are poorly performing charter schools closed down?	95
	Q15. Are most publicly funded charter schools operated by Education Management Organizations and Charter Management Organizations?	102
4	**Standards, Accountability, and Assessment**	111
	Q16. Have standards-based reforms worked to improve the academic performance of American schoolchildren?	112
	Q17. Are the Common Core State Standards a national initiative—and if so, do they amount to a national curriculum?	117
	Q18. Has time that students spend preparing for and taking standardized tests increased dramatically in U.S. public schools?	121
	Q19. Has high-stakes testing improved schools?	129
	Q20. Is it difficult for public schools to fire bad teachers?	136
	Q21. Do assessment systems exist that can accurately capture the value-added impact of teachers on their students' test scores?	144
	Q22. Is the United States lagging behind other nations in K–12 education?	152
	Q23. How are the political interests that shape education policy organized?	158
5	**Teaching and Learning**	165
	Q24. Do later school start times make a difference in children's learning?	165
	Q25. Is bilingual education effective?	171
	Q26. Does homework increase student achievement?	180

6 School Environment — 187

Q27. Are students disciplined disproportionately by race and gender? — 187

Q28. Are small schools better than large schools in providing a quality education to students? — 195

Q29. Are American schools less safe now than in the past? — 200

Q30. Are public and private schools still racially and economically segregated? — 204

Q31. Do today's full-time virtual schools offer a high-quality education for students? — 208

Q32. Do students learn more in smaller classes? — 216

Index — 221

How to Use This Book

Public and Private Education in America: Examining the Facts is part of ABC-CLIO's *Contemporary Debates* reference series. Each title in this series, which is intended for use by high school and undergraduate students as well as members of the general public, examines the veracity of controversial claims or beliefs surrounding a major political/cultural issue in the United States. The purpose of this series is to give readers a clear and unbiased understanding of current issues by informing them about falsehoods, half-truths, and misconceptions—and confirming the factual validity of other assertions—that have gained traction in America's political and cultural discourse. Ultimately, this series has been crafted to give readers the tools for a fuller understanding of controversial issues, policies, and laws that occupy center stage in American life and politics.

Each volume in this series identifies 30–40 questions swirling about the larger topic under discussion. These questions are examined in individualized entries, which are in turn arranged in broad subject chapters that cover certain aspects of the issue being examined, for example, history of concern about the issue, potential economic or social impact, or findings of latest scholarly research.

Each chapter features 4–10 individual entries. Each entry begins by stating an important and/or well-known **Question** about the issue being studied—for example, "Do students in private schools outperform students enrolled in public schools?" Or "Is the United States lagging behind other nations in K–12 education?"

The entry then provides a concise and objective one- or two-paragraph **Answer** to the featured question, followed by a more comprehensive, detailed explanation of **The Facts**. This latter portion of each entry uses quantifiable evidence-based information from respected sources to fully address each question and provide readers with the information they need to be informed citizens. Importantly, entries will also acknowledge instances in which conflicting or incomplete data exists or legal judgments are contradictory. Finally, each entry concludes with a **Further Reading** section, providing users with information on other important and/or influential resources.

The ultimate purpose of every book in the *Contemporary Debates* series is to reject "false equivalence," in which demonstrably false beliefs or statements are given the same exposure and credence as the facts; to puncture myths that diminish our understanding of important policies and positions; to provide needed context for misleading statements and claims; and to confirm the factual accuracy of other assertions. In other words, volumes in this series are being crafted to clear the air surrounding some of the most contentious and misunderstood issues of our time—not just add another layer of obfuscation and uncertainty to the debate.

Introduction

If you are reading this, the odds are pretty good that you once went to school, or are going now. Nearly everyone has a fair amount of experience with schooling. And nearly everyone feels confident that they understand quite a bit about schooling. Opinions may differ—in fact, they often do differ—but people feel that they know what makes a good teacher, or the best way to teach math, or whether children in private schools learn a whole lot more than they would if they had gone to a public school. These opinions and impressions resulting from personal experience are valuable, as well as inevitable. But different people hold conflicting opinions about schooling, and some actually believe things that are not true. Myths about education are prevalent; and, regrettably, contemporary political debates have produced some pernicious lies about the state of American education (Berliner and Glass, 2016).

This volume uses disciplined inquiry to sift through and assess the many conflicting claims about the elements of a good education, as well as the overall state of K–12 education in America today. Sometimes, opinions agree with facts. Sometimes, they do not. This work endeavors to present the most credible facts on a wide range of questions about schools. The facts presented are the result of education research, a form of disciplined inquiry. It's not a hard (physical) science and it's not perfect. But for pursuing the answers to questions about how the nation educates its children, it is the best thing that we have.

Education research is pursued by tens of thousands of individuals across the United States. They work in universities, large school districts, think tanks, and many other places. To the extent possible, they apply principles of objectivity, representativeness, and validity that are honored elsewhere in the pursuit of knowledge.

WHY EDUCATION RESEARCH IS SO DIFFICULT

Many of the issues debated in education—in fact almost everything—are socially derived constructs. Naming and defining terms, places, and events is how humans make sense of the world. In the physical sciences, a carbon atom is a carbon atom, a blood pressure reading is a blood pressure reading. In the social sciences, however, much of what is studied are social constructs: race, student achievement, intelligence, socioeconomic status. Moreover, many concepts and systems in the education world are described categorically—literally as categories—such as public school, charter school, certified teacher, bargaining union, the list goes on. The point here is not to cast aspersions on these constructs or our abilities to sort, understand, and compare them. Our brains need to classify things to make sense of the world. The point is more to caution readers that discerning facts about a subject as complex as education is a challenging undertaking.

Suppose someone is interested in the question "Are public schools better than private schools?" A fair amount of research has been done to answer this question. But the data themselves are limited in terms of what is measured and measurable. In addition, there is not just one type of public school or private school, and the elements that make up each category or construct can blur the boundaries. There are even semi-private schools. These constructs do not stand for monolithic entities. There are many types of charter schools, some of which look very much like traditional schools. There are many so-called traditional schools that look much like an innovative magnet school. There is not one type of homework assignment, and certainly homework looks different across grade levels and subject areas, to say nothing of different school districts and teachers. Nonetheless, it is the job of researchers to make sense of the varieties and similarities of school experiences and outcomes so that they can produce knowledge and insights into programs, policies, and disciplines of American education worth emulating—and those that are not.

Seeking the facts about such things is a complicated business. Researchers are not without bias—far from it. They choose what questions to ask, how to measure things, and are sometimes influenced by who funds their work. Demystifying categorical, unqualified assertions made by advocates of various sorts is one thing this analysis aspires to do. Yes, asking if charter schools are better than traditional public schools is an important question because much is at stake in the education policy arena where battles are fought for resources, credibility, and political clout.

This resource also seeks to illuminate how research findings about school performance, demographics, funding, and other elements can be misused or misunderstood. Due to the complex and myriad influences affecting students and schools, it is challenging to tease out isolated effects of programs, of school types, of interventions. Education is not like the hard sciences or pharmacology. Education researchers are unable to turn to randomized clinical trials of the type required by the Food and Drug Administration (FDA), which by design afford the best chance of determining cause and effect. Controlled clinical trials, while revered in social sciences, including education, are rare due to the impossibility in many instances of random assignment and adequately controlling for extraneous influences. Controlled experiments that are done are usually small and narrowly focused, thus limiting the extent to which their findings can be applied to other populations and settings. The alternatives to randomized experiments often raise more questions than they answer.

This does not mean that education research is not useful. We need research to make sense of data, to make us better understand how programs work, what works, for whom, and under what conditions. Multiple studies on the same topics—done in different settings and across different populations—are valuable in the aggregate. In addition, cause and effect isn't the only knowledge useful to education policy makers and practitioners. Understanding how people experience education can be quite revealing. What meaning do teachers draw from a professional development seminar? How do parents make sense of a complex array of school choice options? What are students feeling when they are required to wear school uniforms? How do educators attempt to translate research findings into practice? These questions necessitate in-depth accounts of phenomena, different ways of knowing, and different research strategies. They also lend participants a voice and some semblance of control over knowledge claims.

Cause and effect research and studies that seek to deepen understanding of the experiences of different participants in the education system—students, parents, teachers, administrators—can be complementary. Experimental studies may be able to demonstrate that an educational intervention caused an effect, but what were the underlying mechanisms that ultimately yielded that effect? Such information is important to know in order to make decisions about taking an intervention to scale. The majority of evidence that is invoked to clarify debates in education derives from large-scale studies or a collection of studies that rely on quantitative data and statistical models to estimate, predict, or explain some relationship or phenomenon.

FURTHER READING

Berliner, D. C., & Glass, G. V (Eds.). (2014). *50 myths and lies that threaten America's public schools: The real crisis in education.* New York: Teachers College Press.

1

Private vs. Public Schools

America has always had a bifurcated education system. Private schools prevailed in colonial times. The public school, or the "common school" as it was called, emerged in the middle of the nineteenth century. By the beginning of the twentieth century, most schooling for children took place in taxpayer-supported public schools, with about 15 percent of the school population in religious schools or private schools for the rich. The private market in education, as some referred to it, held steady for a century at about 15 percent of all students.

As the twenty-first century dawned, the taken-for-granted assumption that public education was the greatest invention of mankind, in the words of Horace Mann, a famed nineteenth-century advocate of public schools, began to be questioned. Corporations started to view public education as a half-trillion-dollar industry that could be tapped for business expansion and new revenue streams. Religious groups began to question why they were denied tax support for their schools when, in their view, they were educating children better than the public schools.

At the dawn of the 2020s, politicians, educators, parents, and many taxpayers were asking questions never seriously addressed before: Are public schools the best way to educate the future citizens of the United States? Why are private schools denied access to public funds? Would the nation's schools—and the students enrolled therein—be better-off if they were run like a business? Answers to these questions are beginning to be formulated, and trillions of dollars and tens of millions of lives hang in the balance.

Q1. DO STUDENTS IN PRIVATE SCHOOLS OUTPERFORM STUDENTS ENROLLED IN PUBLIC SCHOOLS?

Answer: Studies that directly compare performance between public and private schools are based on strong research designs. They are mostly limited to nonexperimental studies that rely on large survey data sets collected for other purposes, although some studies on school vouchers can also inform this question. Unadjusted comparisons almost always show higher average test scores for private school students, but after controlling for sociodemographic characteristics, student achievement differences between the two sectors virtually disappear. Some analyses even favor public schools.

The Facts: The answer to the question of whether private schools outperform public schools depends on who is asking it. Parents, caregivers, policy makers, and politicians have their own individual interests and agendas. Due to the expanded use of policy options that serve to reallocate public funds for private schools (e.g., vouchers, tax credits, education savings accounts), this question is becoming increasingly more relevant today for policy makers and politicians. The long-standing political and empirical debate over whether market competition leads to better schools also bears upon this question. Parents may wonder if the private school is worth the money or if it will help their child win admission into an elite university. Of course, this is posed as an empirical question and does not speak to comparisons among individual schools or take into account parental preferences for different aspects of a private school (e.g., religious instruction, quality facilities) or public school (e.g., diverse student body). But overall evidence suggests that, based on test performance, public schools do as well as private schools when account is taken of the background characteristics of the students they serve.

Good research designs are paramount to making evidence-based claims about school effectiveness. For instance, unadjusted comparisons between private and public school students—on test scores, graduation rates, college enrollment—cannot really say how well one sector performs relative to the other. Such comparisons would be subject to what is referred to in the research arena as "self-selection" bias. Families of students who opt for private schools are different from families of students enrolled in public schools. The families in each group have different backgrounds, social networks, and experiences that influence student academic performance above and beyond the contributions of schools. Without accounting for these differences, researchers could mistakenly conclude that the higher average private school test scores mean that they are superior to public schools. Lacking randomized experiments (as described below), most researchers employ statistical adjustment techniques in an attempt to correct for these preexisting differences.

Experiments are actually best suited to drawing conclusions about causes. Has the type of school, whether public or private, caused a difference in the students' achievement? The typical experimental design is one in which students are randomly assigned to a treatment or control group (or two treatment groups), and then compared over time on some outcome measure. In school research, experiments are relatively rare due to the impossibility of random assignment. Imagine trying to randomly assign students entering kindergarten to either a private or public school. For that to happen for even a single child, both types of schools would have to be relatively near the child's home, the parent(s) would have to accept whichever school their child was assigned, and if a private school was assigned, the parent would have to pay for tuition or the school would have to subsidize it. This scenario is simply not practical.

However, there are a few situations where an experiment can be approximated to compare public and private schools. They occur in the context of school choice programs that need to use lotteries to assign students. For schools of choice that are oversubscribed in sufficient numbers, admission lotteries in essence mimic random assignment. There are a number of studies that compare academic outcomes between students who have an equal chance of either attending a private or public school—most all in the context of a school voucher program (for more information on school vouchers see Q8). One caution in making generalizations about the private education sector performance is the substantial variability in private schools. One could easily make the same point for variability in public schools. Private school options include non-secular schools affiliated with various denominations and secular schools of different sizes, locales, and organizational affiliations (e.g., Montessori schools, which adhere to a specific learning philosophy).

Nonetheless, several independent school lottery studies have shown that, on the whole, there is no clear conclusion that students who use a voucher to attend private schools academically outperform their public school counterparts, although there is some evidence that they have small positive effects on graduation rates and college enrollment (Carnoy, 2017; Epple, Romana, and Urquiola, 2017).

In addition to the school voucher research literature, another body of research aims to directly compare private and public school performance.

This research relies heavily on large-scale survey data collected by state and federal agencies. Some of these survey data are longitudinal, meaning information is collected from the same sample at different points in time. However, most of the data are not collected longitudinally but rather cross-sectionally. An example of cross-sectional educational data would be administering a student survey to sixth, eighth, and tenth-graders at the same time. The studies that analyze survey data typically employ statistical techniques to help control for the abovementioned self-selection bias. The major studies in this category are summarized next.

Private vs. Public School Research

A 2006 study compared math scores of public and private school students using 2003 data from the National Assessment of Educational Progress (NAEP) (Lubienski and Lubienski, 2006). The NAEP is often referred to as the "Nation's Report Card" because it is the only assessment that measures student performance in core academic subjects across the nation and states; the NAEP has been reporting on how U.S. students are performing academically since 1969. The 2006 study's sample consisted of approximately 167,000 students across 6,660 schools at grade four and 131,000 students in 5,375 schools at grade eight. The NAEP data are cross-sectional—not longitudinal—which prevented the researchers from assessing same-student growth over time.

At first look, before any statistical corrections could be made, the private school performance appeared to exceed that of the public schools according to the NAEP data. But the private school students tended to come from higher socioeconomic strata. After statistically adjusting for the socioeconomic characteristics of students and schools, the authors found little difference between public and private school performance. They reported that

> ... the relatively high raw scores of private schools were more than accounted for by student demographics. In fact, after demographic differences had been controlled, the private school advantage disappeared and even reversed in most cases. (Lubienski and Lubienski, 2006, 651)

Another 2006 study conducted a separate analysis of the NAEP test score data, comparing public and private school scores in both math and reading (Braun, Jenkins, and Grigg, 2006). The researchers analyzed fourth-grade math and reading scores from more than 6,900 public school students and more than 530 private school students. They also analyzed eighth-grade math and reading test scores from more than 5,500 public school and more than 550 private schools. Uncorrected comparisons between public and private student test scores favored private school students in all subjects and grade levels. Uncorrected comparisons, however, reveal more about the characteristics of students who self-select into private and public schools than they do about the effectiveness of private versus public education. They do not tell how well each school sector would perform hypothetically if the backgrounds of the two groups of students were equal.

To draw a fairer comparison, the researchers employed statistical techniques that allowed them to correct for differences in student characteristics such as gender, race, ethnicity, socioeconomic status, special education status, and English-language proficiency as well as account for school characteristics such as size, location, teacher experience, and characteristics of the student body (e.g., percentage of students with a disability, family wealth indicators). After controlling for these student and school characteristics, they found virtually no differences in fourth-grade reading scores between private and public schools, but math scores for public schools were higher. In the eighth grade, private school students scored higher in reading but there was no statistical difference in math. As the authors noted, these results cannot be interpreted as causal; that is, one cannot draw the conclusion that private and public schools produce about the same level of student achievement. Their design was not based on randomly assigned students to public and private settings, nor did their data allow them to examine academic gains or growth over time.

Another study from 2008 analyzed student outcome data from the Early Childhood Longitudinal Study (ECLS), which, unlike the NAEP data, are longitudinal (Lubienski, Crane, and Lubienski, 2008). For data to be longitudinal, each student must be tested on more than one occasion, giving researchers more data to examine school effects over time. Analyzing a sample of 9,791 students in 1,273 public and 258 private schools, the authors initially found differences in average student performance in favor of private schools. However, after statistically controlling for differences in student and family characteristics at both the student and school level, the advantages disappeared. In fact, the results suggested that public schools performed better in some ways. An obvious limitation of the study is that it relied on statistical corrections of preexisting groups not randomly assigned, and, hence, was not well-suited for drawing conclusions about causes.

Another study published in 2018 analyzed a representative sample of 1,097 students from the National Institute of Child Health and Human

Development (NICHD) Study of Early Child Care and Youth Development (Pianta and Ansari, 2018). The data were collected longitudinally, meaning students were tracked over time. The researchers explored the extent to which private school enrollment explained academic, social, and personal outcomes from kindergarten through age 15. Uncorrected score comparisons showed that students enrolled in private schools outperformed students in public schools on almost all outcomes assessed by ninth grade. However, once researchers statistically adjusted for demographic characteristics among students and their families, all of the advantages of private school attendance disappeared. Indeed, they found "no evidence that private schools, net of family background (particularly income), are more effective for promoting student success" (Pianta and Ansari, 2018, 430). Based on the results, they concluded there was "no evidence for policies that would support widespread enrollment in private schools, as a group, as a solution for achievement gaps associated with income or race" (431).

The comparison of the effectiveness of public and private schools is fraught with problems of conducting experiments in the real world. No one is going to allow the flip of a coin to determine which school they will attend, so the gold standard of scientific research—the randomized experiment—is not an option. Various methods of trying to equate two groups of students with statistical techniques produce results with unknown levels of success. After decades of research and debate, then, there is no clear answer to the question, "Which are better, private or public schools?" If either is better, it's probably not by much.

FURTHER READING

Abdulkadiroğlu, A., Pathak, P. A., and Walters, C. R. 2018. "Free to choose: Can school choice reduce student achievement?" *American Economic Journal: Applied Economics*, 10(1), 175–206.

Braun, H., Jenkins, F., and Grigg, W. 2006. *Comparing private schools and public schools using hierarchical linear modeling (NCES 2006–461)*. U.S. Department of Education, National Center for Education Statistics, Institute of Education Sciences. Washington, DC: U.S. Government Printing Office.

Carnoy, M. 2017. *School vouchers are not a proven strategy for improving student achievement*. Washington, DC: Economic Policy Institute. Retrieved from https://tinyurl.com/ybss9lvr

Epple, D., Romano, R. E., and Urquiola, M. 2017. "School vouchers: A survey of the economics literature." *Journal of Economic Literature*, 55(2), 441–492.

Lubienski, C. A., and Lubienski, S. T. 2013. *The public school advantage: Why public schools outperform private schools.* Chicago, IL: University of Chicago Press.

Lubienski, C., Crane, C., and Lubienski, S. T. 2008. "What do we know about school effectiveness? Academic gains in public and private schools." *Phi Delta Kappan,* 89(9), 689–695.

Lubienski, S. T., and Lubienski, C. 2006. "School sector and academic achievement: A multilevel analysis of NAEP mathematics data." *American Educational Research Journal,* 43(4), 651–698.

Pianta, R. C., and Ansari, A. 2018. "Does attendance in private schools predict student outcomes at age 15? Evidence from a longitudinal study." *Educational Researcher,* 47(7), 419–434.

Ravitch, D. 2014. "Erin Osborne: Keep profiteers out of the classroom!" DianeRavitch.com, March 8, 2014. https://dianeravitch.net/2014/03/08/erin-osborne-keep-profiteers-out-of-the-classroom

Q2. ARE POLITICAL CONSERVATIVES AND CORPORATIONS THE BIGGEST SUPPORTERS OF PRIVATIZATION OF THE AMERICAN K–12 SCHOOL SYSTEM?

Answer: Yes. The movement to pivot away from the nation's traditional system of public education in favor of private schools has been primarily led by conservative and neoliberal reformers and corporations—the latter of whom stand to benefit financially—from diverting public funds to private schools. Neoliberal reformists favor the privatization of public domains, such as schools, through deregulated and market-oriented systems. Education historian Diane Ravitch termed this partnership of reformers and corporations as "Goliath," for it is indeed a giant wielding great power (Ravitch, 2020). Supporters of school vouchers and voucher-like policies (e.g., private school tuition tax credits) that shift tax dollars to support private education say that such options support individual liberty, one of the core values of the U.S. Constitution. Critics counter that those options have the potential to undermine two other important values—equality and democracy.

The Facts: Public and private education have coexisted for centuries; but in the modern day, public education has been challenged by a host of efforts to divert public funds to private schools through school vouchers and voucher-like policies. The introduction of charter schools in the mid-1990s foreshadowed the modern-day privatization movement. Although charter schools are technically public schools, many confuse them with private schools, and indeed they often operate like private entities. Charter schools are not typically governed by a locally and democratically elected school board, and they can be operated by for-profit corporations. (For more in-depth discussions of U.S. charter schools, see Q10–Q15 in this volume.)

In 2017, the arrival of the Trump administration added fuel to the school privatization movement. President Trump appointed Betsy DeVos, a steadfast supporter of charter schools, school vouchers, and the privatization of public education, to the post of U.S. Secretary of Education. News accounts reported that Secretary DeVos' main agenda was to expand school choice and divert public funding to the private education sector (Green, 2019; Strauss, Douglas-Gabriel, and Balingit, 2018). Although the Obama and George W. Bush administrations, to a significant degree, also adhered to tenets of neoliberalism—market competition through school choice, measuring educational quality, and issuing consequences for poor performance and rewards for high performance—the change from a Democratic White House to a Republican White House in 2017 brought with it new momentum for the privatization movement. A flurry of state and federal school voucher or voucher-like legislative proposals was submitted during the first two years under DeVos (Berends, 2018). Many of the state proposals originated in Republican-leaning "red" states, such as Arizona, Oklahoma, South Carolina, South Dakota, Tennessee, and Utah. Some of the proposals passed, while others did not.

In February 2017, the Trump administration proposed a federal voucher plan. Senator Ted Cruz (R-TX) and Representative Bradley Byrne (R-AL) sponsored legislation to support the plan, naming it the Education Freedom Scholarship and Opportunity Act (S.634/H.R.1434). Similar to the state tuition tax credit plans, it called for the establishment of a private nonprofit entity that would serve as the fiscal agent and distribute funds, called scholarships, to parents of children attending private and religious schools. The proposed Senate bill (S.634) called for tax credits to individuals of no more than 10 percent of adjusted gross income and tax credits for corporations not to exceed 5 percent of taxable income, and capped annual spending at $10 billion. Neither the Senate or House bill ever made it past the introductory stage, as (a GOP-controlled) Congress did not want to issue appropriations for its price tag. According to the govtrack.us website as of March 2020, the artificial intelligence platform Skopos Labs gave 2 percent odds of the Senate bill being enacted (GovTrack.us, 2020). Resistance to a nationwide voucher program comes from both Democrats and Republicans.

Critics on the left worry such a program will further erode support for public education, while critics on the right object to the idea of increased involvement of the federal government in shaping education policy—a responsibility that has historically rested primarily with individual states.

Despite a lack of interest by Congress to support federal tuition tax credits, the Trump administration's 2021 fiscal year budget proposal called for $5 billion annually to support state-designed education scholarship programs—programs that would subsidize tuition for private schools (Office of Management and Budget, 2020, 40). Although these subsidies are called scholarships, there is no intention to award them on the basis of academic promise or past performance. As with the nation's original tuition tax credit program, Arizona's "empowerment scholarships," the awards are meant for families willing to take their children out of a public school and enroll them in a private one. Recent Congressional attitudes toward a national voucher system suggest this budget item is unlikely to survive.

A 2017 50-state analysis done by the Education Commission of the States found 25 voucher programs operating in 14 states and the District of Columbia (Wixom, 2017). In addition, other policy instruments mimic the intent of vouchers without adopting the name, such as tuition tax credits and Education Savings Accounts. (For more on school vouchers and voucher-like policies, see Q8 and Q9). These voucher-like policies effectively redirect public education monies to support private education, both sectarian and religious. At the beginning of this century, they achieved relatively more legislative success because they were not as blatant as school vouchers, which are politically controversial (Welner, 2000). Critics, however, assert that they operate as "stealth vouchers" attempting to fly under the radar of Constitutional provisions explicitly mandating separation of church and state. Religion and government are to remain separate according to the "establishment clause" of the Constitution's First Amendment, which states, "Congress shall make no law respecting an establishment of religion, or prohibiting the free exercise thereof . . ."

Large urban school districts that have struggled over the years have seen a substantial shift toward investments in charter schools, many of which have been operated by for-profit companies. Because charter schools often function like private schools and can be managed by private, for-profit corporations, the door for privatization efforts in the public education arena has been opened wide. Detroit and Flint, Michigan, were witness to major charter school reform, which, according to a 2016 National Alliance for Public Charter Schools' report, had more than half of their public school students enrolled in a charter school by 2016 (David, Hesla, and Pendergrass, 2017). The *Detroit Free Press* reported that in 2017, 61 percent of Michigan's charter schools were managed by for-profit companies (Higgins, 2017). A 2015 study indicated that following the devastating impacts of Hurricane Katrina in 2005, 90 percent of the district of New Orleans was converted to charter schools (Adamson, Cook-Harvey, and Darling-Hammond, 2015).

Supporters of Neoliberal Education Reform

The privatization movement is driven by the ideology of individual choice and a belief in the economic efficiency of competitive markets. These are not just the basic tenets of conservatism but of neoliberalism as well. Advocates for privatization believe that parents deserve the right to use public tax revenue for their own individual ends. They assert that public schools have an ostensible monopoly on the K–12 education market, and that this monopoly has led to complacency, inadequate responses to serving low-performing students, and other negative results. Buttressed by economist Milton Friedman's belief in the power of the free market (Friedman, 1997), neoliberal reformers argue that the solution to America's school woes should be to open the education market up to competition and let consumers (i.e., students and families) choose which school they wish to attend. Proponents of public school education find education to be one of the last remaining public institutions that serves the important function of preparing citizens for a democracy. They worry that if education is left to free markets, disadvantaged and impoverished communities and families will be left even further behind. They advocate for greater investments in schools, while also addressing root causes of socioeconomic inequality that make it harder for many students from disadvantaged backgrounds to excel academically.

Education historian Diane Ravitch refers to the underwriters of education privatization as "corporate disrupters." Ravitch was once the U.S. Assistant Secretary of Education under the George H. W. Bush administration and, at that time, a strong proponent of accountability through testing and market-based school choice. After seeing the impact of those policies firsthand, she became an avid defender of public schools and critic of attempts toward their privatization (Ravitch, 2010). To the list of profit-making corporations, she added the names of billionaires whose faith in their own ability to succeed in business led them to believe that they also have the solution to the problems of education:

> [School reform became] the work of some of the richest people in the nation: the Walton family, Bill Gates, Betsy DeVos, the Koch brothers, Michael Bloomberg, Laurene Powell Jobs, Reed Hastings, Eli

Broad, and a bevy of other billionaires most of whom had made their fortunes on Wall Street, in Silicon Valley, or in the tech industry. (Ravitch, 2020, 4)

Ravitch, though, emphasizes that schools are not discount stores or housing developments, and she claimed that powerful business elites have foisted upon public schools a set of ineffective and damaging neoliberal reforms, including evaluating teachers based on flawed techniques, shutting down or firing staff at low-performing schools without regard for the merits and dedication of individual teachers and administrators, and testing students on narrow academic standards.

Tensions among Core Values: Liberty vs. Equality

The United States was founded on core values that still shape who its citizens are as a society. Those core values are expressed in the governing framework with fundamental commitments to democracy, equality, and individual liberty. These values are meant to exist in a healthy balance, each preventing domination by the others. Advocates of public schools say that public education reflects these values, or at least strives to (Cobb and DeMitchell, 2006). The goals of public education are to serve both the greater good and the individual. It offers democracy an educated citizenry capable of participating wisely and responsibly in a government powered by the people. At the same time, it provides the freedoms for individuals to pursue their lives and does so with the intention of every child receiving equal opportunity to secure its benefits.

Public education thus generates both public and private goods in the eyes of its defenders. In contrast, public education proponents argue that private education treats schooling as a private good, and prioritizes the preparation of individuals over serving the common good. Some supporters of privatization respond to this claim by arguing that certain religious private schools promote the public good by advancing their particular religious doctrines. A more common defense offered by supporters of privatization, though, is that individuals should have the opportunity and freedom to maximize the value of education for themselves, and that well-educated individuals contribute to the common good in numerous ways. They also believe that market competition will create better schools than an education system without such pressures to improve. Schools that must compete for students will make themselves better, according to conservative and neoliberal theory, which, in turn, will produce higher-skilled workers and more responsible and productive citizens.

Conservatism is not the exclusive domain of the private sector, however. Public schools, now more than ever, operate under conservative and neoliberal policies of competitive school choice, high-stakes testing, and punitive accountability systems. Further, public schools have always been asked to solve—or been blamed for—economic downturns and shortcomings in U.S. global competitiveness. Without a government-led system of education for the public, the values of equality of opportunity and democratic governance are subordinated to the value of individual liberty. Education historian David Labaree argues that U.S. schooling today is almost exclusively viewed as a private commodity. He reasons that treating education as a private good exacerbates disparities and is bad for the country:

> All but gone is the assumption that the purpose of schooling is to benefit the community at large. Less and less often do Americans conceive of education as a cooperative effort in nation-building or a collective investment in workforce development. Increasingly, rather, school comes to be viewed as an intense competition among individuals to get ahead in society and avoid being left behind. It has begun to look, to a great extent, like a means of creating winners and losers in the pursuit of academic merit, with the results determining who becomes winners and losers in life. (Labaree, 2018, 11)

Supporters of public education, which is free and open to children of all racial, ethnic, socioeconomic, and religious backgrounds, say that it has different goals than setting American children in competition against one another. They assert that its focus is on reducing inequities in class, race, language, and immigrant status in American society and preparing *all* students to be informed participants in American democracy.

FURTHER READING

Abrams, S. E. 2016. *Education and the commercial mindset.* Cambridge, MA: Harvard University Press.

Adamson, F., Cook-Harvey, C. M., and Darling-Hammond, L. 2015. *Whose choice? Student experiences and outcomes in the New Orleans school marketplace.* Stanford, CA: Stanford Center for Opportunity Policy in Education.

Anderson, G. L., and Donchik, L. M. 2016. "Privatizing schooling and policymaking: The American Legislative Exchange Council and new political and discursive strategies of education governance." *Educational Policy, 30*(2), 322–364.

Berends, M. 2018. "The evolving choice landscape in the U.S." In R. Papa and S. Armfield (Eds.), *Handbook of education policy*, Hoboken, NJ: Wiley-Blackwell.

Center for Media and Democracy. 2013. *ALEC at 40: Turning back the clock on prosperity and progress*. Retrieved from http://www.alecexposed.org/wiki/What_is_ALEC%3F

Cobb, C. D., and DeMitchell, T. A. 2006. "Fundamental values and policy making." *The SAGE encyclopedia of educational leadership and administration*, Vol. 2, 770–772. Thousand Oaks, CA: SAGE Publications.

David, R., Hesla, K., and Pendergrass, S.A., 2017. *A growing movement: America's largest public charter school communities*. Washington, DC: National Alliance for Public Charter Schools. https://www.publiccharters.org/sites/default/files/documents/2017-10/Enrollment_Share_Report_Web_0.pdf

Friedman, M. 1997. "Public schools: Make them private." *Education Economics*, 5(3), 341–344.

GovTrack.us. 2020. *S. 634—116th Congress: Education Freedom Scholarships and Opportunity Act*. Retrieved from https://www.govtrack.us/congress/bills/116/s634

Green, E. L. 2019. "Betsy DeVos backs $5 billion in tax credits for school choice." *New York Times*. February 28, 2019. Retrieved from https://www.nytimes.com

Higgins, L. 2017. "Report: For-profit run charter schools perform worse." *Detroit Free Press*. June 17, 2017. Retrieved from https://tinyurl.com/uzz7vac

Labaree, D. F. 2018. "Public schools for private gain: The declining American commitment to serving the public good." *Phi Delta Kappan*, 100(3), 8–13.

Lipman, P. 2011. *The new political economy of urban education: Neoliberalism, race, and the right to the city*. New York: Routledge.

Martinez, R. O. 2016. "The impact of neoliberalism on Latinos." *Latino Studies*, 14(1), 11–32.

Office of Management and Budget. 2020. *A budget for America's future*. Budget of the U.S. Government. Washington, DC: U.S. Government Publishing Office. https://www.govinfo.gov/content/pkg/BUDGET-2021-BUD/pdf/BUDGET-2021-BUD.pdf

Ravitch, D. 2010. "Why I changed my mind about school reform." *The Wall Street Journal*. March 9, 2010.

Ravitch, D. 2016. "When public goes private, as Trump wants: What happens." *The New York Review of Books*, 63(19), 58–61.

Ravitch, D. 2020. *Slaying Goliath: The passionate resistance to privatization and the fight to save America's public schools*. New York: Knopf.

Schneider, M. K. 2016. *School choice: The end of public education?* New York: Teachers College Press.

Strauss, V. 2016. "A sobering look at what Betsy DeVos did to education in Michigan—and what she might do as Secretary of Education." *Washington Post*. December 8, 2016.

Strauss, V., Douglas-Gabriel, D., and Balingit, M. 2018. "DeVos seeks cuts from Education Department to support school choice." *Washington Post*. February 13, 2018.

Underwood, J., and Mead, J. F. 2012. "A smart ALEC threatens public education." *Phi Delta Kappan*, 93(6), 51–55.

Warder, G. 2015. "Horace Mann and the creation of the Common School." Disability History Museum. Retrieved from http://www.disabilitymuseum.org/dhm/edu/essay.html?id=42

Welner, K. G. 2000. "Taxing the establishment clause: The revolutionary decision of the Arizona Supreme Court." *Kotterman v. Killian. Education Policy Analysis Archives*, 8(33). Retrieved from https://epaa.asu.edu/ojs/article/view/427/550

Wixom, M. A. 2017. *50-state comparison: Vouchers*. Education Commission of the States. March 6, 2017. Retrieved from https://www.ecs.org/50-state-comparison-vouchers

Yamiche, A. 2017. "Trump's call for school vouchers is a return to a campaign pledge." *New York Times*. March 1, 2017. Retrieved from https://www.nytimes.com

Q3. DO PRIVATE SCHOOLS ACCEPT STUDENTS WITH DISABILITIES?

Answer: Some private schools do accept students with disabilities, but available enrollment data indicate that many private schools accept comparatively few students with disabilities, and that some do not appear to have any students with disabilities (who typically have needs that make instructing them more expensive than other students). Public schools, meanwhile, are legally bound to accept and make accommodations for any students with disabilities who wish to attend.

The Facts: On average, private schools enroll small numbers of students who qualify for special education services. According to the U.S. Department of Education, in fall 2017, 95 percent of students ages 6 to 21 who were served under the Individuals with Disabilities Education Act (IDEA) were accommodated by regular public schools, while 1.4 percent were placed in private schools by their parents (Snyder, de Brey, and Dillow, 2019, table 204.60). The remaining 3.6 percent were accommodated by a separate school for serving students with disabilities, other facilities such as hospitals, and in the home. The IDEA is a federal law that guarantees students with disabilities a free appropriate public education (sites.ed.gov/idea/). In accord with IDEA, public school districts that receive federal funds must serve students with disabilities between ages 3 and 21 in the "least restrictive environment." The least restrictive environment guidance is intentionally broad and depends on individual student learning needs and the severity of the disability.

In the past, many students with physical, learning, or behavioral disabilities were assigned to a "self-contained" classroom, isolated from their peers free of disabilities for the entire school day. The least restrictive environment principle of IDEA guides public schools instead to "mainstream" students with disabilities as much as possible. Mainstreaming, also sometimes referred to as "inclusion," is the process whereby students with disabilities spend as much time as possible with peers free of disabilities.

To determine eligibility for special education services, public school districts are required to assess students to determine whether they qualify. Students who need such services are provided an Individualized Education Plan (IEP), which delineates the services and accommodations that the student should receive. Students with emotional or behavioral problems are exempted from regular disciplinary procedures if their behaviors arise from their disability. Essentially, students with disabilities are afforded the right to an appropriate *public* education under due process.

But, with few exceptions, IDEA protections are not guaranteed for students with disabilities who attend a private school. In fact, students who enter a voucher program in Arizona, Colorado, Florida, Georgia, Oklahoma, Mississippi, Tennessee, or Wisconsin give up their IDEA rights. Even voucher programs that cater specifically to students qualifying for special education services—such as those in Florida, Ohio, and Wisconsin—"are not required to provide an appropriate education for the students they serve. Nor are they required to offer due process hearings when issues of implementation or discipline occur" (Underwood, 2017, 77).

Charter schools, which by law are public schools, must abide by IDEA. Nonetheless, evidence provided by a 2012 Government Accountability Office report and studies published in 2015 and 2017, indicates some charter schools have tended to avoid serving students with disabilities (Government Accountability Office, 2012; Winters, 2015; Winters, Carpenter, and Clayton, 2017). A 2007 analysis found that charter schools have been known to dissuade or otherwise filter out students with disabilities at the admissions stage (Rhim, Ahearn, Lange, and McLaughlin, 2007). In some cases, this is out of necessity, as when a charter school recognizes it is not equipped to serve a student with a disability appropriately. The school might not have adequately trained personnel or proper facilities.

These facts are secondary to the question of whether private schools accept students who have disabilities. Private schools that specifically serve students with disabilities do exist. They have existed for decades—more than a century in some cases. Without question, they welcome students with special needs. But few disabled students even bother to apply to private schools that cater to an elite, wealthy clientele. RespectAbility, a nonprofit organization committed to people with disabilities, conducted a nonscientific yet informative study in 2014 of 90 elite private high schools—ones that they deemed "Ivy League feeder schools" (Appelbaum, 2014). They reviewed the school websites and contacted school officials to assess the degree to which individuals with disabilities were recruited, welcomed, and enrolled. Some of the schools did not respond to multiple attempts to reach them, but among those that did, the analysis turned up only six schools that appeared to embrace inclusion of students with disabilities or committed to doing more to serve, employ, and show respect for people with disabilities.

Significant resources are required to meet the unique learning, behavioral, and physical needs of students with disabilities. Private schools that turn away students with disabilities thus have a large financial advantage over public schools, leaving them more money for other expenditures such as swimming pools and other facilities, groundskeeping, athletic travel budgets, and building maintenance. Cash-strapped public schools, meanwhile, do not (and cannot by law) decline to serve students with disabilities. The 1975 federal Individual with Disabilities Education Act (IDEA) helps state and local governments with the costs of special education, but it has failed to meet specific funding levels laid out in IDEA. Specifically, IDEA committed to fund 40 percent of the average per-pupil expenditure in the United States multiplied by the number of special education students in each state. However, federal funding has consistently fallen far short of that commitment (Blad, 2020). In fact, a 2019 report by the Congressional Research Service found it is only funded at a little over a third of the full amount, leaving states and municipalities to make up the difference (Dragoo, 2019).

Elite private schools are the simple special cases. More troubling is the situation with what can be called the quasi-privates. "Quasi-private school" is a term of art. Some public schools, specifically charter schools, are public by law but they attempt to function like a private school. They project an image of elitism and advertise their rigor. These quasi-private schools that are truly public schools walk a fine line attempting not to violate the federal law that protects disabled students. Critics say that states with large numbers of this type of charter school have shown no interest in holding them accountable.

FURTHER READING

Appelbaum, L. 2014. "Elite private schools and discrimination against children with disabilities." *RespectAbility.* June 12, 2014. https://www.respectability.org/2014/06/elite-private-schools-and-discrimination-against-children-with-disabilities

Blad, E. 2020. "Why the feds still fall short on special education funding." *Education Week, 39*(18), 1.

Dragoo, K. E. 2019. *The Individuals with Disabilities Education Act (IDEA), Part B: Key statutory and regulatory provisions.* CRS Report R41833, Version 19. Updated August 29, 2019. Congressional Research Service.

Glass, G. V. 2014. "Ever hear a Basis Schools sales pitch?" *Education in Two Worlds.* https://ed2worlds.blogspot.com/search?q=Basis

Government Accountability Office. 2012. *Charter schools: Additional federal attention needed to help protect access for students with disabilities.* Washington, DC: Author.

Rhim, L. M., Ahearn, E. M., and Lange, C. M. 2007. "Charter school statutes and special education: Policy answers or policy ambiguity?" *The Journal of Special Education, 41*(1), 50-63.

Snyder, T. D., de Brey, C., and Dillow, S. A. 2019. *Digest of Education Statistics 2018* (NCES 2020-009). Washington, DC: National Center for Education Statistics, Institute of Education Sciences, U.S. Department of Education.

Szumski, G., Smogorzewska, J., and Karwowski, M. 2017. "Academic achievement of students without special educational needs in inclusive classrooms: A meta-analysis." *Educational Research Review, 21,* 33–54.

Underwood, J. 2017. "Under the law: When federal and state laws differ: The case of private schools and the IDEA." *Phi Delta Kappan, 99*(3), 76–77.

Winters, M. A. 2015. "Understanding the gap in special education enrollments between charter and traditional public schools: Evidence from Denver, Colorado." *Educational Researcher, 44,* 228–236.

Winters, M. A., Carpenter, D. M., and Clayton, G. 2017. "Does attending a charter school reduce the likelihood of being placed into special education? Evidence from Denver, Colorado." *Educational Evaluation and Policy Analysis*, 39(3), 448–463.

Q4. ARE PUBLIC AND PRIVATE SCHOOL TEACHERS SIMILAR IN THEIR EDUCATIONAL AND SOCIOECONOMIC BACKGROUNDS?

Answer: Based on available data to conduct comparisons, public school teachers have, on average, considerably more academic training and higher base salaries than private school teachers. Demographic statistics also show that public school teachers are, on the whole, less White relative to their peers in private schools. Data on private school teacher characteristics is restricted, which limits comparisons between the two sectors.

The Facts: Because private schools are less regulated than public schools, access to data on private school teacher characteristics is limited. Only basic sociodemographic variables are available for both workforce sectors. For instance, the U.S. Department of Education's annual *Condition of Education* report mandated by Congress does not include descriptive data on private school teachers. Private school teacher data that are collected from federal surveys does not typically provide separate responses for religious and nonreligious schools, making inferences about private school teachers very general. Due to the limited data on private school teachers, one cannot conclude based on the facts presented below that there are few or no differences between the two workforce sectors. Public schools serve a different population of students than private schools and are also held to different federal regulations, such as ones that require public schools to serve students with disabilities and students whose first language is not English. Such services require public schools to employ specialized teachers and support personnel; not all private schools make the same staff investments.

The National Center for Educational Statistics administers the National Teacher and Principal Survey, which is a nationally representative survey of teachers and principals from public and private schools. Participants voluntarily complete the survey. Based on the survey, the National Center for Educational Statistics estimated there were 3,545,000 public school full-time and part-time teachers and 509,200 private school teachers in 2017–2018 (National Center for Educational Statistics, 2019). Of the more than 3.5 million public school teachers, there were 205,600 charter school teachers. The total number of public and private teachers increased at about the same rate (13 percent) between 1999–2000 and 2017–2018. In both sectors, females represent roughly three-quarters of the teaching population.

In 2017–2018, a higher percentage of private school teachers were White compared to public school teachers (85.1 percent versus 79.3 percent). About two-thirds (68 percent) of charter school teachers were White. Public school teachers were more than twice as likely to be Black versus private school teachers (6.7 percent versus 3.2 percent). About 7.2 percent of private school teachers were Hispanic compared to 9.3 percent in public schools. Private school teachers are slightly older, on average, than public school teachers. For instance, the percentage of private school teachers 60 years old and older was 15 percent relative to 7.4 percent of public school teachers in that age category. The average age of traditional (i.e., non-charter) public school teachers was 43 compared to 44 in the private sector. Public and private school teachers each had, on average, roughly 14 years of teaching experience (Taie and Goldring, 2020).

In terms of highest academic degree earned, traditional public school teachers have a higher percentage of teachers who have completed a master's degree, an education specialist degree or certificate, and doctorate (59 percent) compared to private (48 percent) and charter (46 percent) school teachers. Fifty percent of traditional public school teachers had a master's as their highest degree relative to 39 percent in the charter and 49 percent in the private sectors. Finally, 10 percent of private school teachers had "less than a bachelor's degree" as their highest degree, compared to 3 percent among both traditional and charter school teachers.

In terms of salary, full-time public school teachers had a higher average base salary ($57,900) relative to full-time private school teachers ($45,300) in 2017–2018. Both sectors had similar percentages of teachers who held a job outside their school during the school year (18 percent and 21 percent in public and private schools, respectively). Nearly 8 of 10 public school teachers (78 percent) underwent an evaluation in 2016–2017 compared to 7 of 10 (69 percent) of private school teachers.

FURTHER READING

National Center for Educational Statistics. 2019. "Fast facts: Teacher characteristics and trends." *Digest of Education Statistics, 2018* (NCES 2020-009). U.S. Department of Education, National Center for Education Statistics. Retrieved from https://nces.ed.gov/fastfacts/display.asp?id=28

Taie, S., and Goldring, R. 2020. "Characteristics of public and private elementary and secondary school teachers in the United States: Results from the 2017–18 National Teacher and Principal Survey First Look (NCES 2020-142)." U.S. Department of Education. Washington, DC: National Center for Education Statistics. Retrieved from https://nces.ed.gov/pubsearch/pubsinfo.asp?pubid=2020142

2

School Choice: Competition, Stratification, Homeschooling, and Vouchers

The election of Democrat William Jefferson Clinton as president of the United States in November 1991 marked a surprising *absence* of shift in federal policy. The market-based policies that held sway during the Ronald Reagan and George H. W. Bush era were continued by and large through the remainder of the 1990s. Political analysts speak of the prevailing philosophy of government ushered in by the Clinton administration as "neoliberal." Liberal goals were sought through institutions that functioned as markets with varying degrees of regulation. The federal government further solidified the approach launched during earlier Republican administrations to treat public schools, medical and mental health services, parks, prisons, and a host of other institutions as though they were private businesses.

Proponents of market-based reforms expected public institutions to adopt the procedures of private businesses if they were to survive. In their view, schools, hospitals, prisons, and other institutions should compete for support from their respective constituencies, and the inefficient and ineffective would naturally die out. Supporters said that parents should be free to choose the schools that their children attend just as consumers choose which movie to see or which car to buy. Some similarly asserted that private and religious schools should be given the chance to compete for public funds on a level playing field with the public schools.

However, neoliberal policies applied to an institution like public education raised some special concerns. What would happen to public schools that struggled in this highly competitive environment? Where would the children go when their neighborhood school shut down? And what if it was suddenly discovered that a certain class of family using the opportunity to choose any school resulted in another class of family being left behind? In other words, what if the half-century movement to desegregate public education was reversed, and schools became racially segregated again?

Q5. DO MARKET-BASED REFORMS SUCH AS SCHOOL CHOICE INCREASE COMPETITION AND IMPROVE SCHOOL PERFORMANCE?

Answer: Research on the impacts of school choice on competition does not yield findings that would warrant major investments in choice programs to improve schools. When they exist, the positive effects of school competition are seen by many observers as too small to justify market-based approaches to education. Moreover, studies indicate that competition leads to inequities in access to schools and worsens the circumstances of racially and economically segregated schools.

The Facts: Supporters of market-based school reforms contend that school choice creates healthy and productive competition that ultimately benefits students. As the market-based theory goes, schools that compete with one another for students—and the school funding benefits that follow them—will respond by offering a better product in the form of better instruction and higher academic achievement. The "invisible hand" of the market, as eighteenth-century philosopher Adam Smith called it, will sort winners and losers among schools, leading to system-wide improvements and greater efficiencies (Stiglitz, 2000). Schools that do not adequately respond will suffer the consequences of shrinking enrollments or possibly even close. The winners, on the other hand, will be those schools nimble and innovative enough to meet the demands of discerning consumers. This is the ideal scenario for market-based education reformers who believe in the power of the free market over the entire system of schools—although Smith himself believed that the best system of elementary education is one funded by the public with only a small private school sector (Thomas, 2017).

Skeptics, however, do not see market theory applying well to education (Levin, 2020). They believe that if market theory is forced on schools, the result will be significant inequities, further separating students by race and socioeconomic class (Brathwaite, 2017). Free markets also rest on the assumption that consumers have equal and complete access to information on the products and services, and that, further, will act rationally on that information. But detractors assert that neither of these assumptions stands up well in the real world of public education. Parents have access to different social networks and also vary in their understanding of how to navigate complex school choice systems. Because education is compulsory, it is different "from most market goods: some parents and students are likely to be passive choosers who will be disadvantaged in a marketplace where others are active choosers" (Gill and Booker, 2015, 211). Parents also make school choice decisions for idiosyncratic reasons and those unrelated to academic quality or market signals. Convenience of location is one powerful influence on parents' choices of schooling options for their children. In reality, education markets operate more like "quasi" markets (Linick, 2014; Lubienski, 2003).

Market-Induced School Closures

Opponents of privatization acknowledge that calls by market reformers to "weed out low-performing schools" may sound sensible at first glance. After all, no one is in favor of schools that are not doing right by children. But they emphasize that the process of closing an inefficient or ineffective school does not happen as easily as pulling a weed—or without major consequences to children, families, and communities. Furthermore, school closures occur most often due to under-enrollment during tight budget times; and they disproportionately affect low-income communities of color (Lee and Lubienski, 2017). The shifting demographics of a city are one of the main reasons that some schools are consolidated or shut down altogether. Because school closings are so disruptive, they do not happen often and certainly not at the rate that market theory would predict.

Neighborhood schools serve the communities around them for many pragmatic reasons. Travel distances to school are a concern, especially to parents of young children. Schools, whether public or private, operate in the service of children and their families who rely on their stability. Furthermore, academic performance is seldom the only or even a principal consideration in school closures. Chicago Public Schools (CPS), for example, opted not to close some high schools in the early 2010s because students would have to cross gang lines to get to a newly assigned school (Chicago Public Schools, Commission on School Utilization, 2013).

Coincidentally, CPS made the headlines in 2013 with the abrupt closure of 50 schools, a decision led by mayor Rahm Emmanuel. The 50 schools were almost exclusively those serving children of color and alleged to be consistently poor performing. The options for families whose children had attended the closed schools were to send them to distant public schools or charter schools. Although free market theory predicted that the students would find alternatives better than the schools that were closed, studies by the Consortium on School Research of the University of Chicago were able to find few benefits for these students. A 2018 Consortium report concluded that:

> In this and other previous studies on the effects of school closures, we have seen that academic outcomes, on average, do not improve after students' schools were closed. Studies that find positive effects on displaced students only happened in cases with fewer disruptions, such as phase-outs, or when students attended top-performing schools. The affected schools included in this study closed immediately and the majority of students did not attend top-performing schools. [Twenty-one percent of displaced students attended a Level 1 or "excellent standing" school.] At the same time, student performance on average did not go down as much as some feared. (Gordon et al., 2018, 59)

In another study that looked at school closures in Philadelphia, researchers reported that, despite increased achievement among students who were transferred to a higher-performing school, on average the closures had no overall effect on the achievement of displaced students. The researchers also found that impacts depended on the concentration of displaced students enrolled in their new schools. The higher the concentration, the lower the academic benefits. They also found that "displaced students missed more days of school and received more suspension days the farther they traveled to their new school following closure" (Steinberg and MacDonald, 2019, 25).

Market-Induced School Improvement

Traditional public schools are not necessarily structured to respond to market pressures (Hanushek and Rivkin, 2003). Instead they are more accustomed to responding to political signals (Hess, 2002). When faced with new entrants to their "market," traditional public schools may lack the capacity or resources to respond in ways that translate to immediate gains in student achievement (Betts, 2009). Moreover, there are no assurances that schools respond to market forces with genuine improvements in quality. For instance, competition over students may divert their attention to superficial aspects like advertising as opposed to improving academic programming. In fact, several studies have found this to be the case (Jabbar, 2016; Loeb, Valant, and Kasman, 2011; Lubienski, 2007). For poor, low-performing schools, competition is more likely to sink them even lower. As the economist Kenneth Boulding observed, America's schools do not conform to any reasonable conception of a market.

> Schools may be financed directly out of school taxes, in which case the school system itself is the taxing authority and there is no intermediary, or they may be financed by grants from other taxing authorities, such as states or cities. In any case, the persons who receive the product—whether this is knowledge, skill, custodial care, or certification—are not the people who pay for it. This divorce between the recipient of the product and the payer of the bills is perhaps the major element in the peculiar situation of the industry that may lead to pathological results. (Boulding, 1972, 134–135)

To Adam Smith, the free market would lead to improved products and services by means of a transfer of information. Buyers, dissatisfied with Service A would inform Provider A of their unhappiness as well as inform other buyers about the quality of Provider A's service. Provider A would be forced either to improve the service or go out of business when buyers sought services from Provider B.

Boulding argued that these information exchanges, essential to the theory of the free market, simply do not exist in the case of the education of children. For one reason, the recipients of the service—that is, teaching—are children, mostly incapable of evaluating the value of the service they receive or even communicating their response to it to the adults in their lives. Furthermore, the majority of the purchasers of the service of schooling are a general public who have no children receiving the service; hence, they are not even privy to the imperfect feedback of school children. For reasons such as this, Boulding called public education a "possibly pathological section of the American economy" (Boulding, 1972, 129).

Measuring School Competition and Its Effects

One cannot deny that there is at least some competition among schools. Traditional public schools have long competed with both private and religious schools, and vice versa. If competition were the cure-all that some reformers argue, why then are they not satisfied with the schools that a century of competition has produced? They may believe that competition created by money-follows-the-child school choice programs will be different.

However, capturing competition and its effects through research is another question. School choice researchers have conceptualized the potential for competitive effects as either "first order" or "second order." First-order effects are those that might accrue to students who engage in school choice (e.g., enroll in a charter school). Second-order effects are presumed to occur *among* schools that are in competition. Elsewhere in this volume, the evidence on first-order effects, such as the effects of homeschooling, charter schools, and school vouchers on student achievement is evaluated. Here, the focus is on what the research says about second-order effects.

Systematic reviews of the research on second-order effects conducted over the last two decades indicate that the findings are generally mixed; that is, the effects of competition on student achievement and graduation rates are either small, nonexistent, or mildly negative (Austin, 2020; Belfield and Levin, 2002; Gill and Booker, 2015; Jabbar et al., 2019; Ni and Arsen, 2010). In one review of 41 studies that examined the relationship between school competition and school outcomes, researchers reported an overall "modest" positive correlation between competition and education quality (Belfield and Levin, 2002, 297). However, the researchers cautioned policy makers about using the findings to guide public policy, because many of the studies that they reviewed lacked statistical significance and the majority were based on correlational (not experimental) research designs. An age-old maxim in the research world is that correlation does not imply causation.

A more recent meta-analysis of school competition research added to the 41 studies reviewed by Belfield and Levin (2002). A meta-analysis is a comprehensive synthesis of quantitative research findings. The newer meta-analysis reviewed a total of 92 published and unpublished studies done between 1992 and 2015 (Jabbar et al., 2019). The researchers concluded that "[c]onsistent with prior reviews (e.g., Belfield and Levin, 2002; Ni and Arsen, 2010), we find that, in general, the effects of school competition on achievement are very small and, on average, the effects are positive" (Jabbar et al., 2019, 21). They also reported significant variation in results across different contexts and populations and because of this warned policy makers "to use caution when implementing such policies, as it is unclear whether a particular choice model will have the expected competitive effects" (22). Accordingly, they are careful "not to overstate the impact of competition, that 'a rising tide lifts all boats,' given that the effects are too small to have a major impact on educational quality and inequality on their own" (25).

A number of researchers have issued cautions about the methods used to detect competition among schools, noting a lack of consistency in measuring across studies (Arsen and Ni, 2012; Creed, 2015; Linick, 2014) and also the challenges associated with validly capturing the construct "competition." One researcher suggested that this might be why the overall findings are mixed.

> It is important that the education reforms that tout the use of economic concepts such as competition and efficiency as drivers of educational improvement be examined as accurately as possible. However, the true impact of these reforms is obscured by inconsistency in measurement and definition. Future research must bring clarity to these concepts, and perhaps answer other important questions about the potential impacts of market-based reforms. (Linick, 2014, 11)

As an example, some studies have used school-specific measures of competition based on the percentage of students in a given traditional public school who left for a charter school (e.g., Cremata and Raymond, 2014; Winters, 2012). However, this measure may not actually reflect competition but instead may reflect an outcome of charter school entry (Cordes, 2018). In other words, students who are not academically succeeding at a traditional public school may leave for greener pastures at a nearby charter school. Any observed gains in the overall performance of the traditional public school could be due to compositional changes in students and not real school performance gains. Competition is not that easy to measure, let alone attribute to systemic outcomes.

Even if competition is accurately measured, another major challenge is providing evidence that schools responded to this competition. School performance may improve within a competitive policy context, but it is difficult to know if it was really competition that led to the improvement and not some other influence that would cause public schools to improve (Epple, Romano, and Urquiola, 2017). The question remains of "whether these studies capture the true effects of competition and not simply the effects of choice, autonomy, or policy-specific context" (Linick, 2014, 3). How would one disentangle the effects of state or district accountability pressures or investments in academic programming and teacher training? Much of the research estimating competitive effects on schools relies on risky assumptions of what motivates administrators, teachers, parents, and students. Here, as with so many questions raised about how to improve schooling, the methods of education research have only limited capacity to analyze and assess the impact of a single policy or initiative on an institution as complex as public education.

Open Enrollment as a Form of Competition: Do the Gains Outweigh the Losses?

Research on school competition not only examines its potential positive effects on school outcomes, but also reveals some of the losses and side effects. One major concern with competitive school choice is whether all students benefit when there are any benefits at all. Does a rising tide really lift all boats? One researcher studied CPS's open enrollment program from the perspective of students who applied to a selective enrollment school (Phillippo, 2019). CPS students always have a spot reserved at their neighborhood assigned school, but they may apply to other district high schools. The selective enrollment high schools conduct competitive admissions, judging students on indicators such as seventh-grade test scores, a high school entrance exam, portfolios, and interviews. Admission standards are very high, so many students do not qualify. The researcher discovered through her comparative, longitudinal case study that the competitive school choice:

> [c]ontinues to sort students across an entrenched hierarchy of schools and to give young citizens good reasons to mistrust our public institutions and their representatives, even as they accept the policy as fair. Students feel (and are) responsible for getting the best education they can, responsible if they beat out their peers, responsible if they "lose" ... no one comes away unscathed. No one in this situation is really a winner. (Phillippo, 2019, 166)

Another drawback of competitive school choice, according to critics, is the negative outcomes for schools and communities that are among the losers in the competition. Michigan's open enrollment policy permits students to enroll in any public school inside or outside a student's home district. School funding follows the child to the receiving school. This policy has in effect gutted the Detroit Public Schools Community District (DPSCD) and drained its already limited resources. In the 2017–2018 school year, nearly 48 percent of Detroit's 103,928 public school resident students were enrolled in a charter school and another 10 percent were attending schools in metropolitan Detroit's inner- and outer-ring districts. Only 5 percent of DPSCD's 46,530 students came from outside the district, resulting in a net loss of 57,398 students. Despite this mass exodus of students, DPSCD schools remain open to serve the students who live there.

Southwest of Detroit is the River Rouge School District, a small, predominantly White, working-class suburb. River Rouge aggressively advertises for students because it has lost many students itself; it has become a landing spot for Detroit resident students to the point where it has become a majority-Detroit-resident district (Strauss, 2019). In 2017–2018, 61 percent of River Rouge's student enrollment came from outside the district, mostly from nearby Detroit. At the same time, parents in River Rouge are sending their children out of the district or to charter schools in high numbers. In 2017–2018, 35 percent of public school students residing in River Rouge attended a school outside the district, and another 9 percent attended a charter school. Open enrollment has thus led to a busy market in metropolitan Detroit, but not an especially efficient or equitable one.

By whatever name—magnet schools, specialty schools, selective enrollment—data indicate that open enrollment policies have resulted in flight from diverse schools to more homogeneous majority schools. In 1994, for example, the Boulder Valley School District, Colorado, announced a new open enrollment policy whereby any student could enroll in any K–8 school if space was available. An early warning of an upheaval appeared the first morning that online choice was made available to the district's families. The computers crashed under the weight of a slew of logins. After six years of families exercising their free choice, the twenty K–8 schools that enrolled 30 percent minority students in 1994 were majority-minority (more than 50 percent minority) in 2000. White students in schools with only 20–40 percent minority students had fled to even Whiter schools. This upper-middle-class school district in a predominantly White county in a predominantly progressive state experienced White flight from schools with even modest numbers of minority students. What more might be expected in ethnically and racially diverse communities? Research evidence points to markedly increased racial segregation in states and districts offering unregulated school choice.

In schools that are punished by the competition of open enrollment, like those in Boulder, DPSCD, and even River Rouge, there are always students left behind who are dependent on them. As other scholars have argued:

> Because schooling is compulsory (unlike most market goods and services), there will always be a population of "non-choosers" whose fate is left to the conventional public school (or to other schools of last resort, whatever they might be). Those students and their schools might be left substantially worse off if all of the most motivated and best informed families have exited to schools of choice. (Gill and Booker, 2015, 213)

Free market public schooling has been justified on the grounds that it would produce competition among schools; and competition, it is argued, would make all schools better—more efficient, more innovative, more effective. But competition is achieved through choice, and choice has resulted in a resegregating of public education like never before. After the Supreme Court decision in 1954 in *Brown v. Board of Education*, "academic academies" sprung up in some Southern states as a means for some White students to escape integrated schools. Critics of school choice contend that far too often, school choice is producing a twenty-first century version of those academies.

FURTHER READING

Arsen, D., and Ni, Y. 2012. "The competitive effect of school choice policies on public school performance." In K. G. Welner, P. H. Hinchey, W. J. Mathis, and G. Miron (Eds.), *Exploring the school choice universe: Evidence and recommendations*. Charlotte, NC: Information Age Publishing, 193–209.

Austin, M. J. 2020. "Charter school competition." In M. Berends, Primus, A., and Springer, M. G. (Eds.), *Handbook of research on school choice*. New York: Routledge, 146–159.

Belfield, C., and Levin, H. 2002. "The effects of competition between schools on educational outcomes: A review for the United States." *Review of Educational Research, 72*, 279–341.

Betts, J. 2009. "The competitive effects of charter schools on traditional public schools." In M. Berends, M. G. Springer, D. Ballou, and H. Wahlberg (Eds.), *Handbook of research on school choice*. New York: Routledge, 195–208.

Boulding, K. E. 1972. "The schooling industry as a possibly pathological section of the American economy." *Review of Educational Research, 42*(1), 129–143.

Brathwaite, J. 2017. "Neoliberal education reform and the perpetuation of inequality." *Critical Sociology, 43*(3), 429–448.

Chicago Public Schools, Commission on School Utilization. 2013. "Interim report: Commission on School Utilization," March 6.

Cordes, S. A. 2018. "In pursuit of the common good: The spillover effects of charter schools on public school students in New York City." *Education Finance and Policy, 13*(4), 484–512.

Creed, B. M. 2015. "Defining and evaluating measures of school competition: Towards a theoretically grounded, empirically refined measure of school competition." Paper presentation at the Annual Conference of the *Association for Education Finance and Policy*. Washington, DC.

Cremata, E. J., and Raymond, M. E. 2014. "The competitive effects of charter schools: Evidence from the District of Columbia." In *Association for Education Finance and Policy Conference Working Paper*. March 2014.

Davis, T. 2013. "Charter school competition, organization, and achievement in traditional public schools." *Education Policy Analysis Archives*, 21(88). https://doi.org/10.14507/epaa.v21n88.2013

Epple, D., Romano, R. E., and Urquiola, M. 2017. "School vouchers: A survey of the economics literature." *Journal of Economic Literature*, 55(2), 441–492.

Fabricant, M., and Fine, M. 2015. *The changing politics of education: Privatization and the dispossessed lives left behind.* New York: Routledge.

Gill, B., and Booker, K. 2015. "School competition and student outcomes." In H. Ladd and E. B. Fiske (Eds.), *Handbook of research in education finance and policy.* 2d ed. New York: Routledge, 211–227.

Gordon, M. F., de la Torre, M., Cowhy, J. R., Moore, P. T., Sartain, L. S., and Knight, D. 2018. *School closings in Chicago: Staff and student experiences and academic outcomes.* Chicago, IL: University of Chicago Consortium on School Research.

Hanushek, E., and Rivkin, S. 2003. "Does public school competition affect teacher quality?" In C. Hoxby (Ed.), *The economics of school choice.* Chicago, IL: University of Chicago Press, 23–48.

Hess, F. M. 2002. *Revolution at the margins: The impact of competition on urban school systems.* Washington, DC: Brookings Institution Press.

Jabbar, H. 2016. "Selling schools: Marketing and recruitment strategies in New Orleans." *Peabody Journal of Education*, 91(1), 4–23.

Jabbar, H., Fong, C. J., Germain, E., Li, D., Sanchez, J., Sun, W.-L., and Devall, M. 2019. "The competitive effects of school choice on student achievement: A systematic review." *Educational Policy.* https://doi.org/10.1177/0895904819874756

Lee, J., and Lubienski, C. 2017. "The impact of school closures on equity of access in Chicago." *Education and Urban Society*, 49(1), 53–80.

Levin, H. M. 2020. "Market competition and school vouchers." In M. Berends, M. Springer, D. Ballou, and H. Wahlberg (Eds.), *Handbook of research on school choice.* New York: Routledge, 214–225.

Linick, M. A. 2014. "Measuring competition: Inconsistent definitions, inconsistent results." *Education Policy Analysis Archives*, 22(16). http://dx.doi.org/10.14507/epaa.v22n16.2014

Linick, M., and Lubienski, C. 2013. "How charter schools do, and don't, inspire change in traditional public school districts." *Childhood Education*, 89(2), 99–104.

Loeb, S., Valant, J., and Kasman, M. 2011. "Increasing choice in the market for schools: Recent reforms and their effects." *National Tax Journal*, 64, 141–164.

Lubienski, C. 2003. "Innovation in education markets: Theory and evidence on the impact of competition and choice in charter schools." *American Educational Research Journal*, 40(2), 395–443.

Lubienski, C. 2007. "Marketing schools." *Education and Urban Society*, 40, 118–141.

Ni, Y., and Arsen, D. 2010. "The competitive effect of charter schools on public school districts." In C. Lubienski and P. Weitzel (Eds.), *The charter school experiment: Expectations, evidence, and implications.* Cambridge, MA: Harvard Education Press, 93–120.

Phillippo, K. 2019. *A contest without winners: How students experience competitive school choice.* Minneapolis, MN: University of Minnesota Press.

Ravitch, D. 2020. *Slaying Goliath: The passionate resistance to privatization and the fight to save America's public schools.* New York: Knopf.

Steinberg, M. P., and MacDonald, J. M. 2019. "The effects of closing urban schools on students' academic and behavioral outcomes: Evidence from Philadelphia." *Economics of Education Review*, 69, 25–60.

Stiglitz, J. E. 2000. "The contributions of the economics of information to twentieth century economics." *The Quarterly Journal of Economics*, 115(4), 1441–1478.

Strauss, V. 2019. "A different kind of school-choice mess in DeVos's home state of Michigan." *Washington Post.* July 3, 2019. https://www.washingtonpost.com/education/2019/07/03/different-kind-school-choice-mess-devoss-home-state-michigan

Thomas, A. M. 2017. "Adam Smith on the philosophy and provision of education." *Journal of Interdisciplinary Economics*, 30(1) 105–116.

Winters, M. A. 2012. "Measuring the effect of charter schools on public school student achievement in an urban environment: Evidence from New York City." *Economics of Education Review*, 31(2), 293–301.

Q6. DO SCHOOL CHOICE PROGRAMS CONTRIBUTE TO THE RESEGREGATION OF AMERICAN SCHOOLS?

Answer: It depends on the specific program. Controlled school choice policies that aim to integrate schools along the lines of race or ethnicity and socioeconomic status are most often successful in achieving that goal. Unregulated systems of school choice, however, tend to exacerbate school segregation (Cobb and Glass, 2009).

The Facts: School choice programs differ in the extent to which decisions over student assignments are regulated. The simplest distinction separates "controlled" school choice and "unregulated" school choice plans. Controlled school choice attempts to desegregate or integrate schools to promote more equitable peer environments. Numerous research studies point to the harmful influences of minority and class-based isolation endemic in so many of America's schools as a result of residential segregation. At the same time, research also shows the benefits of racially and economically integrated schools that help foster cross-racial understanding, enhance critical thinking skills and academic achievement, and promote better life opportunities (Linn and Welner, 2007).

Controlled school choice programs consider a variety of student and school characteristics with the ultimate goal of balancing school enrollments by race, family wealth, and student achievement. School districts that are under court orders to desegregate may use race or proxies for race to achieve their goals. Such plans often involve magnet schools (i.e., special interest schools such as the arts or science) designed to attract students from diverse backgrounds. Even under court orders to desegregate, modern-day plans rely on voluntary participation by families. The last district with court ordered busing, Charlotte-Mecklenburg in North Carolina, ended it officially in 1999.

School choice plans that are not under any legal mandates to desegregate may choose, voluntarily, to help integrate schools. These voluntary school choice programs were once freely able to consider the race of students who chose to participate. In other words, they were controlled choice plans that could explicitly take race into account. But following a momentous 6–5 Supreme Court decision in 2007 (*Parents Involved in Community Schools v. Seattle School District,* 2007), voluntary district student integration plans suffered a major setback. The court severely limited the use of race-based considerations in the assigning of students to schools. The court's ruling pressured districts with voluntary racial integration plans to either abandon them or attempt to desegregate by using race-neutral characteristics such as family income. Unfortunately, race-neutral policies are not very effective at achieving racial integration (U.S. Department of Education, 2003).

Charter Schools and Segregation

Charter schools operate by and large under conditions of unregulated school choice. Although some state charter school policies (such as those in California) encourage charter schools to strive for racial diversity—a goal made easier by their lack of traditional school attendance boundaries—this is rarely monitored by either the schools themselves or state agencies. Consequently, as several studies have shown, most charter schools end up more racially and economically homogeneous than the surrounding traditional public schools (Bifulco and Ladd, 2007; Cobb and Glass, 1999, 2001; Frankenberg, Siegel-Hawley, and Wang, 2011; Kotok et al., 2017). Two different charter school demographic profiles can be easily recognized: charter schools that predominantly serve students of color in urban communities, and charter schools that enroll predominantly White students, particularly in racially diverse communities. The latter scenario is strongly suggestive of "White flight" or "White exodus" where parents leave racially diverse schools so that their children can attend schools that are less diverse, more racially homogeneous. Research that examines parental preferences and decision-making in schools attests to this phenomenon (e.g., Billingham and Hunt, 2016). White flight was common during the era of court-ordered desegregation; but as this de jure integration waned, White flight was replaced by other more subtle means of achieving the same ends.

Research is mixed on the enrollment of low-income students in charter schools. Some studies reported that charter schools enroll more poor students than nearby traditional public schools (Carnoy et al., 2005; Epple, Romano, and Zimmer, 2016) while others found lower proportions of poor students relative to nearby traditional public schools (Hoxby, Murarka, and Kang, 2009; Tuttle et al., 2010; Saporito, 2003). Finally, there is consistent evidence that charter schools sort students in other ways. While a very small number of charter schools aim to serve certain subpopulations, charter schools on the whole under-enroll English language learners and students with disabilities (Heilig et al., 2016; Mavrogordato and Harris, 2017). A new elite type of charter school has been recognized by Brown and Makris (2018), who referred to them as "prestige" charter schools because they disproportionately serve students from advantaged backgrounds. This volume describes the types of charter school more completely in Q10.

Intra- and inter-district open enrollment policies have also been found to increase social stratification (Holme and Richards, 2009). These programs are generally unregulated, and those that aspire to promote integrated schools have been hamstrung by the 2007 *Parents Involved* Supreme Court decision. For instance, a 2009 study of race-neutral choice policies in Durham, North Carolina, found that they worsened school racial segregation (Bifulco, Ladd, and Ross, 2009). The researchers' analysis of parent choice patterns revealed that White, middle, and upper-middle class parents found ways to enroll their children in the highest performing schools irrespective of school choice policy. Studies of New York City's competitive school choice plans in 2013 and 2018 revealed similar results (Roda and Wells, 2013; Sattin-Bajaj and Roda, 2018).

The demographics of student enrollments in school voucher and neovoucher (e.g., tuition tax credits, education savings accounts) plans may be regulated depending on the state or city policy they operate under. Most conventional school voucher programs limit participation to low-income families or students with disabilities. Neovoucher programs, such as education tax credits and education savings plans, run the gamut from virtually no regulation to some restrictions based on family income. A 2017 analysis of Louisiana's voucher program, which allows low-income and mostly students of color from low-performing public schools to attend a private school, found that a large majority of voucher students reduced racial isolation of the public schools that they left but marginally increased segregation in the private schools they attended (Egalite, Mills, and Wolf, 2017). Another study done in 2010 estimated the effects of a universal voucher program in California based on voting data from a statewide ballot initiative (Brunner, Imazeki, and Ross, 2010). The researchers found that White parents of children in public schools were more supportive of the voucher program if their children attended schools with high percentages of non-White students; this was also true for non-White households with children in public schools.

In sum, the evidence shows that if school choice programs cannot or do not pay attention to social class and race, they generally increase segregation among schools. That is, racially and ethnically diverse schools become less diverse under unregulated choice plans. Parents who enjoy social and economic advantages manage to maintain those advantages, especially in unregulated school choice programs. School choice policies consistently provide an advantage to the dominant cultural group (Cobb and Irizarry, 2020). As one education scholar recognized:

> . . . in choice systems advantage-seeking parents are able to use their relevant capitals to negotiate diverse forms of provision and fuzzy rules of access. In this sense school choice may be considered as a class strategy, a mechanism for reproducing social advantage, a means of "doing" class (cf. Ball 2003) in a very practical way. (Ball, 2003, 83, from Ball and Nikita, 2014)

FURTHER READING

Ball, S. J., and Nikita, D. P. 2014. "The global middle class and school choice: A cosmopolitan sociology." *Zeitschrift für Erziehungswissenschaft, 17*(3), 81–93.

Bifulco, R., and Ladd, H. F. 2007. "School choice, racial segregation, and test-score gaps: Evidence from North Carolina's charter school program." *Journal of Policy Analysis and Management*, 26(1), 31–56.

Bifulco, R., Ladd, H. F., and Ross, S. 2009. "Public school choice and integration: Evidence from Durham, North Carolina." *Social Science Research: A Quarterly Journal of Social Science Methodology and Quantitative Research*, 38, 71–85.

Billingham, C. M., and Hunt, M. O. 2016. "School racial composition and parental choice: New evidence on the preferences of white parents in the United States." *Sociology of Education*, 89(2), 99–117.

Brown, E., and Makris, M. V. 2018. "A different type of charter school: In prestige charters, a rise in cachet equals a decline in access." *Journal of Education Policy*, 33(1), 85–117.

Brunner, E., Imazeki, J., and Ross, S. 2010. "Universal vouchers and racial and ethnic segregation." *The Review of Economics and Statistics*, 92(4), 912–927.

Carnoy, M., Jacobsen, R., Mishel, L., and Rothstein, R. 2005. *The charter school dust-up*. Washington, DC: Economic Policy Institute.

Cobb, C. D., and Glass, G. V. 1999. "Ethnic segregation in Arizona charter schools." *Education Policy Analysis Archives*, 7(1). https://epaa.asu.edu/ojs/article/view/536

Cobb, C. D., and Glass, G. V. 2001. "U.S. charter schools and ethnic segregation: Inspecting the evidence." *International Journal of Educational Reform*, 10(4), 381–394.

Cobb, C. D., and Glass, G. V. 2009. "School choice in a post-desegregation world." *Peabody Journal of Education*, 84(2), 262–278.

Cobb, C. D., and Irizarry, J. 2020. "Private interests and the common good: Conflicting priorities in a school choice world." In R. Papa (Ed.), *Handbook on promoting social justice in education*. Basel, Switzerland. Springer International Publishing AG.

Egalite, A. J., Mills, J. N., and Wolf, P. J. 2017. "The impact of targeted school vouchers on racial stratification in Louisiana schools." *Education and Urban Society*, 49(3), 271–296.

Epple, D., Romano, R., and Zimmer, R. 2016. "Charter schools: A survey of research on their characteristics and effectiveness." In E. A. Hanushek, S. J. Machin, and L. Woessmann (Eds.), *Handbook of the Economics of Education*. Amsterdam, The Netherlands: Elsevier, 139–208.

Frankenberg, E., Siegel-Hawley, G., and Wang, J. 2011. "Choice without equity: Charter school segregation." *Educational Policy Analysis Archives*, 19(1). http://epaa.asu.edu/ojs/article/view/779

Heilig, J. V., Holme, J. J., LeClair, A. V., Redd, L. D., and Ward, D. 2016. "Separate and unequal: The problematic segregation of special populations in charter schools relative to traditional public schools." *Stanford Law and Policy Review, 27*(2), 251–293.

Holme, J., and Richards, M. 2009. "School choice and stratification in a metropolitan context: Inter-district choice and regional inequality." *Peabody Journal of Education, 84*(2), 150–171.

Hoxby, C. M., Murarka, S., and Kang, J. 2009. "How New York City's charter schools affect achievement." Second report in series. Cambridge, MA: New York City Charter Schools Evaluation Project, 1–85.

Kotok, S., et al. 2017. "School choice, racial segregation, and poverty concentration: Evidence from Pennsylvania charter school transfers." *Educational Policy, 31*(4), 415–447.

Linn, R. L., and Welner, K. G., eds. 2007. *Race-conscious policies for assigning students to schools: Social science research and the Supreme Court cases.* Washington, DC: National Academy of Education.

Mavrogordato, M., and Harris, J. 2017. "*Eligiendo Escuelas:* English learners and access to school choice." *Educational Policy, 31*(6), 801–829.

Orfield, G., Frankenberg, E., and Garces, L. M. 2008. "Statement of American social scientists of research on school desegregation to the U.S. Supreme Court in *Parents v. Seattle School District* and *Meredith v. Jefferson County.*" *The Urban Review, 40*(1), 96–136.

Parents Involved in Community Schools v. Seattle School District No. 1, 551 U.S. 701 (2007).

Roda, A., and Wells, A. S. 2013. "School choice policies and racial segregation: Where White parents' good intentions, anxiety, and privilege collide." *American Journal of Education, 119*(2), 261–293.

Rotberg, I. C. 2014. "Charter schools and the risk of increased segregation." *Phi Delta Kappan, 95,* 26–30.

Saporito, S. 2003. "Private choices, public consequences: Magnet school choice and segregation by race and poverty." *Social Problems, 50*(2), 181–203.

Sattin-Bajaj, C., and Roda, A. 2020. "Opportunity hoarding in school choice contexts: The role of policy design in promoting middle-class parents' exclusionary behaviors." *Educational Policy, 34*(7), 992–1035. https://doi.org/10.1177/0895904818802106

Tuttle, C. C., et al. 2010. *Student characteristics and achievement in 22 KIPP middle schools.* Washington, DC: Mathematica Policy Research, Inc.

U.S. Department of Education. 2003. *Evaluation of the Magnet Schools Assistance Program, 1998 Grantees.* Washington, DC: Policy and Program Studies Service.

Q7. DOES HOMESCHOOLING LEAD TO BETTER OUTCOMES FOR STUDENTS THAN TRADITIONAL PUBLIC SCHOOLS?

Answer: While homeschooling may work well for some students and their families, there is no credible evidence that homeschooling is better than traditional public schooling. For example, although some reports show that homeschool students score higher on achievement tests than their public school counterparts on average, this does not mean that the practice of homeschooling *caused* the differences. Differences in student outcomes between homeschooled students and public school students may be due to a wide range of family and community factors and not attributable, at least solely, to the homeschooling experience itself.

The Facts: Homeschooling occurs when a parent opts out of sending a child to a formal school setting and instead assumes responsibility for their child's education. Although homeschooling is a form of school choice, it has not been a major part of that conversation; it tends to fly under the radar of public opinion and policy debates because so much of it happens outside the public eye.

Interest in homeschooling increased rapidly at the turn of the last century. Between 1999 and 2012, the percentage of homeschooled students doubled, increasing from 1.7 percent to 3.4 percent of the total public and private school population (U.S. Department of Education, 2016). Since that spike, participation rates have remained mostly flat. Recent estimates reveal around 1.7 million students being homeschooled, which accounts for 3.3 percent of the total school population.

Although parents may choose homeschooling or private schooling for their child, this does not mean that the state does not still have a responsibility to ensure that each child receives an adequate education. All 50 states and the District of Columbia (DC) have policies on homeschooling or home-based education, although they differ in the level of oversight that they exert. Overall, state regulations on homeschooling are fairly minimal. About a fourth of all the states and DC require home instructors to have certain minimum qualifications, such as a high school degree or the equivalent (Wixom, 2015). The state of Washington, known for having one of the nation's more regulated homeschooling policies, requires instructors (i.e., parents) to meet at least one of the following: (1) have completed 45 quarter units of college level credit, (2) attend a parent qualifying course, (3) work with a certified teacher who meets with the student an hour per week on average, or (4) be deemed qualified to provide home-based instruction by the district superintendent (Washington Homeschool Organization, 2021). Twenty states monitor academic progress of students through a standardized exam or alternative form of assessment. Twenty-three states and DC have explicit attendance policies for homeschoolers, usually in the form of days or hours of instruction per year or some combination that is equivalent to the amounts required in traditional public schools. Alabama, Maryland, and North Carolina do not require a specific number of days or hours of instruction that a student should receive, but instead ask that it takes place on a regular basis during the school year.

Who Homeschools and Why?

Although parents may choose to homeschool for a variety of reasons, research suggests they generally fall in one of two main camps. A seminal 1991 study of homeschooling parents in the Southeast drew the distinction between the "ideologues" and the "pedagogues" (Van Galen, 1991). These categories represent a hallmark for distinguishing between two major motivating factors for homeschooling parents. Ideologues are parents who object to what is taught in schools and prefer to teach life lessons through the family. They are likely to hold conservative political and social beliefs and follow Christian fundamentalism (Rothermel, 2003). Families holding similar values will commonly network, which can lead to a more radicalized set of shared interests, "coming to believe they are following God's will by accepting an imposed responsibility for their children" (Rothermel, 2003, 77). In contrast, pedagogues choose homeschooling more for educational reasons. They are dissatisfied with formal school options and seek to broaden their child's interest in learning through an alternative approach. Other scholars have recast the *ideologue-pedagogue* typology as "heaven based" and "earth based" to underscore the distinction between religious and secular homeschooling groups (Stevens, 2001).

A Growing Industry

There is no single model of homeschooling, and students' experiences differ widely depending on the homeschooling approach, as well as the laws that govern education where they live. Conventional notions of homeschooling (e.g., the parent teaching their child at the kitchen table) have given way to several new variants. The internet has fundamentally changed the homeschooling landscape. Homeschooling curricula, lesson plans, and other learning materials are readily accessible for download and purchase online for those who can afford them. Parent networks have organized online to share curricular resources, teaching responsibilities, and paid instructors. Increasing numbers of homeschoolers are enrolling part time in state online education programs or virtual charter schools (Huerta, Gonzalez, and d'Entremont, 2006). Where permissible by state and local policies, homeschooled students may also enroll in courses at their neighborhood-assigned public school (see, e.g., Wixom, 2015). Occasionally, a request will be received by a public school from homeschooling parents for their child to participate in a school-sponsored extra-curricular activity, such as math club, chorus, or lacrosse.

Despite being a relatively quiet, behind-the-scenes practice, homeschooling is a polarizing public issue. A number of organizations have spoken out against homeschooling, claiming that it harms the academic and social development of children. Others are concerned that it erodes support for public schooling and ignores the need to educate future American citizens on the basic pillars and institutions of democracy. In contrast, homeschooling advocates such as the Home School Legal Defense Association and the Christian Home Educators Association of California argue that homeschooling is a parent's right. They also assert that homeschooling is just as successful in educating children as traditional public schooling. Advocates commonly reference research reports that suggest homeschooling students do better academically, in college, and even enjoy life better (Lubienski, Puckett, and Brewer, 2013). But are these claims warranted by the empirical evidence?

Unfounded Claims

Much of the research on homeschooling has been pursued over the last three decades. Unfortunately, most of it has been based on weak designs and methods that are ill-suited to address cause and effect. Furthermore, some of the research has been sponsored by homeschooling organizations or produced by researchers affiliated with those organizations, leading to concerns over conflicts of interest and potential bias (Lubienski, Puckett, and Brewer, 2013). One early example was the widely publicized study on homeschooling done in 1999 by academic researcher Lawrence Rudner. The study was sponsored by the Home School Legal Defense Association, an advocacy group that hired professor Rudner as an independent researcher. It was one of the first major studies of homeschooling in the United States.

Rudner examined an impressively large number of students—20,000 children—and used as its outcome measure the ubiquitous Iowa Test of Basic Skills and the Tests of Achievement and Proficiency. The analysis revealed that the average homeschooled children scored better than 70 to 80 percent of public school students and roughly a full grade level higher on average. Homeschooling advocates pointed to this result as proof that homeschooling worked, and worked better than traditional public schools.

However, significant criticisms have been leveled against the study's design limitations and sampling choices. The study lacked an experimental design—that is, there was no random assignment of students to treatment (homeschool) and control (traditional public school) groups—and thus was ill-suited to make causal claims. Moreover, the homeschooling sample did not accurately represent the larger population of homeschoolers. Only about half the parents in the homeschooling sample responded to the survey, and those who did were disproportionally represented by parents of higher scoring test takers. Furthermore, this same group of respondents had significantly higher median incomes and had completed more education, on average, than the typical U.S. family. Detractors claim that the advantages reflected by these family characteristics also contributed to the higher test scores for the homeschoolers. Finally, Rudner (1999) himself cautioned that the study "was not a controlled experiment" [and that it] "does not demonstrate that home schooling is superior to public or private schools" (Willard and Oplinger, 2004).

Nonetheless, the high-profile report gained considerable traction and began to shape a promising narrative, albeit a misleading one, on the merits of homeschooling. "The biggest annoyance," Rudner later said, "was a large number of reporters that had read previous articles and never went to the original source and read the caveats" (Willard and Oplinger, 2004). Another homeschooling researcher bemoaned that Rudner's study was "perhaps the most misrepresented research in the homeschooling universe" (Kunzman, 2009b, 97).

In another example, a 2010 study sponsored by the Home School Legal Defense Association and conducted by the National Home Education Research Institute reported that homeschoolers performed better than their public and private school peers, scoring "34–39 percentile points higher than the norm on standardized achievement tests" (Ray, 2009, 3). However, like many other studies on homeschooling, it relied on descriptive methods, which cannot yield valid causal inferences about the effectiveness of homeschooling. The study also included a large sample (11,739) of homeschool students and no comparison group participants. Students were included in the sample if parents indicated on a survey that they were "taught at home within the past twelve months by his/her parent for at least 51 percent of the time" (4). The author worked through testing companies to obtain test score data and linked scores to survey data from parents who completed them. Response rates were estimated to be 11 percent from the set of small testing companies and 19 percent from the four largest test companies. Because the tests were different from one another, a standard score was created to represent how far above or below from the average score each student scored. The standard scores were then averaged across all homeschooling students by grade level and subject tested. Each of these average scores was then compared to the national norm score on the tests, which, by definition is the 50th percentile. Although the report aptly cautions that readers "should be careful about assigning causation" (29), it nevertheless concludes:

> One could say, as Rudner (1999) wrote: "This study simply shows that those parents choosing to make a commitment to home schooling are able to provide a very successful academic environment." On the other hand, it may be that something about the typical nature and practice of home-based education causes higher academic achievement, on average, than does institutional state-run schooling (Ray, 1997; 2000, 91–100; 2005). (29)

In the absence of randomized assignment to treatment and control groups, causal inferences are virtually baseless. Of course, random assignment of students to homeschooling and public school conditions is not feasible; parents make these choices. Families who choose to and are able to homeschool are undoubtedly qualitatively different than parents who do not homeschool. In the homeschooling sample in Ray's (2010) study, nearly 98 percent of the parents were married. The family median income of the sample was at the nationwide median for married couples with one or more children under 18 ($75,000–79,000); only 4.8 percent of families had an income of $29,999 or less. Nearly 92 percent of the homeschooled students in the study were White/not-Hispanic. The family characteristics of this homeschooling sample do not mimic those of the average public school family and these differences make it impossible to make any direct comparison between the two groups. As other scholars have noted, "Outcomes such as increased achievement and engagement may simply be a reflection of the advantages that homeschooling families typically bring to their children—advantages that would make it likely that these students would succeed academically and in life even if they were educated in schools" (Lubienski, Puckett, and Brewer, 2013, 384).

COVID and Homeschooling

In 2020, the world turned upside down. A deadly virus that originated in China in late 2019 swept the world in a matter of months. More than

180 nations saw their economies shut down temporarily or worse. In March and April of 2020, nearly every governor in the United States ordered K–12 public schools to close, almost all through the remainder of the academic year. Almost overnight, home-based education became a reality to tens of millions of U.S. families.

Some 15,000 school districts reacted by searching for ways to continue the nation's children's education by any means possible. Most sought to deliver assignments, if not instruction, via the internet to students confined to their homes. The emergency exposed fault lines in the landscape of public schooling. Many families had no access to the internet. Some had no computers. In New York City, a group of children huddled in a parking lot attempting to connect to the Wi-Fi of a neighboring business. Schools made special efforts to identify children without internet access, and mail them assignments on paper. Equity issues, apparent even in traditional instruction in brick-and-mortar schools, became glaringly obvious when students were confined to their homes.

The pandemic exposed surprising reactions of the general public to public education. Parents, charged with facilitating their children's work on assignments, suddenly discovered a new respect for the profession of teaching. The stress felt by carrying this new responsibility was sometimes relieved by sharing experiences through social media or by humor. Facebook users expressed their admiration for the job that teachers were doing daily: "I've . . . never been more appreciative of our country's teachers. This really puts into perspective the amazing work you all do" (Berkus, 2020). One parent, Shonda Rhimes, tweeted: "Been homeschooling a 6-year-old and 8-year-old for one hour and 11 minutes. Teachers deserve to make a billion dollars a year. Or a week." And others joked about their own ineptitude in assuming the role of homeschooling teacher: "If you see my kids locked outside the house mind your own business, we are having a fire drill" (Denly, 2020).

FURTHER READING

Berkus, N. (@NateBerkus). I've also never been more appreciative of our country's teachers. This really puts into perspective the amazing work you all do. March 20, 2020, 3:05 pm. https://twitter.com/NateBerkus/status/1245064791548235776?s=20

Denly, J. (@joed1986). If you see my kids locked outside the house mind your own business, we are having a fire drill. March 23, 2020, 4:58 am. https://twitter.com/joed1986/status/1242012774517157889?s=20

Huerta, L. A., Gonzalez, M., and d'Entremont, C. 2006. "Cyber and home school charter schools: Adopting policy to new forms of public schooling." *Peabody Journal of Education, 81*(1), 103.

Isenberg, E. 2007. "What have we learned about homeschooling?" *Peabody Journal of Education*, 82, 327–409.

Kunzman, R. 2009a. "Understanding homeschooling: A better approach to regularization." *Theory and Research in Education*, 7, 311–330.

Kunzman, R. 2009b. *Write these laws on your children: Inside the world of conservative Christian homeschooling.* Boston, Beacon Press.

Kunzman, R., and Gaither, M. 2013. "Homeschooling: A comprehensive survey of the research." *Other Education*, 2(1), 4–59.

Lubienski, C., Puckett, T., and Brewer, T. J. 2013. "Does homeschooling 'work'? A critique of the empirical claims and agenda of advocacy organizations." *Peabody Journal of Education*, 88(3), 378–392.

Ray, B. D. 1997. *Strengths of their own—Home schoolers across America: Academic achievement, family characteristics, and longitudinal traits.* Salem, OR: National Home Education Research Institute.

Ray, B. D. 2000. "Home schooling: The ameliorator of negative influences on learning?" *Peabody Journal of Education*, 75(1 & 2), 71–106.

Ray, B. D. 2005. "A homeschool research story." In Bruce S. Cooper (Ed.), *Home schooling in full view: A reader,* 1–19. Greenwich, CT: Information Age Publishing.

Ray, B. D. 2009. *Homeschool progress report 2009: Academic achievement and demographics.* Purcellville, VA: Home School Legal Defense Association. Retrieved from http://www.hslda.org/docs/study/ray2009/default.asp

Ray, B. D. 2010. "Academic achievement and demographic traits of homeschool students: A nationwide study." *Academic Leadership: The Online Journal*, 8(1), 1–31. https://scholars.fhsu.edu/alj/vol8/iss1/7

Rhimes, S. (@shondarhimes). Been homeschooling a 6-year old and 8-year old for one hour and 11 minutes. Teachers deserve. March 16, 2020, 1:12 pm. https://twitter.com/shondarhimes/status/1239600550515101696?s=20

Rothermel, P. 2003. "Can we classify motives for home education?" *Evaluation and Research in Education*, 17(2–3), 74–89.

Rudner, L. 1999. "Achievement and demographics of home school students: 1998." *Education Policy Analysis Archives*, 7, 8. https://doi.org/10.14507/epaa.v7n8.1999

Stevens, M. L. 2001. *Kingdom of children: Culture and controversy in the homeschooling movement.* Princeton, NJ: Princeton University Press.

U.S. Department of Education. 2016. Parent Survey of the National Household Education Surveys Program, 1999 (NHES). *Parent and Family Involvement in Education Survey of the NHES, 2003, 2007, 2012, and 2016.* National Center for Education Statistics.

Van Galen, J. 1991. *Home schooling: Political, historical, and pedagogical perspectives.* Norwood, NJ: Ablex Publishers.

Welner, K. 2002. *Exploring the democratic tensions within parents' decisions to homeschool.* New York: National Center for the Study of Privatization in Education, Columbia University.

Willard, D. J., and Oplinger, D. 2004. "Claims of academic success rely on anecdotes, flawed data analysis." *Akron Beacon Journal.* November 15, 2004.

Wixom, M. A. 2015. "State homeschool policies: A patchwork of provisions. 50-state reviews." *Education Commission of the States.*

Q8. DO SCHOOL VOUCHERS PRODUCE BETTER STUDENT OUTCOMES?

Answer: Several studies have reported small positive effects of school vouchers on student test scores, and there is some recent evidence of positive effects on high school graduation and college enrollment rates. But there are also studies that find no effects and even negative effects on student achievement, as well as high rates of student attrition from such programs.

The Facts: Vouchers are certificates that can be exchanged for goods and services. School vouchers are issued by funding agencies—in this case, states—that can be redeemed for tuition at private or religious schools. The voucher amount may not cover the full tuition of the private or religious school; it depends on the voucher dollar figure and of course depends on school tuition, which varies widely across the private sector. Private and religious schools are under no obligation to admit students under publicly funded voucher programs.

In 1990, the Wisconsin state legislature approved the first major school voucher program, designed for low-income families in Milwaukee. A decade later, Florida launched the McKay Scholarships Program for Students with Disabilities. In 2004, Washington, DC, enacted the first federally funded voucher program, giving priority to students from low-performing public schools. Other cities and states have also initiated voucher programs, including Utah, Indiana, and Louisiana as well as Cleveland and Dayton, Ohio. Indiana's was the first statewide voucher plan targeting students from low-income families.

As of June 2017, according to a policy analysis by the Education Commission of the States, there were 25 voucher programs operating in 14 states and DC (Wixom, 2017). Most voucher programs in the United States limit participation to certain student subgroups, such as low-income families, military families, or students with disabilities. In Gallup surveys of samples of American adults in 2002 and 2004, only 29 percent and 22 percent favored the use of school vouchers (https://news.gallup.com/poll/1612/education.aspx). Because of a lack of widespread public support for voucher programs, they frequently operate under assumed names: Arizona has the Empowerment Scholarships; several states have enacted education savings accounts; and scholarship tax credit accounts are still a third label used for school vouchers flying under the radar. Education policy expert Kevin Welner viewed these programs as vouchers by another name and called them "neovouchers" in a 2017 article in *The Conversation* (Welner, 2017). Although these programs are initially targeted on special subgroups of children (e.g., children of active military families, on reservations, with disabilities), the initial authorizing legislation is frequently followed by the introduction of bills to expand the program scope.

The National Center for Education Statistics reported that in 2017, there were 11 school voucher programs in 9 states for students with a disability, including 3 separate programs in Minnesota (see https://nces.ed.gov/programs/statereform/tab4_7.asp). According to estimates by Kevin Welner, approximately 3.3 percent of the nation's private schools had enrolled voucher recipients in 2017 (Welner, 2017). Furthermore, the majority of participating private schools are religiously affiliated; for instance, 97 percent of Ohio's vouchers went to religious schools.

Wisconsin's Voucher Programs

Today, the state of Wisconsin oversees school voucher programs in the cities of Milwaukee and Racine, as well as statewide under the Wisconsin Parental Choice Program (https://dpi.wi.gov/sms/choice-programs). In 2019–2020, the Milwaukee program enrolled 28,978 voucher participants in 120 private schools. Racine enrolled 3,650 students in 27 different schools. Student eligibility is based on family income and residency in the state. As is the case with most U.S. voucher plans, participation is restricted to low-income families. The amount of payments varies across program. For instance, the 2020–2021 voucher payment for students in the Choice program is $8,300 for students in grades K–8, and $8,946 for students in high school. Private schools receiving vouchers are not allowed to charge additional tuition to K–8 students; however, they may charge tuition in addition to the state voucher if the student is in a high school and their family income is greater than 220 percent of the federal poverty level (e.g., for a family of two, the 2020–2021 threshold is $37,202). Choice private schools may also charge students, irrespective of family income, certain fees including for school uniforms, transportation, social and extracurricular activities, musical instruments, and meals provided at the school.

With respect to serving students with disabilities, the Private School Choice Programs *Frequently Asked Questions for Parents*-2021–22 School Year website indicates that choice private schools "may not discriminate against a student with special educational needs during the admissions process for the Choice program" and that they are "required to offer only those services to assist students with special needs that it can provide with minor adjustments" (Wisconsin Department of Public Instruction, n.d., 13). Few studies exist of how private schools handle this latter requirement—for example, whether they rely on it to limit provision of services or whether they go beyond the minimal expectation expressed by the policy.

Do Vouchers Produce Better Outcomes?

Under the typical school voucher program, students who are enrolled in or would otherwise be assigned to a public school may apply to receive a voucher to attend a private school. When applications exceed the number of spots or vouchers available, voucher recipients are sometimes chosen by random lottery. School voucher studies that have been able to take advantage of these randomized student admissions provide the most robust opportunities to draw causal conclusions about the effects of using a publicly funded voucher to attend a private school. The lottery designs are not as clean as they may sound. For instance, not all lottery winners end up using the voucher. Further, applicants who are denied a voucher may not end up attending a traditional public school, thereby skewing the control group. Similarly problematic is the case where a voucher student exits the private school sometime after enrolling. Despite these challenges, researchers have strategies at their disposal to help account for them.

A 2002 evaluation of voucher programs in three cities—New York City, Washington, DC, and Dayton, Ohio—reported positive effects of vouchers on the test scores of African American students, but not for any other ethnic group (Howell et al., 2002). Another 2004 study reanalyzed data from the New York City voucher program, the largest private school voucher experiment at the time (Krueger and Zhu, 2004). The researchers' analysis reaffirmed a voucher benefit, but one of less magnitude than previously reported after more accurately coding ethnicity and readmitting students to the sample who did not have a pretest score.

Early evaluations of Milwaukee's school voucher program (Milwaukee Parental Choice Program), which was enacted in 1990, took advantage of overages in applications and ensuing lotteries to conduct experiments. But in 1994, changes in income eligibility and the inclusion of Catholic schools limited the need for lotteries. A five-year study of the effect of Milwaukee vouchers following its expansion in the mid-1990s revealed few consistent effects on tests scores (Witte et al., 2012). Two other studies done in 2011 and 2013 found positive test score effects based on years of schooling; the more years in a voucher-supported private school, the higher the student test score gains (Witte et al., 2011; Cowen et al., 2013). There were some subtle differences in the two studies. For example, the 2013 study reported modest benefits to reading but none to math achievement (Cowen et al., 2013). In a 2017 review of the research on vouchers, researchers cautioned that the positive effects could not be validated by other statistical techniques, and speculated whether 2002 federal legislation requiring reporting of high-stakes tests results was the true cause of test score gains (Epple, Romano, and Urquiola, 2017).

Although most of the research on school vouchers examines effects on standardized tests, some studies have looked at the potential effects on education attainment. Using a nonexperimental statistical matching technique, a 2013 analysis found a positive relationship between exposure to the Milwaukee voucher program and high school graduation rates and college enrollment and persistence in a four-year college (Cowen et al., 2013). Another 2015 study tracked New York School Choice Scholarships Foundation voucher students who were participants in the late 1990s in the program as elementary students (Chingos and Peterson, 2015). Researchers were able to obtain college enrollment information for nearly all of the original approximately 2,700 students. They found "no significant impacts of the voucher offer on college enrollment or degree attainment" but did report a significant effect for racial/ethnic minorities. However, these differential effects were relatively modest. The researchers found that 46 percent of students who did not take advantage of a voucher entered college, and 50 percent of voucher users did (Chingos and Peterson, 2015).

A 2013 evaluation of the Washington, DC, Opportunity Scholarship Program took advantage of an experimental design (Wolf et al., 2013). The initial sample was roughly 2,300 students, 60 percent of whom were offered a voucher while the remainder served as the control group. Of those students offered a voucher, 77 percent used it to attend a private school. In terms of achievement benefits, the authors reported "a marginally statistically significant positive overall impact of the program on reading achievement after at least four years" [and that] "[n]o significant impacts were observed in math" (261). In terms of education attainment, the students receiving a voucher offer were more likely to graduate from high school by 12 percentage points (82 percent versus 70 percent). Those who actually used the voucher were 21 percentage points more likely to graduate. A separate experimental evaluation of the DC voucher program conducted in 2017 found that after one year it had "a statistically significant negative impact on the mathematics achievement of students offered or using a scholarship" (Dynarski et al., 2017, xiii).

A 2018 random assignment experiment of the first year of the Louisiana Scholarship Program (LSP) found that participation substantially reduced academic achievement in math, reading, science, and social studies (Abdulkadiroğlu, Pathak, and Walters, 2018). In math, the effect was particularly large, with enrollment in a voucher-supported private school increasing the chances of a failing math score by 50 percent. The authors note the negative effects may be due to the eligible pool of private schools, which charged below-average tuition and appeared to be of lower quality among all privates. A 2017 follow-up randomized study of the LSP, but over a two-year span, found a negative effect of enrollment in a voucher-supported private school on math and no effect on reading (Mills and Wolf, 2017).

Indiana enacted the first statewide voucher program in 2011, opening it up to 3,911 low-income (against a cap of 7,500) students attending a public school. Indiana soon expanded eligibility requirements, removing student caps on qualifying students, and including students with special needs and those located in attendance zones of state graded "F" or failing schools. With the additional pathways, participation rose to 36,290 students and 329 schools in 2018–2019 (Indiana Department of Education, 2019). Notably, in 2018–2019, 58.2 percent of all participating voucher students had no record of attending an Indiana Public School. This figure increased by roughly 2 percent each of the prior three years, much of it likely attributable to returning voucher students (Indiana Department of Education, 2019, 15).

A 2019 longitudinal study of the Indiana voucher program analyzed math and English language arts scores on a state exam administered to both public and private school students (Austin, Waddington, and Berends, 2019). They found "significant achievement losses for students who switch from a public to a private school with a voucher" (20). The decrease in math achievement for Indiana voucher students who switched from a public to a private school was validated by two 2018 studies that used alternative estimation techniques (Berends and Waddington, 2018; Waddington and Berends, 2018). The negative results are also consistent with nonexperimental studies done in 2016 on voucher programs in Ohio (Figlio and Karbownik, 2016) and 2017 and 2018 studies of Louisiana's program (Abdulkadiroğlu, Pathak, and Walters, 2018; Mills and Wolf, 2017).

What to Make of the Research Evidence?

Two comprehensive reviews of the research on school vouchers clarify the question of their impact. The first, published in 2017, focused on econometric studies of voucher programs:

> Overall, the evidence on the U.S. points to non-existent or not very robust effects of vouchers on test scores, except perhaps for Black students. In contrast, more robust evidence has accumulated regarding positive impacts on graduation probabilities, again particularly for Black students. (Epple, Romano, and Urquiola, 2017, 33)

The second research synthesis was also done in 2017 (Carnoy, 2017). The author of that study found an overall lack of compelling evidence of voucher program effects on student outcomes. His review describes studies that show some small positive effects, some negative effects, findings that are mixed or peculiar (e.g., African Americans being the only racial group to benefit in otherwise racially and ethnically diverse voucher settings), and studies that suffer from high student attrition rates. The researcher concluded:

> In the few cases in which test scores increased, other factors, namely increased public accountability, not private school competition, seem to be more likely drivers. And high rates of attrition from private schools among voucher users in several studies raises concerns. The second largest and longest-standing U.S. voucher program, in Milwaukee, offers no solid evidence of student gains in either private or public schools. (1)

And further:

> In the only area in which there is evidence of small improvements in voucher schools—in high school graduation and college enrollment rates—there are no data to show whether the gains are the result of schools shedding lower-performing students or engaging in positive practices. Also, high school graduation rates have risen sharply in public schools across the board in the last 10 years, with those increases much larger than the small effect estimated on graduation rates from attending a voucher school. (1)

Virtually none of the studies on voucher effects explore what underlies the treatment—what actually happens to students beyond the offer to use or the actual use of a voucher to attend a private school. Where positive effects on test scores or education attainment are detected, what is it that the schools were doing that presumably caused them? While experimental studies provide the most rigorous test of program effects, they "deliver a 'reduced form' answer that does not fully reveal what *mechanisms* [italics in the original] account for the effects—a further reason for why extrapolation is difficult" (Epple, Romano, and Urquiola, 2017, 31).

In addition, highly contentious topics like voucher programs heighten the stakes for both proponents and opponents, and no evaluator is devoid of bias or ideological leanings. This reality should be kept in mind when reading media accounts and reports of research concerning school vouchers.

A final note on the relevance of education research may be in order here. The consumer of such research often feels frustrated by the recitation of mixed results. For example, "Jones (2000) found that phonics works great; but Garcia (2001) found that phonics was a total failure." Education research is at a very early stage. No science of groups of adults and children in schools exists, or perhaps, ever will. Occasionally a strain of research will hit on a useful and important generalization. Punishing children who perform poorly on tests, as was done more than 100 years ago, has negative effects everywhere, all the time. Researchers B. F. Skinner and Edward Thorndike proved as much, long ago. But researching a phenomenon as complicated as school voucher systems or court-ordered integration is a different matter.

FURTHER READING

Abdulkadiroğlu, A., Pathak, P. A., and Walters, C. R. 2018. "Free to choose: Can school choice reduce student achievement?" *American Economic Journal: Applied Economics*, 10(1), 175–206.

Austin, M., Waddington, R. J., and Berends, M. 2019. "Voucher pathways and student achievement in Indiana's Choice Scholarship Program." *RSF: The Russell Sage Foundation Journal of the Social Sciences*, 5(3), 20–40.

Belfield, C., and Levin, H. M. 2005. "Vouchers and public policy: When ideology trumps evidence." *American Journal of Education*, 111(4), 548–567.

Berends, M., and Waddington, R. J. 2018. "School choice in Indianapolis: Effects of charter, magnet, private, and traditional public schools." *Education Finance and Policy*, 13(2), 227–255.

Carnoy, M. 2017. *School vouchers are not a proven strategy for improving student achievement*. Economic Policy Institute. Retrieved from https://

www.epi.org/publication/school-vouchers-are-not-a-proven-strategy-for-improving-student-achievement/

Chingos, M. M., and Peterson, P. E. 2015. "Experimentally estimated impacts of school vouchers on college enrollment and degree attainment." *Journal of Public Economics, 122,* 1–12.

Cobb, C. D., and Irizarry, J. 2020. "Private interests and the common good: Conflicting priorities in a school choice world." In R. Papa (Ed.), *Handbook on promoting social justice in education.* Basel, Switzerland. Springer International Publishing AG.

Cowen, J. M., et al. 2013. "School vouchers and student attainment: Evidence from a state-mandated study of Milwaukee's parental choice program." *Policy Studies Journal, 41*(1), 147–168.

Dynarski, M. 2016. "On negative effects of vouchers." *Brookings Institution. Evidence Speaks Reports, 1,* 18.

Dynarski, M., Rui, N., Webber, A., and Gutmann, B. 2017. *Evaluation of the DC Opportunity Scholarship Program: Impacts after one year (NCEE 2017-4022).* Washington, DC: National Center for Education Evaluation and Regional Assistance, Institute of Education Sciences, U.S. Department of Education.

Epple, D., Romano, R. E., and Urquiola, M. 2017. "School vouchers: A survey of the economics literature." *Journal of Economic Literature, 55*(2), 441–92.

Figlio, D., and Karbownik, K. 2016. *Evaluation of Ohio's EdChoice Scholarship Program: Selection, competition, and performance effects.* Columbus, OH: Thomas B. Fordham Institute.

Howell, W. G., Wolf, P. J., Campbell, D. E., and Peterson, P. E. 2002. "School vouchers and academic performance: Results from three randomized field trials." *Journal of Policy Analysis and Management, 21,* 191–217.

Indiana Department of Education. 2019. *Choice Scholarship Program Annual Report: Participation and payment data.* Indiana Department of Education, Office of School Finance. Retrieved from https://www.doe.in.gov/sites/default/files/choice/2018-2019-choice-scholarship-program-report-final-040219.pdf

Krueger, A. B., and Zhu, P. 2004. "Another look at the New York City school voucher experiment." *American Behavioral Scientist, 47*(5), 658–698.

Mills, J. N., and Wolf, P. J. 2017. "Vouchers in the bayou: The effects of the Louisiana Scholarship Program on student achievement after 2 years." *Educational Evaluation and Policy Analysis, 39*(3), 464–484.

Waddington, R. J., and Berends, M. 2018. "Impact of the Indiana Choice Scholarship Program: Achievement effects for students in upper elementary and middle school." *Journal of Policy Analysis and Management*, 37(4), 783–808.

Welner, K. 2017. "Tax credits, school choice and 'neovouchers': What you need to know." *The Conversation*. April 14, 2017. Retrieved from theconversation.com/tax-credits-school-choice-and-neovouchers-what-you-need-to-know-74808

Wisconsin Department of Public Instruction. n.d. *Private school choice programs "Frequently Asked Questions for Parents-2021–22 School Year."* Retrieved from https://dpi.wi.gov/sites/default/files/imce/parental-education-options/Choice/Student_Application_Webpage/PSCP_FAQ_2021-22.pdf

Witte, J. F., et al. 2012. *MPCP longitudinal educational growth study fifth year report*. School Choice Demonstration Project, 77. Fayetteville, AR: University of Arkansas.

Witte, J. F., Cowen, J. M., Fleming, D. J., and Wolf, P. J. 2011. *Student attainment and the Milwaukee Parental Choice Program*. School Choice Demonstration Project, Report 29. Fayetteville, AR: University of Arkansas.

Wixom, M. A. 2017. "Policy analysis: Voucher programs." *Education Commission of the States*. June 2017. Retrieved from https://files.eric.ed.gov/fulltext/ED574527.pdf

Wolf, P. J., et al. 2013. "School vouchers and student outcomes: Experimental evidence from Washington, DC." *Journal of Policy Analysis and Management*, 32(2), 246–270.

Q9. DO EDUCATION TAX CREDITS AND EDUCATION SAVINGS ACCOUNTS DIVERT MONEY FROM PUBLIC TO PRIVATE SCHOOLS?

Answer: Several states permit individuals and corporations to make donations up to a certain amount to designated nonprofit organizations, which then repackage and distribute the funds as private school vouchers. Typically, donors receive a state tax credit in the amount equal to the charitable contribution. These are called education tax credits. A tax credit is a dollar-for-dollar reduction of a person's state income tax liability, unlike a deduction that only reduces the tax burden by a percentage. Education savings accounts (ESAs) operate similarly to flexible health or childcare spending accounts where parents can draw on state funds to pay for private school tuition and other related expenses. States with ESAs deposit public funds annually into parents' accounts, so long as their child leaves a public school. Both education tax credits and ESAs divert taxpayer money intended for public schools to support private schools.

The Facts: Due to a lack of public support for school vouchers, voucher proponents have had to find alternative ways to use public taxpayer money for private schools. Those have come in the form of what education policy scholar Kevin Welner referred to as neovouchers (Welner, 2008). There are two types of neovouchers: education tax credits and ESAs.

Education Tax Credits

Arizona was the first state to adopt a tuition tax credit policy in 1997. The Arizona Original Individual Tax Credit Scholarship Program allows Arizona taxpayers to donate to a private, nonprofit-certified School Tuition Organization (STO), which serves as fiscal steward. The school tuition organization is then authorized to grant funds selectively to parents to help offset private or parochial school tuition. In effect, Arizona's Original Individual Income Tax Credit program is a backdoor pathway to school vouchers. The taxpayer who made the donation receives a commensurate tax credit from the state. In the first year of its operation, the maximum donation in Arizona was $500. For the 2020 tax year, taxpayers may claim a dollar-for-dollar tax credit of up to $590 filing as single or married filing separate filers and $1,179 for married filing joint filers. In 2012, Arizona adopted a second, "switcher" individual tax credit scholarship program. Arizona taxpayers who first maximize their contributions to the Original Individual Income Tax Credit ($569 individual, $1,138 joint in tax year 2019) may claim the switcher credit. "Switcher" refers to public school students switching to private schools. Arizona offers a separate tax credit program for corporations, which can donate on behalf of low-income families to attend private and parochial schools.

The Arizona tuition tax credit program has not escaped criticism. From its inception, a Scholarship Tuition Organization has been owned by the former president of the state senate, Steve Yarborough (Republican). As is the case with most other state tuition tax credit plans, STOs in Arizona are allowed to keep 10 percent of the donations to cover administrative costs. According to a 2013–2014 IRS filing, Yarbrough's Arizona Christian School Tuition Organization has diverted $116 million from the state treasury through individual tax-credit donations since 1998 (Roberts, 2015). Doing the math on 10 percent overhead is simple. In 2013–2014 alone, the Arizona Christian School Tuition Organization took in about $17 million in tax-credit donations—amounting to $1.7 million in overhead. IRS filings indicate that Yarborough paid himself nearly $146,000 in compensation. As with other market reforms of public education, tuition tax credit programs are the object of little oversight by state government.

STOs in general are strange creations of state governments. STOs are private corporations empowered by state governments to distribute private school tuition vouchers to individuals of their choice. State statutes do set some guidelines on how the money can be allocated. For instance, one common rule is money donated by a family is not to be returned to that family to pay for part of their private school tuition. Another basic rule is STOs shall not limit the availability of scholarships to students of one school. Unfortunately, there is no research that looks into STO practices because most of STOs operate with little transparency to the public. In Arizona, for example, the state "discloses only how many scholarships are allocated, not how many students participate in this program. Many students receive multiple scholarships and often from more than one non-profit STO" (Rau, 2017).

Critics of STOs contend that the money they bring in, combined with inadequate public and regulatory oversight, has resulted in clear corruption. A 2014 expose by *NC Policy Watch*, a project of the North Carolina Justice Center, reported fraud by some people taking advantage of the system (Wagner, 2014). A 2015 report found that Arizona STOs diverted $140 million from the state treasury to support the tuition tax credits program (Roberts, 2015). A 2016 audit of one STO, the Arizona Private Education Scholarship Fund, Inc., showed donations received in the amount of $6,047,769 and scholarships awarded were $4,758,072. Total costs for administering the program, including fundraising, was $526,217 and the STO carried forward $763,480. The numbers illustrate that a large portion of the donations that year was not turned into scholarships, at least for that year. Over 21 percent of donations went to either administrative expenses (8.7 percent) or was saved for future use (12.6 percent).

Critics of the Arizona tuition tax credit program charged that the program was playing fast and loose with the establishment clause of the U.S. Constitution. The establishment clause prohibits the government from establishing an official religion, as well as from taking any action that favors one religion over another. The Arizona Constitution echoes the U.S. establishment clause: "no public money . . . shall be applied to any religious worship, exercise, or instruction or to the support of any religious establishment." The state's program was challenged in the case known as *Kotterman v. Killian* (1999). The state Supreme Court ruled against the challenge in a 3–2 vote, arguing that since the money was sent from the taxpayer directly to the Scholarship Tuition Organization, it never was the state government's money. The decision was viewed as a distortion of reality by liberal scholars (Welner, 2000). The Arizona Supreme Court decision paved the way for the creation of other tuition tax credit programs throughout the nation.

According to a 2017 policy report published by the National Education Policy Center, 21 tuition tax credit programs operated in 17 states (Huerta and Koutsavlis, 2017). By definition, tuition tax credits divert monies intended for public education to private and faith-based schools. Voucher proponents argue that private schools run more efficiently and that tuition tax credits also end up being a net savings to states (e.g., Lueken, 2016). They make the case that since school funding is tied to public school enrollment, when public school students leave for private schools by way of a voucher, the state can keep the funds originally allocated to those students—a purported savings. Skeptics find the calculus as faulty and misleading, arguing that public schools end up losing more than they "gain" by not having to educate those students. For one thing, there are certain fixed costs such as keeping the lights on and maintaining buildings. For another, the departure of a few students from a classroom doesn't mean the school can eliminate the teacher and their salary—there are still students to be educated. Studies on the financial effect of charter schools taking away students from district public schools show that districts cannot reduce costs to keep up with revenue losses they experience without reducing services to the remaining public school students (Bifulco and Reback, 2014). Skeptics also assert that tuition tax credits provide particular advantages to students and families that are already well-off (Welner, 2008). In 2011, the National Education Policy Center issued guidance for policy makers and researchers to assess the costs or savings from tax credit voucher policies, and urged caution in assessing the claims of legislators who fail to provide defensible evidence in support of their arguments (Welner, 2011).

In 2015, the Center for Tax and Budget Accountability, a self-described bipartisan, nonprofit research, and advocacy thinktank, reviewed the research on school vouchers and financial data from Indiana's school choice legislation. Indiana's comprehensive school choice program was introduced in 2013 through three major bills, which included school vouchers, state income tax deductions, and tuition tax credits. The Center's review of the evidence showed no indications that the voucher programs saved money. In the 2014–2015 school year alone, Indiana spent $115 million of public dollars on school vouchers—funds that were otherwise destined to support the state's public schools. Their analysis of Indiana expenditures further indicated that the School Expenditure Deduction (state tax deduction) cost Indiana municipalities $1.4 million annually in local tax revenue (Center for Tax and Budget Accountability, 2015).

Republican leaders have expressed interest in launching a federal voucher plan, including tuition tax credits. Such ideas have shown up in legislative White House budget proposals as "Education Freedom Scholarships," although none have made it beyond the proposal stage.

Education Savings Accounts

Education savings accounts (ESAs) are a relatively new form of neovoucher. ESAs are "private savings accounts funded by a deposit from the state government and managed by a parent" (Wixom, 2017). The accounts are similar to flexible spending plans that are available for medical and childcare expenditures. Qualifying expenses vary by state, but generally parents are allowed to use their ESA to pay for private school tuition, tutoring, online courses, textbooks, homeschool curriculum materials, and sometimes transportation. The maximum annual deposit also varies by state but usually falls near the state average public per pupil expenditure. A basic condition of participation is that parents cannot enroll their child in a public school. Most states also limit eligibility to certain subgroups, such as students with disabilities or those attending low performing schools. As of 2021, ESAs operated in the six states of Arizona, Florida, Mississippi, North Carolina, Tennessee, and West Virginia.

FURTHER READING

Bifulco, R., and Reback, R. 2014. "Fiscal impacts of charter schools: Lessons from New York." *Education Finance and Policy,* 9(1), 86–107.

Budget of the U.S. Government, Office of Management and Budget. 2020. *A Budget for America's future.*

Center for Tax and Budget Accountability. 2015. *Analysis of Indiana School Choice Scholarship Program.* Chicago, IL: Center for Tax and Budget Accountability.

GovTrack.us. 2020. *S. 634—116th Congress: Education Freedom Scholarships and Opportunity Act.* Retrieved from https://www.govtrack.us/congress/bills/116/s634

Huerta, L. A., and d'Entremont, C. 2007. "Education tax credits in a post-Zelman era: Legal, political and policy alternative to vouchers?" *Educational Policy,* 21(1), 73–109.

Huerta, L. A., and Koutsavlis, S. 2017. "Review of 'The tax-credit scholarship audit: Do publicly funded private school choice programs save money?'" Boulder, CO: National Education Policy Center. Retrieved from http://nepc.colorado.edu/thinktank/review-tax-credits

Lueken, M. F. 2016. "The tax-credit scholarship audit: Do publicly funded private school choice programs save money?" *EdChoice*. Retrieved from http://files.eric.ed.gov/fulltext/ED570441.pdf

Rau, A. B. 2017. "Controversial Arizona tax-credit scholarship program grants $1B to students." *AZ Central*. August 20, 2017. Retrieved from https://www.azcentral.com/story/news/politics/arizona-education/2017/08/18/controversial-arizona-education-tax-credit-scholarship-program-gives-students-1-billion/554058001

Roberts, L. 2015. "Senator Steve Yarbrough makes out like a . . . legislator . . . on tax-credit tuition program." *AZ Central*. July 28, 2015. Retrieved from https://www.azcentral.com/story/opinion/op-ed/laurieroberts/2015/07/28/steve-yarbrough-tax-credit-private-school-tuition/30760847

Wagner, L. 2014. "School vouchers: A second look at fraud and abuse." *NC Policy Watch*. October 16, 2014. Retrieved from http://www.ncpolicywatch.com/2014/10/16/school-vouchers-a-second-look-at-fraud-and-abuse

Welner, K. G. 2000. "Taxing the Establishment Clause: The revolutionary decision of the Arizona Supreme Court in *Kotterman v. Killian*." *Education Policy Analysis Archives*, 8(36). https://doi.org/10.14507/epaa.v8n36.2000

Welner, K. G. 2008. *NeoVouchers: The emergence of tuition tax credits for private schooling*. New York: Rowman and Littlefield.

Welner, K. 2011. *How to calculate the costs or savings of tax credit voucher policies*. NEPC Policy Memo. University of Colorado, National Education Policy Center.

Wixom, M. A. 2017. "School choice glossary." *Education Commission of the States*. https://www.ecs.org/wp-content/uploads/School_Choice_Glossary-3.pdf

3

School Choice: Charter Schools

In 1974, a professor at the University of Massachusetts surveyed the American public education system and asked a momentous question: Why couldn't a school board make a contract—a charter—with the teachers of a school to innovate and reach a set of great new goals, and then have those teachers report directly to the board without middle managers like principals or superintendents involved? The idea appealed to the head of the American Federation of Teachers (AFT), who gave it full-throated public support. And in Minnesota in 1992, the first charter school was born. At that time, charter schools were heralded by supporters who said that they would be hot beds of innovation and discovery, free of bureaucratic interference. Thirty years later, however, the charter school movement has produced something very different.

The charter school movement was, by and large, swept up in the privatization movement during its first two decades of development. Large corporations swept up charter schools teetering on the brink of closure and created many new ones. By 2020, half of all charter school students attended schools run by private, profit-making companies—"education management organizations," as they have come to be called. These companies, which number far fewer than 100 nationwide, collect billions of dollars in revenues and have emerged as a powerful lobbying force at both state and federal levels.

To their advocates, modern charter schools provide a welcome alternative to ineffective and impersonally large traditional public schools. But just like traditional public schools, the system of charter schools offers some excellent, many mediocre, and some poorly operated schools.

America's charter schools face a controversial future. They are legally public schools, but do they truly operate as public schools? Are they open to every child? Do they purposely project an image of being private? Do they act like public schools at some times and like private schools at others? As a major player on the menu of school choice options, are they contributing to the resegregation of public education? Are they innovative? Are they better?

Q10. DO CHARTER SCHOOLS HAVE SIGNIFICANT VARIATIONS IN STRUCTURE, OPERATIONS, AND PERFORMANCE FROM SCHOOL TO SCHOOL?

Answer: Yes. Although there are some commonalities among charter schools, they are not uniform in demographics, structure, governance, or operation. Different state legislation contributes to different types of charter school with different levels of autonomy. The purpose of any given charter school is also an important consideration. Among the various types of charter school are corporate versus standalone charters, profit-making versus nonprofit charters, "elite" charters, "White flight" charters, and virtual or cyber charters, among others.

The Facts: It is important to understand the history, origins, and politically charged context surrounding charter schools in the United States. In 1988, Albert Shanker, president of the American Federation of Teachers, spoke of empowering teachers to lead schools of innovation. Shanker learned of the charter concept from Ray Budde, a University of Massachusetts professor interested in organizational behavior. Budde first raised the notion of school district reorganization in a 1974 paper titled "Education by Charter" (Kolderie, 2005). He introduced the idea of reorganizing existing schools within a district to be led and run by teachers as opposed to central district administrators. Instead of teachers reporting to the district administration, they could report directly to the district school board. In 1988, Budde reintroduced the idea in a formal academic paper. His idea was largely ignored until Shanker gave it a prominent place in the discussions of school reform, including describing the charter concept in a 1988 *New York Times* article.

Shanker proposed creating new schools bound by performance contracts, or charters. He believed that if these "chartered" schools were allowed to operate more autonomously, it would lead to innovations that would eventually be adopted by traditional public schools, thereby enhancing the entire public schooling enterprise. Central to Shanker's plan was the idea that these schools should be run mainly by teachers under fewer bureaucratic regulations than typically found in other district schools. Such freedom, he claimed, would allow them to serve as education laboratories for innovation from which other district schools could eventually benefit. A rising tide would lift all boats, it was hoped. Moreover, the new charter schools would offer parents a choice for their children, thus creating competition among schools that would boost academic performance across the board.

Shanker's original concept quickly changed into something quite different. The charter school concept was favored by strong school choice advocates who wanted to give parents alternatives to neighborhood-assigned schools. Charter schools also appealed to neoliberal education reformers who believed public education, as well as many other institutions, would function more efficiently and effectively as a market. Consumer demand would dictate the quality and supply of schools, and competition among schools would spur improvement across the entire system. They believed that explicit contractual arrangements—a charter—setting explicit performance goals would lead to greater school accountability (see Garn and Cobb, 2012).

Improving America's Schools Act

Prior to the passage of the first state charter school legislation, proposals were advanced to introduce highly controversial school vouchers into the public school reform arena. School voucher programs grant parents a tax-supported "voucher" to pay for tuition at a private school. Then-president Ronald Reagan made several attempts to get federal school voucher programs through Congress, but they all failed because the voucher concept proved too controversial. A compromise supported by both Democrats and Republicans soon emerged: charter schools. In 1994, President Bill Clinton signed into law the Improving America's Schools Act, which provided flow-through federal funds to states to establish publicly funded charter schools. The charter movement had begun in earnest.

Officially, the first charter school opened in 1992 in Minnesota and, gradually, more states came on board with their own legislation. As of 2020, 45 states as well as the District of Columbia and the U.S. territories of Puerto Rico and Guam have charter school legislation. According to the National Alliance for Public Charter Schools, 3.2 million students are enrolled in 7,000 charter schools (publiccharters.org) in the United States.

Even though not all states have charter school enabling legislation, at least one charter school exists in each of the 50 states.

A few states account for a large proportion of charter schools and charter school students. For the 2017–2018 school year, California led all states with 1,275 charter schools enrolling 630,000 students, approximately 10 percent of the entire K–12 public school population.

Of course, states differ greatly in population. When numbers of charter school students are expressed as a percentage of K–12 public school enrollment, Arizona has approximately 20 percent—1 in 5—public school students enrolled in charter schools.

New Orleans made headlines after Hurricane Katrina by becoming a charter-only district in 2005; it is the only large city in the United States without a traditional public school. In Detroit and Flint, Michigan, more than half of all students were enrolled in charter schools as of 2017–2018. In contrast, states such as Iowa, Virginia, and Washington each have fewer than 10 charter schools.

Charter School Accountability

Charter schools are publicly funded and tuition-free to families. They generally are exempted from some of the regulations governing other public schools in their district or state. Unlike traditional public schools, they are not overseen by democratically elected governing boards. States pass laws governing how charter schools can be created, funded, and regulated. Depending on the state, charter schools can be authorized by multiple entities, including districts, state boards, state departments of education, or universities. Charter schools in nearly every state may be operated by for-profit management organizations or by nonprofits that may contract for services with for-profit companies.

Although charter school laws differ across states, the basic nature of the charter agreement is the same. A charter contract is established between a school and a state-designated charter school authorizer. The charter contract describes the school and how it will operate, including information on its mission, instructional programming, staffing, projected enrollment, and budget.

Accountability requirements for charter schools differ across states (see ecs.org/charter-school-policies for state-by-state comparisons). Many states require specific performance goals to be identified in the charter school application. All states require charter schools to take state tests, and 11 states and the District of Columbia set minimum performance standards that can trigger sanctions or even closure if not met (Cookson et al.,

2018). Only 16 states require charter school teachers to be certified, another 16 states require that some charter teachers be certified, and a handful of states permit some sort of waiver of this requirement.

The charter school industry has organized in most states to lobby legislatures against strong accountability measures focused on charter schools.

An often-overlooked aspect of charter school accountability is accountability for the charter authorizers themselves. Some states more than others monitor the oversight provided by charter authorizers. States adopt different forms of accountability as well.

Equity Issues

State policy and laws influence educational equity (Mead and Green, 2019). In the year 2000, during the early stages of the charter school movement, a California study revealed that many charter schools required parents to sign a contract prior to enrolling their children in the school (Nakagawa, 2000). The contracts typically stipulated a number of hours of parent involvement and the types of involvement favored by the school. The researcher reported that "one contract requires 3 hours of participation a week in activities such as assisting in the classroom, doing other activities at the school (office work, site maintenance, repairs, cleanup), or working on a committee" (Nakagawa, 2000, 464–465). Notably, some contracts threatened expulsion for students whose parents did not meet participation requirements.

A 2019 analysis by The Century Foundation found that only five states out of 43 specifically bar charter schools from requiring parent volunteer hours, the implication being that students from low-income families who cannot get to the school due to work obligations or lack of transportation are disproportionately excluded (Potter and Nunberg, 2019). The report also found that fewer than half the states with charter laws require schools to provide transportation for students. A national chain based in Arizona—and ranked twice among top 10 high schools by *U.S. News and World Report*—is reported to require $1,500 donations to its foundation from all accepted families. The chain's owners used foundation money and their salaries to buy a condominium in Manhattan (Montini, 2018).

Public policies can contribute to inequities by creating barriers to access, but so, too, can unwritten policies and practices, for example:

> In December 2017, the American Civil Liberties Union of Arizona released the results of its investigation of 471 charter schools, which found that 56 percent had enrollment policies that clearly violate

the law or discourage at-risk students. For example, Spanish is the most commonly spoken language after English, but only 26 percent of these schools provide enrollment documents in both languages. Attrition rates—that is, how many students drop out of a school or class in a given period—are strikingly high for high-testing charters. In 2006, [CEO Eva] Moskowitz launched Success Academy Charter Schools, Inc., with 73 first-graders. In 2018, this class became the first to graduate from the academy's high school, but only 17 of the early enrollees remained—an attrition rate of 77 percent. (Barkan, 2018, 107)

Charter School Growth

Some states are considered more charter-friendly than others. For instance, in Arizona, five different entities may sponsor a charter school: the state board for charter schools, the state board of education, a school district, one of three major universities (Arizona State University, University of Arizona, Northern Arizona University), or specified community college districts (asbcs.az.gov/how-does-charter-school-get-charter). In 2017–2018, Ohio had the sixth-largest charter school enrollment in the United States, partly due to five eligible authorizers: school districts, 501(c)3 organizations, regional education service centers, universities, and the state department of education (oapcs.org). Notably, half of Ohio charter schools have been sponsored by groups not affiliated with a public agency (Cookson et al., 2018).

Other states have approached charter schools with more government oversight. For instance, some states place caps on the number of charter schools or restrict the growth of individual schools. These less friendly charter states behave cautiously due to state budget concerns, fears of profiteers raiding public tax dollars, or strong pressure from teachers' unions wary of diverting limited resources from traditional public schools. In June 2019, after a highly contentious battle, West Virginia became the 45th state to pass a charter school law permitting growth only incrementally, allowing three new charter schools in 2021 with three more in 2023, and three more every three years after that.

Charter Types

The original charter idea conceived of charter schools as being autonomous, operated mainly by teachers, and freed from the bureaucratic requirements that prevented schools from being more innovative. Charter schools have evolved somewhat differently, which, as noted above, has been a function of differing state politics giving rise to differing regulations; for example, more or less oversight, loose or tight restrictions on charter authorizers, and allowing or prohibiting for-profit charter operators.

The different types of charter school that exist today, some 30 years after their inception, are also greatly influenced by the motivations of their sponsors. The research literature has described charter schools a number of ways, including:

- corporate charter schools (in cases where a corporation manages them or a network of them, sometimes in multiple states);
- stand-alone charter schools;
- district-run charter schools;
- Education Management Organizations (EMO)-run charter schools;
- for-profit and nonprofit charter schools;
- virtual, cyber, or online charter schools;
- "elite" charter schools, which enroll predominantly high-achieving students;
- "White-flight" charter schools (in scenarios where charter enrollments are predominantly White but located in racially diverse areas); and
- minority-serving charter schools, which aim to enroll predominantly students of color in low-income communities.

These charter school types illustrate the fact that U.S. charter schools are not all the same, and their differences are not attributable only to innovations or diversity with respect to academic theme or instructional approach.

FURTHER READING

Barkan, J. 2018. "Death by a thousand cuts: The story of privatising public education in the USA." *Soundings*, 70(70), 97–116.

Budde, R. 1988. *Education by charter: Restructuring school districts. Key to long-term continuing improvement in American education*. Andover, MA: Regional Laboratory for Educational Improvement of the Northeast and Islands. ERIC 295298.

Cookson, P. W., Jr., Darling-Hammond, L., Rothman, R., and Shields, P. M. 2018. *The tapestry of American public education: How we can create a system of schools worth choosing for all?* Palo Alto, CA: Learning Policy Institute.

Garn, G., and Cobb, C. D. 2012. "School choice and accountability." In W. Mathis, G. Miron, P. Hinchey, and W. Mathis (Eds.) *Exploring the school choice universe: Evidence and recommendations*. Charlotte, NC: Information Age Publishing, 89–104.

Kolderie, T. 2005. Evolving education newsletter. *Updates and Insights*, 1(6). https://www.educationevolving.org/newsletters/vol-1-no-6#ray_budde_origins

Mead, J. F., and Green, P. 2019. *Advancing intentional equity in charter schools*. The Century Foundation. March 7, 2019. Retrieved from tcf.org/content/report/advancing-intentional-equity-charter-schools

Montini, E. J. 2018. "Montini: Did you buy Basis Charter School founders an $8.4 million NYC condo?" *Arizona Republic*. May 7, 2018. Retrieved from https://www.azcentral.com/story/opinion/op-ed/ej-montini/2018/05/07/basis-charter-school-owners-8-4-million-nyc-condominium/587234002

Nakagawa, K. 2000. "Unthreading the ties that bind: Questioning the discourse of parent involvement." *Educational Policy*, 14(4), 443–472.

Potter, H., and Nunberg, M. 2019. *Scoring states on charter school integration*. The Century Foundation. Retrieved from https://tcf.org/content/report/scoring-states-charter-school-integration

Shanker, A. 1988. "Convention plots new course—A charter for change." *New York Times*, July 10, 1988.

Q11. ARE CHARTER SCHOOLS ACTUALLY PUBLIC SCHOOLS?

Answer: Yes, technically. Charter schools do not charge parents tuition. Instead, they are funded by taxpayers and are subject to city, state, and federal laws. Hence, they are public schools. However, in many ways, charter schools do not behave as public schools do and are therefore more appropriately described as public school "variants." Charter school owners have sometimes claimed the privileges of private companies to take advantage of opportunities not available to public entities. Moreover, charter schools often self-consciously project an image of being private, a strategy that reflects a recognition that many American families perceive private schools as superior to public schools. In the eyes of the general public, and remarkably even among some charter school employees, charter schools are often incorrectly considered private. This misperception has much to do with the way that many charters are advertised or the policies that they maintain that exclude certain students.

The Facts: K–12 public schools are taxpayer-funded, government-regulated, free of tuition, and open to all children in a prescribed enrollment or catchment area. Public schools are intended to serve the public, no matter who the public is. In the United States, public schools provide the critical function of educating a democratic citizenry. The public school system is far from perfect; but in its traditional form, it strives to educate all students regardless of their background, wealth, or religion.

Traditional public schools are government-regulated, government-funded, tuition-free schools. Charter schools are also funded by public tax revenues and tuition-free, and they are therefore legally public schools. However, charter schools operate under different rules than traditional public schools. Charter schools receive funding primarily based on how many students they enroll; therefore, their budget is determined by how many students they attract. Market theorists believe that this is a valuable incentive; if charter schools will compete for students, only the good schools will survive. But incentives for charter schools to enroll students and to perform well academically can result in competing interests. Charter schools might be incentivized to enroll students who will make them look good on state assessments, or who are easier to educate. Alternatively, simply adding more and more students creates the likelihood that some of those additional students will drag down scores on the state assessment. Adding profit incentives to the mix for charters operated by for-profit corporations introduces more conflicting interests. Here again, market theorists and neoliberal reformers contend that profit-taking and quality schooling are not at odds and instead view them as mutually reinforcing. The evidence, however, does not suggest that the market approach to public education necessarily serves everyone in the public well.

Charter schools have had a complicated existence. They have been both lauded and decried by politicians on both sides of the aisle. They have been both championed and criticized by powerful equity-conscious organizations. There are numerous factions for and against charter schools, others for "good" charter schools, and still others who find them destructive of the notion of a quality education for all citizens. In some cases, the charter school market appears to be working, effectively serving consumer demand. A number of charter schools across the country are quite popular as evidenced by waiting lists and lotteries for entry, even though the veracity of some of the claims made by charter schools surrounding demand has been called into question (Welner and Miron, 2014). In many other instances, however, charter schools have behaved in predictable ways under intense pressures to increase enrollments as well as boost performance. By and large, charter schools do not exist for the purpose of profiteering or to serve exclusionary ideologies. Many are trying to do right by children. But there are also some that cause harm at the expense of children in need. Consider, in the following sections, the ways in which some charter schools may operate in an "un-public school" manner.

Publicly Funded, Privately Governed and Operated

Ohio has the fifth-largest number of charter schools in the nation. Ohio's charter schools—called "community schools"—operate independently from school districts. Charter school sponsors, in Ohio and elsewhere, are agencies that open new charter schools, manage contracts, make renewal and closure decisions, and provide oversight and technical assistance for their schools. A 2018 report published by the Learning Policy Institute found that half of Ohio charter schools have been sponsored by entities with no affiliation to a public agency (Cookson et al., 2018).

Charter schools are often allowed to be run by private individuals and overseen by a board of trustees composed of unelected private citizens. The privatization of public services is not new to this country. For the last three decades, both Republican and Democratic administrations have endorsed privatization in the hope of achieving some combination of increased efficiency, higher quality services, and lower cost. Airports, prisons, hospitals, transportation, and even trash removal have been privatized. In the realm of education specifically, President Obama's Race to the Top program launched in 2009 greatly increased charter school presence in states. To receive funds, states were required to pass laws to increase the number of charter schools operating under private management.

Funding
Private-public tensions have resulted in challenges to the public nature of charter schools. For instance, a coalition of appellants contested Washington state's original 2012 charter law on the grounds that it "improperly diverts public school funds to private organizations that are not subject to local voter control" (Collingwood, Jochim, and Oskooii, 2018, 88). In 2015, after a yearlong deliberation, the state Supreme Court ultimately sided with the plaintiffs by a 6–3 vote, ruling that charter schools were unconstitutionally funded by the state's common school (general) fund to support public education. The Court also determined that charter schools, in essence, were not public because their governing boards were not democratically elected. Soon after the ruling, however, the charter school law was temporarily restored after the state legislature created a separate funding source from state lottery revenue. This move in effect negated the

constitutional concerns over funding. After another prolonged legal battle, the state Supreme Court issued a 2018 ruling that upheld the charter school law. Opponents—in particular the state's largest teachers' union—expressed deep disappointment with the decision, asserting that they "still believe it is wrong to divert public funds to privately run organizations that are not accountable to local voters" (Prothero, 2018).

Oversight
In terms of governance and oversight by the public, charter schools and traditional public schools are quite different. Traditional public schools are governed by local education agencies (LEAs), or school districts, which are overseen by locally elected school boards. Charter schools, on the other hand, are by and large governed by boards populated by persons who are not democratically elected. Traditional public school boards are accountable to all citizens of the city or municipality that the school district serves, while charter school boards are responsible to their "customers" and charter authorizer. The exceptions are charter schools that are sponsored directly by public school districts.

Traditional LEAs work with their school boards to decide whether and where to open new schools. Some states also allow LEAs to open charter schools. Depending on state statute, a charter board of directors may be permitted to choose a private, even for-profit, entity to operate or manage multiple charter schools. Such entities are often referred to as Education Management Organizations (EMOs) or Charter Management Organizations (CMOs). The Knowledge is Power Program (KIPP) and Achievement First are examples of CMOs that operate schools in multiple states. The distinction between EMOs and CMOs is not altogether clear; however, the National Alliance for Public Charter Schools describes EMOs as for-profit and CMOs as nonprofit organizations. CMOs provide more functions than EMOs, such as assisting with hiring, professional development, data management, advocacy, and private fundraising. Fundraising by some CMOs has raised concerns among public school advocates regarding potential conflicts of interest and undue influence over what is supposed to be public schooling (Reckhow, 2013). In the end, the research literature seems to view EMOs and CMOs as much the same.

For many of the reasons already mentioned, many legal and policy scholars view charter schools as public school "hybrids." Technically, "hybrid" is not the appropriate term, because it connotes a mix of two elements; charter schools are more of a "variant" of public schools rather than a mix of two parts. Unlike traditional public schools, charter schools, especially in states with little government oversight, can sidestep certain state and federal regulations designed to protect employees and students.

Several studies have reported these occurrences (e.g., Baker and Miron, 2015; Green, Baker, and Oluwole, 2013; Lubienski, 2016; Scott and DiMartino, 2010). In essence, some charter schools can behave as private organizations even though they are legally public institutions.

Labor Laws
Charter schools at times have wanted to have it both ways. When challenged legally, CMOs and EMOs claim they are private contractors and, unlike public schools, are not subject to many state and federal labor laws. A 2016 legal review by the National Labor Relations Board (NLRB) ruled that charter schools are employers subject to the National Labor Relations Act (NLRA) under most conditions. The NRLA is designed to protect the rights of employees and employers and encourage collective bargaining. At the time, the matter seemed settled that charter schools were to be subject to state-based collective bargaining regulations; states with collective bargaining agreements, by rule, should allow charter school employees to unionize. But in February 2019, the NLRB voted to reconsider whether charter schools were subject to federal labor law. On March 25, 2020, the NLRB issued its decision not to decline jurisdiction over charter schools as a class and instead make decisions on its jurisdiction over charter schools on a case by case basis. Currently, the vast majority of charter schools are nonunion, which union supporters contend leads to overworked, underpaid teachers and high teacher turnover.

Charter schools benefit from public school status by receiving public funds, typically on a per pupil basis. When charter schools recruit students, they can offer a tuition-free education, like all public schools. Charter schools are also recipients of state agency support. Even though state departments of education are often viewed unenthusiastically as slow-reacting bureaucracies, they still offer tax-funded supports such as teacher training, curriculum assistance, and federal monies for high poverty schools.

School Choice or Schools' Choice?

Part of what makes public schools public is that they are open to all families residing in their local catchment area. A key difference between charter schools and traditional public schools is that the latter group cannot turn students away because there is not enough space or because they cannot adequately meet a particular student learning need.

In some communities, charter schools are in such high demand that lotteries determine who gets a seat. Magnet schools, which are public schools with a special theme (science, music, art) and a goal of bringing together students from diverse backgrounds, may also allocate seats based on a lottery. Magnet schools were created by the Nixon administration in the early 1970s in order to circumvent de jure racial integration.

In effect, using lotteries when applications exceed seats allows magnet and charter schools to restrict access. In contrast, traditional public schools must take all students seeking admission, regardless of space or their ability to meet students' needs. In instances where there literally are not enough seats, traditional public schools add modular or temporary classrooms, or districts build new wings and sometimes new schools to meet demand.

Charter schools are in a position where they must attract enough students to operate, because they receive funding based on enrollments. Many charter schools already face financial pressure due to limited state funding, especially for capital expenditures like school buildings. Some states provide more public funds than others for charter school building or renovation projects. States vary in how they fund charter schools, but generally do so by allocating a fixed amount (e.g., the state average per student expenditure) based on a charter school's enrollment as of October 1 each year.

Most states consider student learning needs when allocating per pupil funding. In those instances, students who qualify for special services, such as special education or English language learning assistance, will receive a per pupil funding allocation that is marginally higher than the state average. While charter schools face pressure to perform well academically, of more immediate concern is meeting enrollment targets to maintain operation. Charter school advocates frequently tout long waiting lists among charters as evidence they are in high demand, but this isn't the case for every, or even most, charter schools.

Characteristics of Enrollment

If charter schools' continued existence depends on enrollment, then one would expect that good performance is paramount to this existence. Charter schools operate under both market-based and test-based accountability (Garn and Cobb, 2012). Families choose charter schools for a variety of reasons, and states hold all schools accountable for their student outcomes—with measurement of performance relying almost exclusively on test scores. This dynamic sets up situations where charter schools may be rewarded for attracting students with stronger test-taking ability and good behavior, and penalized for enrolling poor test-takers and high-needs students. Some states have included provisions in their charter school policies to prioritize serving at-risk or low-performing students (see, e.g., Tuttle, Gleason, and Clark, 2012). Such provisions are evident in state charter school laws and their application requirements (Education Commission of the States, 2018). However, it is unclear whether these requirements are monitored or enforced.

Considerable evidence has been found that some charter schools work to shape their student populations, either encouraging or discouraging certain types of students. For instance, several studies have found that some charter school leaders explicitly, or more subtly through word-of-mouth marketing, strive to structure school enrollment (Bulkley and Fisler, 2002; Hernández, 2016; Lubienski, 2007; Wilson and Carlsen, 2016). Some charter schools seek to enroll low-performing students or so-called "at-risk" students. In other cases, however, charter schools look to enroll students who are less costly to educate or who are from families of at least middle-class economic backgrounds. Kevin Welner, executive director of the National Education Policy Center housed at the University of Colorado, building off the investigative reporting by Simon (2013) in *Reuters*, reported on 12 such charter school structuring practices (Welner, 2013) and later expanded it to 14 (see Table 5.1 in Mommandi and Welner, 2018, for this list along with case examples). According to the authors of this expanded list, such influential practices can occur prior to, during, or after enrollment (Mommandi and Welner, 2018).

The authors of the 2018 report repeatedly heard of four ways that charter schools limited access through the application process: lengthy and onerous applications, required in-person visits, entrance exams, and restrictive application deadlines (Mommandi and Welner, 2018). Another inhibitive policy included requiring parents to volunteer a minimum number of hours at the school. Even after students were enrolled, some charter schools engaged in "counseling out" of students who performed poorly or who presented disciplinary issues. In 2010, a lawsuit was filed by the Southern Poverty Law Center and other advocacy groups against the Louisiana State Department of Education for violating the rights of New Orleans public school students with disabilities. Charter schools, in particular, were accused of steering prospective students with special needs toward other schools. In the 2008–2009 school year, students with disabilities were 12.6 percent of the student population in the state-operated School Recovery District (post-Hurricane Katrina), compared to 7.8 percent in local charter schools; eleven charter schools reported that 5 percent or less of their population included students with disabilities. The case was eventually settled in 2015, requiring new or renewing charter schools to provide descriptions of their plans for offering "the full array of related services to students with qualifying disabilities who are or may come to be enrolled at the charter school" (P. B. et al. v. Pastorek, 2015). In addition, the settlement agreement called for the annual calculation of provision rates for special education services in each local education agency (or school district) in New Orleans—such rates would be used as a basis for identifying individual schools for targeted monitoring.

Although charter schools are subject to the requirements of the Individuals with Disabilities Education Act (IDEA) and Section 504, there have been documented instances in which charter schools dissuade parents of a student with a disability from enrolling. In fact, a 2007 survey of charter school authorizers found that many charter schools told families that their child may be better served at a traditional public school (Rhim et al., 2007). In other cases, parents are aware that an underresourced charter school may not be the best option for their child with special needs, so they seek or remain at a traditional public school.

The end result is that charter schools, on the whole, serve a disproportionately low percentage of special education students in comparison to traditional public schools (Government Accountability Office, 2012; Rhim et al., 2007; Winters, 2015; Winters, Carpenter, and Clayton, 2017). Research has also consistently demonstrated that charter schools enroll smaller percentages of English language learners (ELLs) than traditional public schools (Finnigan et al., 2004; Heilig et al., 2016; Miron, Urschel, Mathis, and Tornquist, 2010).

Skimming

The pushing out of low-performers and creaming of high-performers is not the case in all charter school settings. In education, "creaming" refers to the selection of higher ability students who tend to perform well academically and cost less to teach. In a 2005 study, researchers found no evidence of cream-skimming in their analysis of California and Texas charter schools, noting that "[i]n both states little evidence can be found that charter schools are systematically cream-skimming high-performing students, and indeed in Texas the opposite appears true" (Booker, Zimmer, and Buddin, 2005, 22). In another study done in 2013, researchers analyzed data from an unnamed large urban district and also did not find evidence of charter schools pushing out low-performing students (Zimmer and Guarino, 2013).

To be sure, traditional public schools can and do use some of these practices to shape their own enrollments (Heilig and Darling-Hammond, 2008). However, regulations and oversight preclude them from subverting their open enrollment mandate. Due to their separate admissions processes, charter schools are more easily able to shape their school enrollment. Although not a widespread phenomenon, there is enough evidence of charter schools choosing students, rather than the reverse, to make it problematic for policy makers interested in promoting education equity. The pushing out and cream-skimming of students for the purpose of scoring well on performance assessments flies in the face of the nation's espoused values of diversity and inclusion (Mommandi and Welner, 2018; Simon, 2013; Welner, 2013).

Niche Schools and Selective Admissions

In traditional public schools, selective admissions are relatively rare. Some magnet schools that focus on specialized courses of study such as dramatic arts, screen students based on performance portfolios or auditions even though they are public schools. Likewise, prominent public "exam" schools, such as the Boston Latin Academy and Boston Latin School, Chicago's 11 selective enrollment schools, and New York City's Bronx High School of Science and Stuyvesant High School, admit students based on competitive exams.

In some cases, charter schools conduct selective admissions. A 2000 survey funded by the U.S. Department of Education found that 59 percent of charter schools had primary control over their admissions (RPP International, 2000). In some cases, parents or students were required to interview prior to being admitted. Further, in many instances, admission and continued enrollment were contingent on parental involvement contracts or student behavior expectations.

In contrast to traditional public schools, charter schools are more apt to condition admissions or continued enrollments-based parental involvement contracts or student behavior expectations. As noted above, charter schools may advertise or market themselves in ways to attract particular families at the exclusion of others (Bulkley and Fisler, 2002).

Charter schools that offer niche programming, whether it be "no excuses," gifted and talented, technology, arts, or military, will draw niche enrollments. Incidentally, "no excuses" charter schools remain one of the most conspicuous and controversial models, as they operate with strict codes of conduct, high academic rigor relying heavily on repetition, and longer school days. Charter school organizations such as the knowledge is power program (KIPP) have famously aligned with the "no excuses" approach, which has its proponents and detractors due to the manner and context in which instruction is delivered, and the fact that they almost exclusively serve students of color from high-poverty backgrounds. In a

2000 survey of charter school directors, 26 percent cited serving special populations as a primary reason for starting their school (Nelson, 2000). Many charter proponents justify selecting or targeting specific student populations based on a charter school's curricular theme or geographic location, especially if that is what parents say they prefer. For example, charter school operators whose primary mission is to serve underprivileged populations will position new charter schools in or near high-poverty areas. Charter proponents also argue that magnet schools do the same kind of targeting of specific student populations and that such specialization can lead to improved student outcomes. Targeting certain segments of the population is not a bad thing unless others in need are denied the same opportunity—such targeting makes charter schools less "public" in terms of accessibility (Fabricant and Fine, 2015).

Are Charter Schools Public or Are They Small Businesses?

During the COVID-19 pandemic, the federal government sought to rescue the crumbling U.S. economy through a variety of economic stimulus initiatives. In mid-April of 2020, Congress passed the $349 Billion Payroll Protection Act. The act allocated grants and loans to small businesses to maintain the payrolls and avoid terminating employees. At least 75 percent of the allocation had to go directly to employees. The National Alliance for Public Charter Schools and lobbyists for charter school corporations urged charter schools to apply for the funds (Blad, 2020). Since the Act limited applications to private businesses, critics said that the stance adopted by NAPCS and corporate lobbyists raised serious ethical issues. These critics charged that it showed once again how charter schools identify themselves as public on some occasions and as private on others, depending on which identity might be most advantageous to them. By and large, charter schools during the pandemic continued to receive tax money from the state and local districts because they were continuing instruction online.

The Committee for a Responsible Federal Budget, a self-described nonpartisan nonprofit organization led by former Congressional leaders from both sides of the aisle, reported that of the estimated $42 billion of COVID-19 federal relief funds that were disbursed to the education sector (including higher education), nearly $6 billion went to private and charter K–12 schools. (The breakdown between private and charter schools was not specified.) Their analysis also found that:

> Among the money made available for K-12 education, over 70 percent went to public schools and 30 percent went to private or charter schools. By comparison, roughly 85 percent of K-12 students attend

public school, compared to 15 percent in private or charter schools.... Importantly, the PPP data includes forgivable loans to charter schools, which were eligible to participate in the program owing to their quasi-public-private structure, but it excludes many forgivable loans paid to churches and other institutions that may have schools as part of their organization. (Committee for a Responsible Federal Budget, 2020)

FURTHER READING

Baker, B., and Miron, G. 2015. *The business of charter schooling: Understanding the policies that charter operators use for financial benefit.* Boulder, CO: National Education Policy Center. Retrieved from http://nepc.colorado.edu/publication/charter-revenue

Blad, E. 2020. "Charter schools eye coronavirus relief aimed at small businesses." *Education Week*, April 7, 2020. Retrieved from https://mobile.edweek.org/c.jsp?cid=25920011&item=http://api.edweek.org/v1/blog/49/index.html?uuid=80513&cmp=SOC-SHR-FB

Booker, K., Zimmer, R., and Buddin, R. 2005. *The effects of charter schools on school peer composition.* RAND Education Working Paper. WR-306-EDU.

Brown, E., and Makris, M. V. 2018. "A different type of charter school: In prestige charters, a rise in cachet equals a decline in access." *Journal of Education Policy, 33*(1), 85–117.

Budde, R. 1988. *Education by charter: Restructuring school districts. Key to long-term continuing improvement in American education.* Andover, MA: Regional Laboratory for Educational Improvement of the Northeast and Islands.

Bulkley, K., and Fisler, J. 2002. *A decade of charter schools: From theory to practice.* Philadelphia, PA: Consortium for Policy Research in Education.

Collingwood, L., Jochim, A., and Oskooii, K. A. 2018. "The politics of choice reconsidered: Partisanship, ideology, and minority politics in Washington's charter school initiative." *State Politics and Policy Quarterly, 18*(1), 61–92.

Committee for a Responsible Federal Budget. 2020. "How much COVID relief have public and private schools received?" Blog, September 1, 2020. http://www.crfb.org/blogs/how-much-covid-relief-have-public-and-private-schools-received

Cookson, P. W., Jr., Darling-Hammond, L., Rothman, R., and Shields, P. M. 2018. *The tapestry of American public education: How we can create a system of schools worth choosing for all?* Palo Alto, CA: Learning Policy Institute.

Education Commission of the States. 2018. "Fifty-State Comparison: Charter Schools." ECS, January 2018. http://ecs.force.com/mbdata/mbquestNB2C?rep=CS1706

Fabricant, M., and Fine, M. 2015. *Charter schools and the corporate makeover of public education: What's at stake?* New York: Teachers College Press.

Finnigan, K., Adelman, N., Anderson, L., Cotton, L., Donnelly, M. B., and Price, T. 2004. *Evaluation of the Public Charter Schools Program: Final report.* PPSS-2004-08. U.S. Department of Education.

Garn, G., and Cobb, C. D. 2012. "School choice and accountability." In W. Mathis, G. Miron, P. Hinchey, and W. Mathis (Eds.), *Exploring the school choice universe: Evidence and recommendations.* Charlotte, NC: Information Age Publishing, 89–104.

Government Accountability Office. 2012. *Charter schools: Additional federal attention needed to help protect access for students with disabilities.* Washington, DC: Author.

Green III, P. C., Baker, B. D., and Oluwole, J. O. 2013. "Having it both ways: How charter schools try to obtain funding of public schools and the autonomy of private schools." *Emory Law Journal, 63*(2), 303–337.

Heilig, J. V., and Darling-Hammond, L. 2008. "Accountability Texas style: The progress and learning of urban minority students in a high-stakes testing context." *Educational Evaluation and Policy Analysis, 30*, 75–110.

Heilig, J., Holme, J., LeClair, A. V., Redd, L. D., and Ward, D. 2016. "Separate and unequal: The problematic segregation of special populations in charter schools relative to traditional public schools." *Stanford Law and Policy Review, 27*(2), 251–294.

Hernández, L. E. 2016. "Race and racelessness in CMO marketing: Exploring charter management organizations' racial construction and its implications." *Peabody Journal of Education, 91*, 47–63.

Jabbar, H. 2016. "Selling schools: Marketing and recruitment strategies in New Orleans." *Peabody Journal of Education, 91*(1), 4–23.

Kolderie, T. 2005. "Ray Budde and the origins of the 'Charter Concept.'" *Education Evolving,* 1–3. Retrieved from www.educationevolving.org/pdf/Ray-Budde-Origins-Of-Chartering.pdf

Ladd, H. F. 2019. "How charter schools threaten the public interest." *Journal of Policy Analysis and Management, 38*(4), 1063–1071.

Lange, C. M., Rhim, L. M., and Ahearn, E. M. 2008. "Special education in charter schools: The view from state education agencies." *Journal of Special Education Leadership, 21*(1), 12–21.

Lay, J. C., and Bauman, A. 2019. "Private governance of public schools: Representation, priorities, and compliance in New Orleans charter school boards." *Urban Affairs Review*, 55(4), 1006–1034.

Lubienski, C. 2007. "Marketing schools: Consumer goods and competitive incentives for consumer information." *Education and Urban Society*, 40(1), 118–141.

Lubienski, C. 2016. "Sector distinctions and the privatization of public education policymaking." *Theory and Research in Education*, 14(2), 192–212.

Miron, G., Urschel, J. L., Mathis, W, J., and Tornquist, E. 2010. *Schools without diversity: Education management organizations, charter schools and the demographic stratification of the American school system.* Boulder and Tempe: Education and the Public Interest Center and Education Policy Research Unit. Retrieved from http://epicpolicy.org/publication/schools-without-diversity

Mommandi, W., and Welner, K. 2018. "Shaping charter enrollment and access." In Rotberg, I. C., Glazer, J. L. (Eds.), *Choosing charters: Better schools or more segregation?* New York: Teachers College Press, 61–81.

Montini, E. J. 2018. "Montini: Did you buy Basis Charter School founders an $8.4 million NYC condo?" *Arizona Republic*. May 7, 2018. Retrieved from https://www.azcentral.com/story/opinion/op-ed/ej-montini/2018/05/07/basis-charter-school-owners-8-4-million-nyc-condominium/587234002

Nelson, B. 2000. *The state of charter schools, 2000: Fourth-year report.* U.S. Government Printing Office.

Nichols-Barrer, I., Gill, B., Gleason, P., and Tuttle, C. 2012. *Student selection, attrition, and replacement in KIPP middle schools.* Mathematica Policy Research.

P. B. et al. v. Pastorek. 2015. Civil Case No. 2:10-cv-04049. https://www.splcenter.org/sites/default/files/d6_legacy_files/downloads/case/pb_v_pastorek.pdf

Prothero, A. 2018. "Washington Supreme Court upholds state's embattled charter schools." *Education Week*. October 25, 2018. Retrieved from https://tinyurl.com/rb9c27q

Reckhow, S. 2013. *Follow the money: How foundation dollars change public school politics.* New York: Oxford University Press.

Rhim, L. M., Ahearn, E., Lange, C. M., and McLaughlin, M. J. 2007. *Survey of charter school authorizers (Report No. 6).* College Park, MD: Institute for the Study of Exceptional Children and Youth.

Rotberg, I. C., and Glazer, J. L. (Eds.). 2018. *Choosing charters: Better schools or more segregation?* New York: Teachers College Press.

RPP International. 2000. *The state of charter schools, fourth year report: National study of charter schools.* Washington, DC: U.S. Department of Education, Office of Educational Research and Improvement.

Scott, G. A. 2012. *Charter schools: Additional federal attention needed to help protect access for students with disabilities.* Report to Congressional Requesters. GAO-12-543. U.S. Government Accountability Office.

Scott, J. T., and DiMartino, C. 2010. "Hybridized, franchised, duplicated, and replicated: Charter schools and management." In C. Lubienski and P. Weitzel (Eds.), *The charter school experiment: Expectations, evidence, and implications.* Cambridge, MA: Harvard Education Press, 171–196.

Simon, S. 2013. "Class struggle: How charter schools get students they want." *Reuters.* February 15, 2013. Retrieved from https://tinyurl.com/rqx7fkv

Tuttle, C. C., Gleason, P., and Clark, M. 2012. "Using lotteries to evaluate schools of choice: Evidence from a national study of charter schools." *Economics of Education Review, 31*(2), 237–253.

Welner, K. G. 2013. "The dirty dozen: How charter schools influence student enrollment." *Teachers College Record.* April 2013.

Welner, K. G., and Miron, G. 2014. Wait, wait. Don't mislead me! Nine reasons to be skeptical about charter waitlist numbers. *NEPC Policy Memo.* Boulder, CO: National Education Policy Center.

Wilson, T. S., and Carlsen, R. L. 2016. "School marketing as a sorting mechanism: A critical discourse analysis of charter school websites." *Peabody Journal of Education, 91,* 24–46.

Winters, M. A. 2015. "Understanding the gap in special education enrollments between charter and traditional public schools: Evidence from Denver, Colorado." *Educational Researcher, 44,* 228–236.

Winters, M. A., Carpenter, D. M., and Clayton, G. 2017. "Does attending a charter school reduce the likelihood of being placed into special education? Evidence from Denver, Colorado." *Educational Evaluation and Policy Analysis, 39*(3), 448–463.

Zimmer, R. W., and Guarino, C. M. 2013. "Is there empirical evidence that charter schools 'push out' low-performing students?" *Educational Evaluation and Policy Analysis, 35*(4), 461–480.

Q12. ARE CHARTER SCHOOLS MORE INNOVATIVE THAN TRADITIONAL PUBLIC SCHOOLS?

Answer: Although charter schools were initially conceived of as laboratories for innovation, they are generally no more instructionally innovative than traditional public schools. The only area where some plausible claims of innovation have been made are with a "no excuses" model delivered by KIPP, a popular charter school network.

The Facts: The initial charter concept set forth in 1988 by the president of the American Federation of Teachers (AFT), the largest teachers' union, and Ray Budde, a university professor, held that chartered schools were to

- be funded publicly;
- be run mainly by teachers;
- be unfettered by bureaucratic regulations governing traditional public schools;
- serve as innovative education laboratories; and
- offer parental choice and competition with traditional public schools. (Shanker, 1988)

Today, there is considerable heterogeneity in the charter school sector (see Q10). New charter schools have been created, while some existing public, private, and religious-affiliated schools have converted to charter status. Former Christian and Jewish day schools have applied for and received charter status, as have former Montessori schools, which adhere to a student-centered, experiential learning philosophy. There are charter schools run by nonprofits, others run by for-profit firms, and still others sponsored by universities and school districts. There are virtual or cyber charter schools enrolling students across state lines and conducting education exclusively online. There are charters that cater to gifted and talented students, to so-called at-risk students, and to those seeking careers in the military.

Numerous charter schools endorse a back-to-the-basics curriculum or adopt a "no excuses" philosophy of schooling. There are charters that screen students with selective admissions and those that require parents to participate in, or even donate to, the school as a condition of enrollment. Some charters in high demand have long waiting lists and lotteries to assign winners, while other charters remain in a constant struggle to fill seats and meet their budget. Notably, the original stand-alone charter sector has given considerable ground to Education Management Organizations (EMOs) and Charter Management Organizations (CMOs) that oversee dozens of charter schools in different locales across the country. One possibly innovative practice that is associated with "no excuses" charter schools, in particular, is intensive student tutoring. Tutoring in charter schools is more intensive and more common than in traditional public schools. Charter schools often depend on paid tutors and may require all students to participate (Chabrier, Cohodes, and Oreopoulos, 2016).

Examining Claims of Innovation Leadership

Although there is considerable diversity among charters, investigations into whether charter schools are more innovative than traditional public schools have yielded mixed results. A 2003 analysis of 56 research studies on charter schools and innovation found the most commonly recognized innovation to be in the area of school governance, rather than in classroom practices or the curriculum (Lubienski, 2003). In a 2012 analysis of the nationally representative National Center for Education Statistics (NCES) Schools and Staffing Survey (SASS), researchers were able to examine practices reported being used at both the level of schools and districts. They examined innovation in staffing policies, academic support services, school organizational structures, and governance across 203 charter and 739 traditional public schools in 36 states. There was some evidence that charter schools employed various forms of scheduling and student grouping at a slightly higher rate than traditional public schools. For instance, block scheduling, looping, and mixed-age classrooms were used slightly more frequently. Although traditional public schools have been engaged in these same practices for years, charter schools did so more frequently. Overall findings, however, revealed that charter schools were no more innovative than traditional public schools (Preston et al., 2012).

For a 2015 study by the American Enterprise Institute, researchers examined the websites of more than 1,500 charters schools in 17 cities. Researchers looked for "descriptive words about their mission, vision, educational philosophy, academic model, or curriculum" to code each school as either "general" or "specialized." Schools identified as specialized were further categorized into more than a dozen types (e.g., "no excuses," STEM, arts, military schools). The researchers reported an "almost exactly even split between general and specialized charter schools, with the most common types of specialized schools being "no excuses" and progressive schools" (McShane and Hatfield, 2015). A subsequent 2015 review of this study, however, found flaws in its methodology and alleged that it offered little utility to the policy debate over charter schools (Danzig and Mathis, 2015).

A similar 2016 analysis was conducted on charter schools in New Orleans, a unique context given that New Orleans ostensibly became a completely charter district following Hurricane Katrina (Arce-Trigatti et al., 2016). In the study, researchers examined the 2014 *New Orleans Parents' Guide to Public Schools* to determine the ways in which charter schools differed from one another. They focused on eight characteristics, none of which directly reflected innovative practices: college-prep mission status; evidence of specific curricular theme; numbers of instructional hours, sports, extracurriculars, and nonacademic support staff; grades served; whether school has open enrollment or selective admissions. Findings indicate that half the schools self-identify as having a college prep mission. A relatively small portion would be considered a niche school—grounded in a particular curricular theme such as arts or STEM—and most of these were high schools. Nearly one-quarter (23 percent) of the New Orleans charter schools conduct selective admissions. Although this study did not compare New Orleans charter school characteristics to that of traditional public schools, the evidence presented did not point to any major innovations.

In another 2016 study, data were analyzed from a matched sample of charter and traditional public schools in six states—Colorado, Delaware, Indiana, Michigan, Minnesota, and Ohio—to examine student ability grouping and how it was related to student learning in math (Berends and Donaldson, 2016). Charter school math classes were slightly more evenly distributed in terms of student ability than those in traditional public schools, which tended to provide separate instruction to groups of high-ability students. This suggests that charter schools may group students more heterogeneously than traditional public schools in math; however, mixed-ability classrooms, while certainly not the norm in math courses, is not considered an innovative practice.

Virtual, or online, schools have proliferated, and as of 2017–2018, about half of them were charter schools. Among the expected benefits of virtual education was that it would place students at the center of their own learning, allow them to progress through curricula at their own pace, expose them to new venues for teaching and learning, and allow teachers to differentiate instruction. Unfortunately, such innovations have not yielded positive results overall (see Q31). By all research accounts, including robust studies done in 2015 and 2017, student outcomes in virtual schools have fallen woefully short of academic performance levels posted by students in other school settings failures (CREDO, 2015; Ahn and McEachin, 2017).

KIPP Schools

One of the often-cited examples of charter school innovation is one large charter school organization with a distinct philosophy. KIPP schools embrace a "no excuses" discipline and compliance-oriented instructional model that emphasizes test preparation. Teachers are trained to conduct classroom instruction in a very strict manner, with high expectations for student engagement, performance, and behavior. Students are required to SLANT: Sit up, Listen, Ask and Answer questions, Nod, and Track the speaker. Silence is expected in the hallways, as are coordinated call-and-response communications in the classroom. School hours are extended during the day and classes sometimes are conducted on Saturdays.

Strict control over the environment and a heightened focus on test preparation and grades for "performance character" have produced strong test results for KIPP and even expanded college-going rates for disadvantaged populations. There are some concerns that patterns of high attrition rates among students may be inflating some of these gains, however. (If low-scoring students drop out or are encouraged to leave, those who persist will obviously exhibit higher performance levels.) For instance, a 2011 study of 30 KIPP schools showed that roughly 40 percent of Black males left between the sixth and eighth grade (Miron, Urschel, and Saxton, 2011). Nevertheless, KIPP schools remain in demand among parents who believe in the culture of "no excuses."

Although KIPP is committed to serving students of color from economically disadvantaged communities, many critics express concern about the extent to which a "no excuses" environment may discourage freedom of expression, pursuit of curiosity, and deep learning (Golann and Torres, 2020). At least two studies, one done in 2013 and another in 2018, reported that former KIPP teachers have expressed serious reservations about how the KIPP strict disciplinary approach ultimately serves children (Goodman, 2013; Kershen, Weiner, and Torres, 2018). Although not specifically targeting KIPP, other critiques have been leveled at "no excuses" models, citing concerns that their instructional models are too focused on testing, lack culturally relevant materials for students of color, and demand ill-founded expectations for how children should act and move their bodies (Sondel, Kretchmar, and Dunn, 2019).

Advocates of charter schools believe that their autonomy allows them the freedom to implement nonconventional practices and that ultimately these practices can be shared and scaled for system-wide improvement. KIPP's more extreme methods of classroom control are uncommon when viewed in the context of the nation's public school system, but the question remains whether these methods constitute an innovation in education. Many elements of their regimen have been present in schools for decades (e.g., Direct Instruction, Direct Instructional System for Teaching and Remediation [DISTAR]). At the very least, KIPP offers an illustration of the institutionalization and scale up of such practices, because the model has expanded to other areas of the country, namely, in impoverished communities populated by families of color.

FURTHER READING

Ahn, J., and McEachin, A. 2017. "Student enrollment patterns and achievement in Ohio's online charter schools." *Educational Researcher*, 46(1), 44–57.

Arce-Trigatti, P., Lincove, J. A., Harris, D. N., and Jabbar, H. 2016. "Is there choice in school choice?" *Education Research Alliance for New Orleans*. April 20, 2016.

Berends, M., and Donaldson, K. 2016. "Does the organization of instruction differ in charter schools? Ability grouping and students' mathematics gains." *Teachers College Record*, 118(11), 1–38.

Center for Research on Education Outcomes (CREDO). 2015. *Online charter school study*. Retrieved from https://credo.stanford.edu/publications/online-charter-school-study

Chabrier, J., Cohodes, S., and Oreopoulos, P. 2016. "What can we learn from charter school lotteries?" *Journal of Economic Perspectives*, 30(3), 57–84.

Danzig, A., and Mathis, W. J. 2015. "Review of "Measuring diversity in charter school offerings." Boulder, CO: National Education Policy Center. Retrieved from http://nepc.colorado.edu/thinktank/review-charter-diversity

Golann, J. W., and Torres, A. C. 2020. "Do no-excuses disciplinary practices promote success?" *Journal of Urban Affairs*, 42(4), 617–633.

Goodman, J. F. 2013. "Charter management organizations and the regulated environment: Is it worth the price?" *Educational Researcher*, 42, 89–96.

Horn, J. 2016. *Work hard, Be hard: Journeys through "no excuses" teaching*. Lanham, MD: Rowman and Littlefield.

Kershen, J. L., Weiner, J. M., and Torres, C. 2018. "Control as care: How teachers in 'no excuses' charter schools position their students and themselves." *Equity and Excellence in Education*, 51(3–4), 265–283.

Knowledge is Power Program. 2008. *Student mobility at KIPP*. San Francisco, CA: KIPP.

Lubienski, C. 2003. "Innovation in education markets: Theory and evidence on the impact of competition and choice in charter schools." *American Educational Research Journal*, 40(2), 395–443.

Macey, E., Decker, J., and Eckes, S. 2009. "The knowledge is power program (KIPP): An analysis of one model's efforts to promote achievement in underserved communities." *Journal of School Choice*, 3(3), 212–241.

McShane, M. Q., and Hatfield, J. 2015. *Measuring diversity in charter school offerings*. Washington, DC: American Enterprise Institute.

Miron, G., Urschel, J. L., and Saxton, N. 2011. *What makes KIPP work? A study of student characteristics attrition and school finance*. New York, NY:

Teachers College, National Center for the Study of Privatization in Education/Kalamazoo: Western Michigan University, Study Group on Educational Management Organizations.

Preston, C., Goldring, E., Berends, M., and Cannata, M. 2012. "School innovation in district context: Comparing traditional public schools and charter schools." *Economics of Education Review, 31*(2), 318–330.

Robelen, E. W. 2007. "KIPP student-attrition patterns eyed." *Education Week, 26*(41), 1–16.

Shanker, A. 1988. "Convention plots new course—A charter for change." *New York Times*, July 10, 1988.

Sondel, B., Kretchmar, K., and Dunn, A. H. 2019. "'Who do these people want teaching their children?' White saviorism, colorblind racism, and anti-Blackness in 'no excuses' charter schools." *Urban Education*. https://doi.org/10.1177/0042085919842618

Q13. DO CHARTER SCHOOLS PERFORM BETTER THAN TRADITIONAL PUBLIC SCHOOLS?

Answer: Some do, some do not, and most perform about the same. The first wave of charter school effectiveness research produced mixed results because scholars found considerable variability in charter school performance. Recent years have seen the increased application of more rigorous "causal" research designs that reveal similar findings, but that have added more details on why some schools do better or more poorly than others. There has been a notable shift from making broad comparisons between charter and traditional public schools to examining why such variability in performance exists. Efforts have focused on whether factors associated with certain charter schools—such as their educational approach or location, who governs and operates them, how they are staffed, and under what state or local policies they operate—play a role in their performance relative to traditional public schools. For instance, urban charter schools have performed slightly better than traditional public schools on standardized math assessments; "no excuses" charter schools have scored appreciably higher than traditional public schools on such tests; and virtual charter schools have done substantially worse.

The Facts: Measurements of charter school effectiveness are of great interest to many stakeholders. Policy makers and politicians want to know whether to invest public tax dollars in schools that exist alongside, or in competition with, traditional public schools. Families and students want to know whether a charter school is a better option than the traditional public school in their community. Educators want to know whether charter schools are working as promised, as do those with a vested political interest in either supporting or challenging the entire concept of charter schools.

So, do charter schools perform better than traditional public schools? Performance can be considered in many different ways, but most people want to know how a school contributes to students' academic learning, life skills, and social-emotional development. Not all valued student outcomes lend themselves to standardized measurement, and not all embodiments of student achievement lend themselves to systematic inquiry studied at scale. For example, research on school choice has found that parents value many aspects of a school beyond test scores (Lareau and Goyette, 2014).

Existing research on charter schools has focused mostly on statewide standardized test scores as a measure of performance. There are limitations to using test scores as a measure of school performance, let alone student achievement. Tests are restricted to certain subject areas and grade levels, and are not really designed to tap critical thinking skills, for example. But they are about the only proxies that measure student achievement on a large scale. A smaller set of studies investigated effects of charter schools on educational attainment, such as graduation rates and postsecondary enrollment and completion. But by far the largest number of studies on charter school effectiveness has focused on student test scores in core subjects like math and reading, relative to a comparison set of traditional public schools. So, the question of whether charter schools "outperform" traditional public schools is confined to this relatively narrow definition of school performance.

The Challenge in Making Fair Comparisons

Any comparisons between charter and traditional public schools, in order to be useful and valid, must be fair. For instance, it is overly simplistic and misleading to compare average annual school test scores (or changes in scores) of charter schools versus traditional public schools in any one state, county, or even city. Such comparisons neglect important mediating factors that are known to influence school test scores. For instance, if a charter school in a city happened to skim off higher-ability students from nearby traditional public schools, then comparing test scores between the two schools tells an incomplete story about how the charter school actually contributed to student achievement. Similarly, a charter school that happened to attract low-scoring students would introduce the same group bias to any question about which school sector performed better.

Researchers from the National Bureau of Economic Research summarized one major challenge of studying charter school effectiveness, namely, selection bias:

> In the case of direct effects, an analysis is complicated by the fact that students and their families choose to attend charter schools. This choice may imply these students are different as they may be more engaged students and families than a typical student attending a TPS [traditional public school]. Alternatively, students attending charter schools could be students who have not had success in traditional settings and are trying charter school as a last resort. Therefore, any observed differences in performance between students in charter and TPSs may not result from weaker or superior educational services in charter schools, but result from different unobserved characteristics of students. If these unobserved characteristics are not accounted for in a research study, they can create a "selection bias" and could lead researchers and policymakers to invalid conclusions. (Epple, Romano, and Zimmer, 2016, 164–165)

There are research designs and statistical controls that attempt to reduce such selection biases. Because random assignment of students to a charter or traditional public school is not practical or feasible, the next best estimations can be done through rigorous research designs and statistical controls.

For example, some researchers have taken advantage of charter school lotteries. When charter school applications are oversubscribed, random admission of students essentially simulates a randomized experiment. Findings from robust lottery-based studies are generally what researchers call *internally* valid because they are not as subject to selection bias. Selection bias would occur when those interested in attending a charter school are qualitatively different from students who don't seek enrollment in a charter school. The differences are usually unknown to researchers who speak of them as "unobservable confounding variables." For instance, parents of charter school seekers could be privy to different information or have more resources than parents of nonseekers; the students themselves could be differentially motivated to excel academically, and so on. If the unobservable, or even observable, characteristics of charter school seekers contribute in some way to their test performance, then any comparisons between charter school seekers and nonseekers would be compromised. The comparisons would not have strong *internal validity*. On the other hand, if there were more charter school seekers than available seats, and the charter school randomly selected students via a lottery, then there is an opportunity for a more valid comparison, provided, of course, that the students not chosen would enroll in a traditional public school.

However, lottery-based studies are few and not without their own set of limitations. Primary among these are limitations in generalizing their findings to other schools and settings. Lottery-based studies can only occur when oversubscription to a school occurs and when sufficient numbers of students are "lotteried out." The lottery "winners" and "losers" create the pseudo treatment and control groups familiar to randomized-control designs. However, the fact that lottery-based studies only occur when there is high demand means that the results cannot be applied to the full population of charter schools. The high demand may be driven by parents dissatisfied with lower-quality traditional public schools near their local charter school. This presents a possible built-in bias among lottery studies and ends up compromising the generalizability of their findings to other, "noncompetitive" settings. In other words, if charter schools subject to oversubscribed lotteries ended up increasing student achievement, it would be difficult to know whether the same effects would be observed if the same charter school were placed near high-performing traditional public schools.

For instance, a 2016 study looked at the effects of student achievement by reviewing 113 studies of lottery-based charter school research (Chabrier, Cohodes, and Oreopoulos, 2016). The researchers found that the effects of charter schools dropped sharply as test scores increased at nearby competing traditional public schools. A 2012 study of 492 charter middle schools located in 35 states between 2005 and 2007 indicated that only 10 to 15 percent were "sufficiently oversubscribed to participate in a lottery-based study" (Tuttle, Gleason, and Clark, 2012, 239).

In terms of other limitations of lottery-based studies, researchers have discovered that not all lotteries are truly random. In many instances, lotteries permit sibling exceptions if they were not randomly drawn. Because the other siblings were not randomly chosen, lottery analyses cannot provide inferences for these children. Furthermore, a 2012 study found that many schools do not keep careful records of lotteries (Tuttle, Gleason, and Clark, 2012). In some cases, lottery rules have been ignored to admit favored students or student-athletes. In 2017, for instance, Connecticut Public Radio reported on Hartford's Capital Prep Magnet School, which was regularly enrolling star athletes outside the lottery to support its championship sports teams (Graziano, 2017).

There are statistical techniques used in lottery-based studies, as well as other quantitative studies, that rely exclusively on sophisticated statistical models, but they are too complex to go into detail here. The quantitative approaches presented here are far from perfect, but they are the best options available for comparing student achievement between charter and traditional public schools. As with the evaluation of so many social programs, definitive experiments are not possible, and the studies that are possible leave many unanswered questions.

Charter School Research

According to a 2015 summary of the research on charter schools, early studies employing quasi-experimental methods have yielded mixed results: the studies showed that charter school students perform academically about the same as traditional public school students (Berends, 2015, 169). A 2013 report published by the Center for Research on Education Outcomes compared charter and traditional public schools in 27 states and found virtually no difference in achievement (Cremata et al., 2013). A 2012 study that analyzed data across seven states also did not find significant achievement differences between charter and public schools (Zimmer et al., 2012).

Academics have also worked to sort through and draw conclusions from the large body of research that has recently emerged in this area by conducting systematic summaries, or syntheses, of research studies addressing this topic. There are even formal techniques called meta-analyses to help derive summary statistics across multiple quantitative studies that address similar research questions (see gvglass.info/papers/meta25.html).

Five research syntheses published between 2015 to 2019 have examined the question of charter school effectiveness. One of the reviews was published in a peer-reviewed journal (Berends, 2015), meaning it was subject to scrutiny by other scholars prior to being published. Peer review is by no means a guarantee that studies are done without bias and deficiencies, but it is the best means available to mitigate those two concerns. The four other syntheses were published in academic handbooks (Epple, Romano, and Zimmer, 2016; Ferrare, 2020) and edited volumes (Betts and Tang, 2019; Gamoran and Fernandez, 2018). All of these four reviews likely underwent some form of peer review, although as with most edited volumes, the process is not transparent.

Based on the constellation of studies that examine charter school performance and reviews of research that summarize findings among larger and more rigorous studies on charter school achievement, the only defensible conclusion is that overall results are mixed. The most consistent finding is the inconsistency in charter school performance and the fact that results vary by charter school type and location. Some charter schools do better than district schools, some do worse, and others perform similarly (Epple, Romano, and Zimmer, 2016).

Two other comprehensive reviews of charter school research published in the mid-2010s come to similar conclusions. These reviews attempt to synthesize the research on charter schools since their inception in 1992. In the *Handbook for Economics of Education* (Hanushek, Machin, and Woessmann, 2016), three quantitative researchers report that findings are mixed. In the *Annual Review of Sociology* (2015), Mark Berends wrote that "findings reveal mixed results where student achievement is concerned (i.e., some positive, some negative, some neutral) and positive results in terms of educational attainment (i.e., high school graduation and college attendance)" (159). A comprehensive analysis of Texas charter schools, published in 2016, reported that its graduates did no better in earning in the early labor market relative to noncharter school graduates (Dobbie and Fryer, 2016).

A 2015 review of charter school studies conducted between 2003 and 2014 (the majority done closer to 2014) is important to highlight here. Because the number of individual studies at their disposal was so large, the researchers chose to highlight "the more prominent studies" and "synthesize by research design because . . . each research design is answering somewhat narrowly defined and different questions with different inferences" (169). The researchers synthesized 12 studies that used a sophisticated econometric technique called a "fixed effects" approach, 7 studies that employed a lottery-based design, and another 7 studies that used statistical matching and regression techniques. In their synthesis, the authors reported:

> It is fair to say that researchers have not come to consensus on charter school effectiveness because [of] [sic] these differences in findings. An interpretation that fits the evidence is that some charter schools, including especially the oversubscribed schools, are in fact much more effective with respect to student achievement than there [sic] counterpart [traditional public schools], while the majority of charter schools are not superior, and some are inferior, to their counterpart[s]. (Epple, Romano, and Zimmer, 2016, 176)

Researcher Mark Berends (2015) noted that, while few studies have focused on charter schools' effects on educational attainment, such as high school graduation, college enrollment, college persistence, and college graduation, those that do, consistently find positive effects. He cautioned that among this small set of studies, the samples were restricted to certain geographic areas, thus limiting the generalizability to other settings.

A 2018 research synthesis focused on the outcomes literature on urban charter schools, in particular (Gamoran and Fernandez, 2018). The authors came to the same conclusion as others noted here, namely, that the research literature on charter school effectiveness mostly focuses on student test scores as the outcome; that rigor of study design varies, but has increased over the years; and that, ultimately, the most consistent finding across all studies is that there is great *variation* in charter school performance relative to traditional public schools.

A 2018 meta-analysis was conducted on 38 studies that used either a lottery-based or a value-added approach that relied on statistically generated comparison groups for a traditional public school comparison (Betts and Tang, 2018). The researchers chose to focus on these two study designs due to their relative rigor and sophistication. The 38 studies were conducted over a range of years, grade levels, and locations, and they judiciously excluded "no-excuse" KIPP charter schools, which were analyzed separately to avoid an undue upward bias on their estimates. The authors concluded that:

> On average, for the limited set of charter schools, locations, and years that have been studied to date, charter schools are producing higher achievement gains in math relative to traditional public schools in elementary and middle but not high schools. For reading achievement charter schools on average are producing higher gains in middle schools but not in elementary or high schools. For both math and reading, middle school studies tend to produce the highest effect sizes of all of the grade groupings. The literature shows a large variation in estimated charter school effects across locations, and some studies also show large variations within a given city or state. (Betts and Tang, 2019, 67–68)

Finally, a 2020 study reviewed the research on charter school impacts on achievement and attainment, prioritizing studies published after 2014 (Ferrare, 2020). The review organized studies by their geographical scope and context: studies of achievement at the national, multistate, state, city, and district levels. The review also examined studies conducted on specific charter school sectors, including those operated by nonprofit and for-profits, virtual charter schools, and "no-excuse" charter schools. The author's conclusion pointed to variability in outcomes across settings, sectors, and student groups. For instance, some charter schools, such as in Boston and New York City, appear to do well at raising test scores and some attainment indicators, while in other contexts findings are mixed or negative, as in Indianapolis and Chicago. There is some evidence that charter school performance improves over time, as in North Carolina; however, there is also evidence of lingering poor performance, as in Arizona. The review cautioned against making any specific policy recommendations at the national level, given the great variation across states. Most of the research has been done on urban charter schools because that is where they are most located; however, more exploration is encouraged in nonurban charters. A 2011 study provided evidence of the underperformance of nonurban charter schools relative to urban charter schools (Angrist et al., 2011).

Meanwhile, virtual charter schools perform consistently and significantly worse than brick-and-mortar charter and traditional public schools (see Q31). A 2015 study of virtual charter schools in 18 states found student performance exhibited annual achievement losses, on average, in both math (−8.50 percentile points) and reading (−3.40 percentile points) (Woodworth et al., 2015). Separate studies on Ohio virtual charter schools showed even greater negative effects on student achievement (Zimmer et al., 2009) and one of those studies reported students in Ohio's virtual charter schools were less likely than their traditional public school peers to pass the state graduation exam (Ahn and McEachin, 2017).

"No Excuses" Charter Schools

Despite the overall mixed findings of charter school impact on student achievement, one area where there have been some strong positive effects are with "no excuses" charter schools such as KIPP and Democracy Prep. Studies published in 2011, 2014, and 2019 all demonstrate significantly higher academic achievement in reading and math among KIPP students (Angrist et al., 2011; Betts and Tang, 2014, 2019). Some of the inferences from these findings have been challenged, however. A 2011 study speculated that KIPP students' high scores on standardized exams might stem in part from high attrition rates for students who struggle to meet KIPP's academic and behavioral expectations (Miron, Urschel, and Saxton, 2011). That study also found that KIPP schools enrolled fewer students with disabilities and students classified as English language learners. A 2016 analysis of a small sample of 19 KIPP middle schools found that attrition rates in KIPPs were not much different than attrition of local school districts; however, the analysis revealed that replacement of those students tended to be higher achieving students—thus raising questions whether higher achievement scores are due to the KIPP model or student selection (Nichols-Barrer et al., 2016).

Finally, a 2016 study done by two Harvard economists analyzed Texas charter schools, which represent 3.5 percent of Texas public students. The researchers describe the Texas charter sector as

> ... one of the largest in the nation ... [that] ... boasts several of the most successful charter school networks. The Knowledge is Power Program (KIPP) and YES Prep schools—both winners of the Broad prize for most effective charter networks—have flagship schools in Houston, and the IDEA Public Schools [are] another exemplar of the charter community. (Dobbie and Fryer, 2016, 1)

The researchers found that, on the whole, Texas charter schools had no impact on test scores and a negative impact on future earnings. "No excuses" charter schools, in contrast, increased test scores and four-year college enrollments but had little impact on earnings. Similarly, a 2016 lottery-based analysis of a subset of "no excuses" charter schools showed large positive effects on academic performance (Chabrier, Cohodes, and Oreopoulos, 2016). The researchers note that because "no excuses" schools tend to be located in urban communities with underperforming schools, one explanation for their large effects is because they are compared to neighborhood schools with poor scores. Digging deeper into the analysis, researchers found that the one component that proved to have a significant impact was intensive tutoring on the part of the charter schools.

FURTHER READING

Ahn, J., and McEachin, A. 2017. "Student enrollment patterns and achievement in Ohio's online charter schools." *Educational Researcher*, 46(1), 44–57.

Angrist, J. D., et al. 2011. "Student achievement in Massachusetts' charter schools." Cambridge, MA: Center for Education Policy Research at Harvard University.

Berends, M. 2015. "Sociology and school choice: What we know after two decades of charter schools." *Annual Review of Sociology*, 41, 159–180.

Betts, J. R., and Tang, Y. E. 2014. *A meta-analysis of the literature on the effect of charter schools on student achievement*. Seattle, WA: Center on Reinventing Public Education.

Betts, J. R., and Tang, Y. E. 2018. *A meta-analysis of the effect of charter schools on student achievement*. San Diego, CA: San Diego Research Alliance.

Betts, J. R., and Tang, Y. E. 2019. "The effects of charter schools on student achievement." In M. Berends, R. J. Waddington, and J. A. Schoenig (Eds.), *School choice at the crossroads: Research perspectives*. New York: Routledge, 69–91.

Chabrier, J., Cohodes, S., and Oreopoulos, P. 2016. "What can we learn from charter school lotteries?" *Journal of Economic Perspectives*, 30(3), 57–84.

Cremata, E., et al., 2013. *National charter school performance study, 2013*. Stanford, CA: Center for Research on Education Outcomes.

Dobbie, W., and Fryer, R. G. 2013. "Getting beneath the veil of effective schools: Evidence from New York City." *American Economic Journal: Applied Economics*, 5(4), 28–60.

Dobbie, W., and Fryer, R. G. 2016. "Charter schools and labor market outcomes." *NBER Working Paper* (w22502). https://doi.org/10.1086/706534

Epple, D., Romano, R., and Zimmer, R. 2016. "Charter schools: A survey of research on their characteristics and effectiveness." In *Handbook of the Economics of Education* (Vol. 5). Elsevier, 139–208.

Ferrare, J. J. 2020. "Charter school outcomes." In M. Berends, Primus, A., and Springer, M. G. (Eds.), *Handbook of research on school choice*. Abingdon, UK: Routledge, 160–174.

Gamoran, A., and Fernandez, C. M. 2018. "Do charter schools strengthen education in high-poverty urban districts?" In I. C. Rotberg and J. L. Glazer (Eds.), *Choosing charters: Better schools or more segregation?* New York: Teachers College Press, 133–152.

Graziano, F. 2017. "Hartford's Capital Prep bypasses lottery, wins championship, raises questions." *Connecticut Public Radio*, May 26, 2017. Retrieved from https://tinyurl.com/y6ppgkd8

Hanushek, E. A., Machin, S., and Woessmann, L. (Eds.) 2016. *Handbook of the Economics of Education*. Amsterdam, The Netherlands: North Holland.

Lareau, A., and Goyette, K. (Eds.). 2014. *Choosing homes, choosing schools*. New York: Russell Sage Foundation.

Miron, G., Urschel, J. L., and Saxton, N. 2011. "What makes KIPP work? A study of student characteristics attrition and school finance." *National Center for the Study of Privatization in Education*. New York: Teachers College.

Nichols-Barrer, I., Gleason, P., Gill, B., and Tuttle, C. C. 2016. "Student selection, attrition, and replacement in KIPP middle schools." *Educational Evaluation and Policy Analysis*, 38(1), 5–20.

Tuttle, C. C., Gleason, P., and Clark, M. 2012. "Using lotteries to evaluate schools of choice: Evidence from a national study of charter schools." *Economics of Education Review*, 31(2), 237–253.

Woodworth, J., et al. 2015. *Online charter school study*. Stanford, CA: Center for Research on Educational Outcomes (CREDO).

Zimmer, R., et al. 2009. *Charter schools in eight states: Effects on achievement, attainment, integration, and competition.* Santa Monica, CA: RAND Corporation.

Zimmer, R., et al. 2012. "Examining charter student achievement effects across seven states." *Economics of Education Review*, 31(2), 213–224.

Q14. ARE POORLY PERFORMING CHARTER SCHOOLS CLOSED DOWN?

Answer: Part of the answer depends on how one defines poor performance. Charter schools guilty of financial malfeasance are more likely to be sanctioned or shut down altogether. Many charter closings are done for budget or financial reasons. It is more difficult to close a charter school for purely academic reasons, although this does happen in states with stricter accountability policies. Education researchers emphasize that charter schools that demonstrate strong operational and instructional plans at the time of authorization are much more likely to be successful.

The Facts: The federally funded National Charter School Resource Center describes the charter school concept of accountability in this way:

> A charter school is a public school that is independently run. It receives greater flexibility over operations in exchange for increased performance accountability. The school is established by a "charter," which is a performance contract describing key elements of the school. The charter contract describes things like the school's mission, instructional program, governance, personnel, finance, plans for student enrollment, and how all these are measured. . . . In exchange for this autonomy, charter schools are subject to periodic performance reviews and may be closed for failing to meet agreed-upon outcomes. (charterschoolcenter.ed.gov/what-charter-school)

Thus, the charter or performance contract dictates terms of a performance agreement between the charter authorizer, or sponsor, and the charter school. State regulations vary in terms of how frequently charter schools are reviewed, by whom, and against which criteria. States also differ in terms of how the authorizers themselves are held accountable.

Renew or Revoke? It Depends on the State

The Education Commission of the States (ECS), a self-described "trusted source for comprehensive knowledge and unbiased resources on education policy issues ranging from early learning through postsecondary education" (ecs.org), regularly updates a 50-state comparison of charter school policies that summarize key regulations by states that have charter school legislation (ecs.org/charter-school-policies). ECS is generally an impartial entity, although any organization may have some hidden biases. The resource compares how each state specifies grounds for closing or nonrenewing a school's charter and also any state policy provisions for charter school closures. In January 2020, according to ECS, every state but Maryland identifies a basis for terminating or not renewing a charter. Maryland leaves it to county boards to determine guidelines and procedures for charter revocation. Regulations for terminating a school's charter look generally similar across states, although some provide more details than others.

For example, in Wisconsin, authorizers may revoke a charter if:

- The charter school violated its contract.
- The pupils enrolled in the charter school failed to make sufficient progress toward attaining the state education goals.
- The charter school failed to comply with generally accepted accounting standards of fiscal management.
- The charter school violated the state's charter school law. (Wis. Stat. Ann. § 118.40)

Arizona statute provides a bit more detail on closure and review timeframes:

A charter school authorizer may deny a charter school's request for renewal if, in its judgment, the charter school has failed to:

- Meet or make sufficient progress toward the academic performance expectations set forth in the performance framework;
- Meet the operational performance expectations set forth in the performance framework or any improvement plans;
- Meet the financial performance expectations set forth in the performance framework or any improvement plans;
- Complete the obligations of the contract;
- Comply with any provision of law from which the charter school is not exempt.

Also, a charter school authorizer must review a charter at five-year intervals using a performance framework adopted by the authorizer and may revoke a charter at any time if the charter school breaches one or more provisions of its charter or if the sponsor determines that the charter holder has failed to:

- Meet or make sufficient progress toward the academic performance expectations set forth in the performance framework;
- Meet the operational performance expectations set forth in the performance framework or any improvement plans;
- Meet the financial performance expectations set forth in the performance framework or any improvement plans;
- Comply with any provision of law from which the charter school is not exempt.

In determining whether to renew or revoke a charter, the authorizer must consider, as one of the most important factors, whether the school is making sufficient progress toward the academic performance expectations set forth in the authorizer's performance framework. (Ariz. Rev. Stat. Ann. § 15–183)

Of course, these policies are all well and good on paper. Consistent interpretation and enactment of them remains a challenge. Determining what constitutes "sufficient progress" is not always black and white, and if there is some doubt, renewal is typically chosen over termination. In fact, pressure to renew even troubled charters is often strong. Termination of a school can be highly disruptive to a charter school's constituents. There are also financial implications; money has to be returned, and assets purchased with public taxpayer funds also need to be returned, a less straightforward process.

Finances and Closures

Early in their history, charter schools were usually closed for financial reasons; either they were not fiscally healthy or were mismanaged. Closures for academic reasons were comparatively rare. Even authorizers who wanted to shut down a charter school that was not helping students learn had trouble doing so.

In 2004, a period in which the charter school movement was steadily growing, the U.S. Department of Education conducted an evaluation of the federal Public Charter Schools Program and reported that:

- Charter schools rarely face formal sanctions (revocation or nonrenewal). Furthermore, authorizing bodies impose sanctions on charter schools because of problems related to *compliance with regulations* and *school finances* rather than *student performance*. Authorizers have difficulty closing schools that are having problems.
- During the time period examined by this study, little difference exists between the accountability requirements for charter schools and traditional public schools. (Finnigan et al., 2004, x)

Advocates of market-based approaches to education believe that the failure of a charter school demonstrates that the market is working and holding schools accountable for their performance.

However, the abrupt closure of a charter school is highly disruptive to students, educators, and families. Some parents who have enrolled their children in charter schools at risk of failing have even filed lawsuits that seek to place a moratorium on school closures and new charter school openings (Clark, 2019). Critics also contend that charter school closures are an inefficient and wasteful use of public tax dollars. The losses are sunk costs, never to be recovered.

Failing traditional public schools, by contrast, are usually allowed to continue under certain conditions, including targeted interventions by the district office or state authorities. These interventions are frequently not successful due to larger structural issues plaguing many schools, such as poverty in the surrounding community. To be sure, on the traditional public school side, returns on investment in schools that persistently perform poorly are also grossly inefficient. Traditional public schools cannot escape being shut down, but their shutdown tends to be a response to declining or shifts in enrollment in a district or due to the prohibitive costs (perceived or otherwise) of renovating schools in need of repair.

A report by the charter school advocacy group, Center for Education Reform (2011b), indicated that during the first 18 years of the charter school movement (i.e., 1992–1993 to 2010–2011 school years), 15 percent of the roughly 6,700 charter schools ever opened later closed their doors. Annually, about 1 to 2 percent of traditional public schools close, although comparing the two sectors is challenging given that the charter results occurred over a span of nearly two decades and the traditional public school numbers are annual. More importantly, the reasons for closings differed across sectors, in part due to the nature of the charter contract, because performance against contractual expectations is the basis for renewal or nonrenewal. Most traditional public school closures are due to enrollment changes in a school's catchment area. The Center for Education Reform cited five main reasons for charter school closures: financial (41.7 percent), mismanagement (24 percent), academic (18.6 percent), district obstacles (6.3 percent), and facilities (4.6 percent). The report concluded that:

> Most charter schools that close for financial or operational deficiencies do so within the first five years, or within their first charter contract. Failing to produce audits, or conduct basic, required oversight is a sure sign that the charter school leaders are not capable of leading a strong organization. Academic closures usually take longer because it takes the whole charter term to gather enough sound data and make proper comparisons. (Center for Education Reform, 2011a)

Closures over Time

Common Core of Data collected by the National Center for Educational Statistics shows that the percentage of charters closing is relatively small and actually on the decline since 2006–2007. The National Association of Charter School Authorizers, a charter school supporter, reported higher numbers of charter closures than the National Center for Educational Statistics and also disaggregated closures that occurred during scheduled renewal periods and unexpected closures prior to that period (qualitycharters .org/policy-research/inside-charter-school-growth/closings/). For instance, between the school years 2010–2011 and 2015–2016, the percentage of overall charter closures ranged between 2.3 and 3.8 percent (for an average of 3.5 percent). The charter closure rate "outside of renewal" ranged from 1.5 to 3.2 percent (for an average of 2.4 percent) during the same time period.

A 2017 National Alliance for Public Charter Schools report indicates that 211 charters closed out of a total of 6,939 (3.0 percent) in 2016–2017 (2017, 4). The report highlights the states with the five largest numbers of closed schools that same year, with California and Texas closing 30 schools each, Florida 25, Ohio 22, and Georgia 17. At the same time, several new charters were opening in those same states: Texas with 64 new schools, California with 56, and Florida with 26 new schools opening.

Charter school closure locations vary across the nation and are appreciably higher in some cities and states. For instance, *The Columbus*

Dispatch reported in 2014 that 29 percent of Ohio's charter schools closed between 1997 and 2013, and that in 2013, 17 charter schools closed (Smith-Richards and Bush, 2014). A 2015 article published in *Michigan Capitol Confidential* showed that between 1994 and 2015, 30 percent of Detroit's 72 charter schools closed for financial, academic, or enrollment reasons (Gantert, 2015).

Proponents of charter schools and market-based education reforms claim that charter closures mean the market is working. During congressional Hearings on the potential appointment of Betsy DeVos as Secretary of Education, DeVos cited the fact that 122 charters had been closed in Michigan, demonstrating charter schools are not given special shields from regulation (Einhorn and Darville, 2017).

The Implications of Charter Closures

Research has shown the negative social effects of closing a school, particularly on students who feel displaced following closures (Engberg et al., 2012; Kirshner, Gaertner, and Pozzoboni, 2010; de la Torre and Gwynne, 2009). In most states, charters that close are not held responsible for helping families find a replacement school; in those situations, families can be left scrambling to find another school. Some states and charter organizations provide more transitional help than others. Students and families can be faced with a new, perhaps longer commute to school. Relationships with students and teachers are abruptly ended. Students, especially those of younger age, may internalize the failure of the school.

Studies of the impact of charter school closures on student achievement have been mixed. A 2014 study of Michigan charter schools showed students displaced from charter closings doing no persistent harm (Brummet, 2014), while a 2016 study of Ohio charter middle schools indicated positive achievement gains for students who were displaced—likely attributable to their move to higher quality schools, which may or may not be another charter school (Carlson and Lavertu, 2016).

Charter school authorizers face a fundamental question: On what basis should closing decisions be made? Closings occur for a range of reasons, the most common being budget concerns associated with some inter-related combination of low enrollment, mishandling of finances, and poor academic performance. The closings that occur unexpectedly midyear are especially disruptive. However, if a school is not serving student needs, something should be done. Its closure should be based on a host of criteria: Is it beyond saving? Are the underlying problems identified and fixable (e.g., leadership turnover)? Is the school physically unsafe for students? Is instruction woefully executed and, again, beyond repair in a timely manner? Is the charter operator acting inappropriately, inefficiently, or illegally?

FURTHER READING

Brummet, Q. 2014. The effect of school closings on student achievement. *Journal of Public Economics, 119,* 108–124.

Carlson, D., and Lavertu, S. 2016. "Charter school closure and student achievement: Evidence from Ohio." *Journal of Urban Economics, 95,* 31–48.

Center for Education Reform. 2011a. CER *press* release: *"Charter schools closure rate tops 15 percent."* December 21, 2011. Washington, DC: Center for Education Reform. Retrieved from https://edreform.com/2011/12/charter-schools-closure-rate-tops-15-percent

Center for Education Reform. 2011b. *The state of charter schools: What we know—and what we do not—about performance and accountability.* Washington, DC: Center for Education Reform.

Clark, J. 2019. "Closing a failing school is normal, but not easy, in charters-only New Orleans." National Public Radio (NPR), September 6, 2019. Retrieved from https://www.kpbs.org/news/2019/sep/06/closing-a-failing-school-is-normal-but-not-easy

de la Torre, M., and Gwynne, J. 2009. *When schools close: Effects on displaced students in Chicago Public Schools.* Chicago, IL: Consortium on Chicago School Research.

Einhorn, E., and Darville, S. 2017. What we learned (and didn't) about Betsy DeVos at her confirmation hearing. *Chalkbeat,* January 18, 2017. Retrieved from https://tinyurl.com/yx5t92pn

Engberg, J., Gill, B., Zamarro, G., and Zimmer, R. 2012. "Closing schools in a shrinking district: Do student outcomes depend on which schools are closed?" *Journal of Urban Economics, 71*(2), 189–203.

Finnigan, K., Adelman, N., Anderson, L., Cotton, L., Donnelly, M. B., and Price, T. 2004. *Evaluation of the public charter schools program: Final report.* PPSS-2004-08. U.S. Department of Education.

Gantert, P. 2015. "No accountability? 30 percent of Detroit's charter schools have closed." *Michigan Capitol Confidential.* August 1, 2015. Retrieved from https://www.michigancapitolconfidential.com/21579

Kirshner, B., Gaertner, M., and Pozzoboni, K. 2010. "Tracing transitions: The effect of high school closure on displaced students." *Educational Evaluation and Policy Analysis, 32*(3), 407–429.

National Alliance for Public Charter Schools. 2017. "Estimated Public Charter School Growth, 2016–2017." NAPCS, February 1, 2017. https://www.publiccharters.org/publications/estimated-charter-public-school-enrollment-2016-17

National Association of Charter School Organizers. 2017. "New Report Examines Slow in Charter School Growth." NACSA, March 15, 2017. https://www.qualitycharters.org/news-commentary/press-releases/inside-charter-school-growth

Paino, M., Renzulli, L. A., Boylan, R. L., and Bradley, C. L. 2014. "For grades or money? Charter school failure in North Carolina." *Educational Administration Quarterly, 50*(3), 500–536.

Smith-Richards, J., and Bush, B. 2014. "Columbus has 17 charter school failures in one year." *The Columbus Dispatch*, January 12. Retrieved from http://www.dispatch.com/content/stories/local/2014/01/12/charter-failure.html

Q15. ARE MOST PUBLICLY FUNDED CHARTER SCHOOLS OPERATED BY EDUCATION MANAGEMENT ORGANIZATIONS AND CHARTER MANAGEMENT ORGANIZATIONS?

Answer: No, although the number has steadily risen since the early 2000s.

The Facts: At the beginning of the movement in the early 1990s, charter schools tended to be independent, stand-alone schools. There were signs of early corporate influence, such as with Edison Schools, Inc., which tried to sell services to charter schools and operated several itself. The modern-day charter arena has seen a dramatic increase in multischool networks run by Education Management Organizations (EMOs) and Charter Management Organizations (CMOs), which can operate in multiple districts and states.

EMOs emerged as part of the market-based education reforms in the late 1990s. The concept, as well as the name, was patterned after Health Management Organizations (HMOs), which came into existence at about the same time. The idea behind these organizations was that privately run businesses or firms could more efficiently and creatively oversee government services. In the case of EMOs, they were expected to be entrepreneurial and nimble in their leadership of schools. EMOs, which can manage either district public schools or charter schools, establish performance contracts with one or more of their schools.

EMOs also can have either for-profit or nonprofit status and can serve single sites, regions, or the entire nation. For instance, some EMOs oversee charter schools in multiple states, such as the Knowledge is Power Program (KIPP) and Achievement First. Most EMOs have historically been for-profit, although the number of nonprofit EMOs has been increasing.

CMOs serve charter schools exclusively and tend to be nonprofit, although they can also contract services with private, for-profit firms. There are not many clear differences between EMOs and CMOs, although EMOs can choose to focus on certain operational aspects of their network, such as administrative services, while CMOs tend to provide multiple functions such as hiring, training, data analysis, and private fundraising.

A 2013 analysis published by the National Education Policy Center reported that as of the 2011–2012 school year, roughly 36 percent of charter schools and about 44 percent of charter school students were in CMO- or EMO-managed schools (Miron and Gulosino, 2013). The same report determined that between 1995–1996 and 2011–2012, the number of for-profit EMOs rose from 5 to 97 and the number of schools they operated soared from 6 to 840. A 2015 study reported that stand-alone charter schools—institutions that do not belong to a CMO or EMO—dropped by about one-quarter between 2010 and 2014 (Mead, Mitchell, and Rotherman, 2015).

As of 2019, about 20 percent of all charter schools were managed by nonprofit CMOs while another 10 percent or so are affiliated with EMOs. Critics of these centrally controlled management organizations say that they are encroaching on the public school district. Although a 2016 study reported that charter school teachers feel like they have more autonomy and freedom in providing instruction than their traditional public school counterparts, charter sector teachers in non-EMO schools reported higher levels of autonomy than those in EMO-managed schools (Oberfield, 2016). The author of that study cautioned that because teachers choose the environment in which they wish to work, the differences in perceived autonomy cannot necessarily be attributed to organizational differences—it could instead be a function of self-selection. In other words, teachers who choose charter schools may particularly value autonomy given that teacher independence is one of the main narratives underlying charter schools.

Capitalism Meets Public Education

Proponents of market-based education and putting public education in the hands of businesses argue that pursuing profits and serving the best interests of students are not mutually exclusive goals. Critics contend that the search for profit and the interests of children are not well aligned, and that the lure of making profits from a taxpayer-funded education system is too great for at least some EMOs. (Even some nonprofit CMOs and EMOs have made arrangements that benefit their owners financially.) For instance, there have been documented instances in which a charter operator (e.g., an EMO) contracts with itself to offer services or assets to its charter schools. Investigative reporting by *ProPublica*, an independent nonprofit news organization, showed that North Carolina charter school entrepreneur Baker Mitchell was profiting from a reciprocal business arrangement.

> Every year, millions of public education dollars flow through Mitchell's chain of four nonprofit charter schools to for-profit companies he controls. The schools buy or lease nearly everything from companies owned by Mitchell. Their desks. Their computers. The training they provide to teachers. Most of the land and buildings. Unlike with traditional school districts, at Mitchell's charter schools there's no competitive bidding. No evidence of haggling over rent or contracts. (Wang, 2014)

A 2018 research article warned of questionable financial deals and intermingling of funds that have occurred in the charter school sector when regulatory oversight is lacking (Green, Baker, and Oluwole, 2018). One of the illustrations offered by the authors is a nonprofit charter EMO, Imagine Schools, responsible for 63 charters schools enrolling more than 33,000 students in 11 states and the District of Columbia. Imagine Schools engaged many of its real estate deals through its subsidiary, for-profit SchoolHouse Finance. They rented space to Imagine Schools at rates far exceeding what charter schools normally pay. A typical charter school spends around 14 percent of its publicly funded budget on rent while Imagine Schools was paying upward of 40 percent.

Every year, the U.S. Department of Education's Office of Inspector General drafts a plan describing its major priorities. Between January 2005 and September 30, 2014, the U.S. Office of Inspector General opened 65 charter school investigations and by 2015 those investigations yielded 41 indictments and 30 convictions of charter school officials (Center for Popular Democracy, 2017, 3). The 2014 Annual Plan cited the "current and emerging risk that charter school relationships with charter management organizations and education management organizations pose" (U.S. Department of Education, 2013, 8).

Investigations ensued, including, according to a 2015 *Hartford Courant* investigative report, the FBI issuing subpoenas to examine business relationships of a Connecticut-based nonprofit charter management company (Kauffman, de la Torre, and Lender, 2015). The Connecticut Department of Education released an investigative report in January 2015 that cited the former CEO of "rampant nepotism" and using school funds to make extravagant modifications to an apartment owned by the charter organization and that he subsequently rented (Dorsey, 2015). The CEO had resigned only months prior in June 2014 after it was revealed that he had misrepresented his academic credentials and failed to report a prior criminal record.

A 2017 *Los Angeles Times* article reported that the FBI and Homeland Security raided Celerity Educational Group's Los Angeles offices, seizing laptops and computer records (Phillips, Blume, and Hamilton, 2017). In May 2019, the founder and ex-CEO of the nonprofit Celerity Educational Group was sentenced to two-and-a-half years in federal prison for conspiring to misappropriate $3.2 million in public education funds allocated to some of her company's schools (U.S. Attorney's Office, Central District of California, 2019).

In July 2020, federal prosecutors charged the former executive director of the for-profit Community Preparatory Academy charter school in California with theft and tax fraud. The director, who was accused of stealing more than $3.1 million from the school to fund personal activities such as Disney cruises and other forms of entertainment, agreed to plead guilty on two felony offenses (U.S. Attorney's Office, Central District of California, 2020). In September 2020, a former charter school principal in Arizona was sentenced to four months in jail and required to repay more than $2.5 million dollars for fake-enrolling students in the now-closed charter school in Goodyear, Arizona (Attorney General, State of Arizona, 2020).

Traditional public schools are not immune to the misuse of public funds and corruption. But there are more safeguards in place to limit and detect such behavior than in the charter sector. Unlike traditional public school districts, EMOs and CMOs operate with less oversight. As organizations that have no links to state and local governments, monitoring their practices requires intentional monitoring such as through annual financial and performance reports and audits. But even these safeguards appear inadequate to deter misbehavior, including misappropriation of public funds (Ertas, 2020). Moreover, charter school regulations vary by state, with some instituting tighter regulatory and accountability policies than others. Charter school proponents generally see more regulations as being at odds with what they believe makes charter schools work—autonomy within a competitive educational market. Skeptics, on the other hand, are concerned that an unregulated institutional environment invite, or at least enable, corrupt behavior. In response to high-profile corruption events, some states have enhanced their guidelines to provide more oversight of the charter sector. In the fall of 2018, for example, California Governor Jerry Brown signed a bill prohibiting for-profit charter schools in his state. The sponsor of the bill, Assemblyman Kevin McCarty, gathered evidence demonstrating how some for-profit corporations running charter schools in California had abused the system. One report to the Education Committee documented the following:

> In California, there are 34 charter schools run by for-profit EMOs or for-profit CMOs enrolling over 25,000 students. In 2016, the largest for-profit EMO, K-12 Inc., which has received over $310 million of taxpayer money over the last 12 years, settled a lawsuit filed by the state for $168.5 million over claims that the corporation manipulated attendance records and overstated students' success. This same for-profit EMO, which is publicly traded on Wall Street, had estimated revenue of $708 million in 2012. The company estimated their profit at $87 million in the same year. They paid their top 6 executives $11 million in compensation while their average teacher salary was $36,000. At the same time, one of the charter schools managed by this for-profit corporation in California had a graduation rate of 36 percent compared to 78 percent statewide. In addition, every year since it began, except 2013, this school had more dropouts than graduates.
>
> If the goal of a for-profit corporation is to maximize profit for the corporation's shareholders, then the Committee should consider whether it is an appropriate use of state taxpayer dollars for for-profit corporations to operate public schools. Additionally, does this for-profit model provide a perverse incentive for these charter schools to limit services for students in order to increase profits? (Kelley, 2017)

Teacher Turnover in EMO and CMO Schools

While there is no single study that has assessed the cost-benefits of EMO and CMO-run schools, there are some indications of the inefficient use of public tax dollars. One of the primary areas of inefficiency is teacher turnover. A 2013 study found that high turnover among teachers can damage school culture and have negative effects on student achievement (Ronfeldt, Loeb, and Wyckoff, 2013). Teacher turnover can lead to high costs associated with rehiring, onboarding, and developing new teachers. For instance, a 2013 *New York Times* article reported that teachers at Achievement First schools in Connecticut, Brooklyn, and Providence, Rhode Island, taught for an average of only 2.3 years (Rich, 2013). One of the more prominent EMOs, KIPP, also has a history of significant teacher turnover. A 2016 publication reviewed the research literature on teacher turnover among CMOs, reporting higher than normal turnover rates (Torres, 2016). An excerpt from that study reads:

> Multi-year averages show that teacher turnover in charter schools is around 20 percent to 25 percent nationally and in various state contexts (Gross and DeArmond, 2010; Miron and Applegate, 2007; Silverman, 2012, 2013; Stuit and Smith, 2010), which is about twice as high as the national average at traditional urban public schools (Stuit and Smith, 2010). Available data show similar turnover rates in CMO schools. Average CMO turnover rates were around 20 percent for the 17 CMO schools funded by the New Schools Venture Fund, and some leaders reported 35 percent annual turnover rates (Furgeson et al., 2011). Twenty-seven percent of teachers in KIPP schools nationwide left their classroom teaching position in 2010–2011 (KIPP Foundation, 2012) and 32 percent did in the 2011–2012 school year (KIPP Foundation, 2013). (Torres, 2016, 895)

To be sure, hiring and retaining teachers in high-poverty areas remains a challenge nationally. Charter schools that locate in such areas are not immune to these difficulties. But the evidence suggests that at least some of the major charter management providers in these districts have greater difficulty retaining teachers than their traditional public school neighbors.

FURTHER READING

Attorney General, State of Arizona. 2020. "Former vice principal of closed Goodyear Charter School sentenced for her role in enrolling fake students." Office of the Attorney General, Arizona. September 23, 2020. Retrieved from https://www.azag.gov/press-release/former-vice-principal-closed-goodyear-charter-school-sentenced-her-role-enrolling

Baker, B., and Miron, G. 2015. *The business of charter schooling: Understanding the policies that charter operators use for financial benefit.* Boulder, CO: National Education Policy Center. Retrieved from http://nepc.colorado.edu/publication/charter-revenue

Berends, M. 2018. "The continuing evolution of school choice in America." In R. Papa and S. Armfield (Eds.), *Handbook of education policy.* Hoboken, NJ: Wiley-Blackwell, 97–118.

Bulkley, K. E., and Henig, J. R. 2020. "Charter school governance and politics." In M. Berends, A. Primus, and M. G. Springer (Eds.), *Handbook of research on school choice*. Abingdon, UK: Routledge.

Center for Popular Democracy. 2017. *The tip of the iceberg: Charter school vulnerabilities to waste, fraud, and abuse*. Center for Popular Democracy. Retrieved from https://populardemocracy.org/sites/default/files/Charter-Schools-National-Report_rev2.pdf

Dorsey, F. L. 2015. *Investigative report for the Connecticut State Department of Education: Investigation of Jumoke/FUSE charter and school turnaround operations*. January 2, 2015. Retrieved from http://blog.ctnews.com/education/files/2015/01/Jumoke-FUSE-Invest-2014-2.pdf

Ertas, N. 2020. "Administrative corruption and integrity violations in the charter school sector." *Public Integrity*. https://doi.org/10.1080/10999922.2020.1758535

Green, P., Baker, B. D., and Oluwole, J. O. 2018. "Are charter schools the second coming of Enron: An examination of the gatekeepers that protect against dangerous related-party transactions in the charter school sector." *Indiana Law Journal*, 93(4), 1121–1160.

Kauffman, M., de la Torre, V., and Lender, J. 2015. "Probe of charter school group blasts 'suspect' conduct, 'rampant nepotism.'" *Hartford Courant*. January 5, 2015. Retrieved from https://www.courant.com/community/hartford/hc-fuse-jumoke-investigation-report-0103-20150102-story.html

Kelley, C. 2017. *Assembly Committee on Education report*. Patrick O'Donnell, Chair AB 406 (McCarty)—As Amended March 23, 2017.

Ladd, H. F. 2019. "How charter schools threaten the public interest." *Journal of Policy Analysis and Management*, 38(4), 1063–1071.

Mead, S., Mitchell, A. L., and Rotherman, A. J. 2015. *The state of the charter school movement*. Washington, DC: Bellwether Education Partners.

Miron, G., and Gulosino, C. 2013. *Profiles of for-profit and nonprofit Education Management Organizations, 2011–2012*. Boulder, CO: National Education Policy Center.

Miron, G., Urschel, J. L., Yat Aguilar, M. A, and Dailey, B. 2011. *Profiles of for-profit and nonprofit Education Management Organizations: Thirteenth annual report—2010–2011*. Boulder, CO: National Education Policy Center.

Oberfield, Z. W. 2016. "A bargain half fulfilled: Teacher autonomy and accountability in traditional public schools and public charter schools." *American Educational Research Journal*, 53(2), 296–323.

Phillips, A. M., Blume, H., and Hamilton, M. 2017. "Federal agents raid Los Angeles charter school network." *Los Angeles Times*. January 25, 2017. Retrieved from https://www.latimes.com/local/education/la-me-edu-celerity-charter-schools-20170125-story.html

Rich, M. 2013. "At charter schools, short careers by choice." *The New York Times.* August 26, 2013.

Ronfeldt, M., Loeb, S., and Wyckoff, J. 2013. "How teacher turnover harms student achievement." *American Educational Research Journal, 50,* 4–36.

Torres, A. C. 2016. "Is this work sustainable? Teacher turnover and perceptions of workload in charter management organizations." *Urban Education, 51*(8), 891–914.

U.S. Attorney's Office, Central District of California. 2019. "Charter school founder and CEO sentenced to 2½ years in federal prison for misappropriating $3.2 million in public education funds." U.S. Department of Justice, May 20, 2019. Retrieved from https://www.justice.gov/usao-cdca/pr/charter-school-founder-and-ceo-sentenced-2-years-federal-prison-misappropriating-32

U.S. Attorney's Office, Central District of California. 2020. "Former head of Community Preparatory Academy admits stealing over $3 million and spending $220,000 on Disney expenses." U.S. Department of Justice, July 17, 2020. Retrieved from https://www.justice.gov/usao-cdca/pr/former-head-community-preparatory-academy-admits-stealing-over-3-million-and-spending

U.S. Department of Education. 2013. Fiscal year 2014 annual plan. *Office of Inspector General.* Retrieved from https://www2.ed.gov/about/offices/list/oig/misc/wp2014.pdf

Wang, M. 2014. "Charter school power broker turns public education into private profits." *ProPublica,* October 15, 2014. Retrieved from https://www.propublica.org/article/charter-school-power-broker-turns-public-education-into-private-profits

Woodworth, J., Raymond, M., Han, C., Negassi, Y., Richardson, P., and Snow, W. 2017. *Charter management organizations.* Palo Alto, CA: CREDO.

4

Standards, Accountability, and Assessment

The word "accountability" entered the vocabulary of the nation's educators in the 1970s. This is not to say that public schools were unaccountable to anyone in the past. They have always faced tough questions from their boards and even from state agencies and accrediting agencies. But with the significant of infusion of federal funds stemming from the 1965 Elementary and Secondary Education Act, accountability became an entity in its own right, attracting the attention of politicians, bureaucrats, academics, parents, and educators everywhere.

At a very basic level, public education accountability revolves around how schools use public funds. Public schools have always been held to this level of accountability. But with the rise of increasing federal support for public schools, a new, more scientific form of accountability was introduced. Schools became responsible for employing methods of scientific management: goals must be articulated; measurement of progress toward goals must be made; feedback on progress must be conveyed to management; corrective action must be taken; and the entire process repeated.

In education, goals take the form of standards, for example: All students will make a minimum of eight months progress in reading each school year. Measurement of progress toward goals has taken the form of nationally standardized written tests, frequently in a form that can be graded by machine.

Increasingly, however, educators and parents are asking whether this system of goal setting and standardized testing best serves the interests of children. Are the goals of American education fully and accurately measured by the standardized tests? Are the test data a useful or even appropriate basis for the many decisions teachers and administrators must make in regards to promotion, graduation, hiring, and firing of staff?

Q16. HAVE STANDARDS-BASED REFORMS WORKED TO IMPROVE THE ACADEMIC PERFORMANCE OF AMERICAN SCHOOLCHILDREN?

Answer: Few argue that academic standards are a bad thing. They can help guide teachers and schools in the process of developing curricula, identifying learning objectives, and delivering instruction. In the United States, however, standards-based reforms have raised concerns about federal overreach in education and complaints about overly prescriptive, narrow, or otherwise disputed learning objectives. In particular, critics say that standards-based instruction is too reliant on student testing.

The Facts: Academic content standards specify what students at grade levels should know and be able to do. They are typically organized by subject area, such as reading and math, and further broken down into smaller subject area strands. For example, a third-grade math standard set by a well-known consortium in 2009 is "Geometric measurement: understand concepts of area and relate area to multiplication and to addition." And in third-grade reading: "Determine the main idea of a text; recount the key details and explain how they support the main idea." Both examples come from the Common Core State Standards, which will be explained below.

In recent decades, subject matter organizations established their own set of academic standards. For instance, the National Council of Teachers of Mathematics (NCTM) drafted *Curriculum and Evaluation Standards for School Mathematics* in 1989 and have revised or updated these standards several times since. The National Council for Teachers of English (NCTE), along with the International Reading Association (IRA), developed standards in English language arts and literacy in 1994 and last updated them in 2009. The National Science Teaching Association (NSTA) led the development of a major overhaul of science and science literacy standards and worked with affiliated groups to build the *Next Generation Science Standards* (NGSS), released in 2013. Educators in other fields such as social studies and geography have also developed standards through their national organizations.

The standards for any one content area contain both knowledge and skills. For instance, the NCTM standards, which are now part of the Common Core State Standards, include both content and process standards. The process standards are mathematical processes, such as problem solving, reasoning and proof, communication, representation, and connections. Here is an example of an eighth-grade math standard from the Common Core State Standards. It is categorized under the *Expressions and Equations* learning strand, which asks of students to "understand the connections between proportional relationships, lines, and linear equations."

CCSS.MATH.CONTENT.8.EE.B.6

Use similar triangles to explain why the slope m is the same between any two distinct points on a non-vertical line in the coordinate plane; derive the equation $y = mx$ for a line through the origin and the equation $y = mx + b$ for a line intercepting the vertical axis at b.

Math or geometry experts may see the value to students of understanding this concept. But the level of difficulty is remarkable to most lay people and, one would assume, to an eighth-grader. Standards like these need a context to be relevant, especially to an eighth-grader. Of course, that is where good teaching comes into play; it takes a skilled educator to make this content come alive in a young child's world. This highlights one of the challenges of standards-based reform: the readiness of districts across the nation to implement the standards in the classroom.

Brief History of Standards

Standards-based reform became popular following the publication of a bellwether report, *A Nation at Risk* (1983), that sounded alarms about the state of American education, especially compared to that of other countries. The authors of the report, a panel of experts organized by Secretary of Education Terrel Bell and collectively known as the National Commission on Excellence in Education, declared that "the educational foundations of our society are presently being eroded by a rising tide of mediocrity that threatens our very future as a nation and as a people" (National Commission on Excellence in Education, 1983).

In response to this bleak warning, most states developed or adopted their own sets of academic standards. In 1989, President George H. W. Bush worked with a coalition of governors to develop a set of education goals for the nation, called America 2000. Although America 2000 did not pass Congressional muster, a revamped version under President Bill Clinton called Goals 2000 later did. Goals 2000 provided a national framework for education reform intended to "promote the research, consensus building, and systemic changes needed to ensure equitable educational opportunities and high levels of educational achievement for all students" (https://tinyurl.com/unkaq2f). It was the first formal federal effort to promote the creation, adoption, and ultimately measurement of academic standards. Although state participation was said to be voluntary, the federal government made some funding dependent on adopting the standards.

Another Clinton-era attempt to introduce academic standards in U.S. schools was initiated by the reauthorization of the federal Elementary and Secondary Education Act (ESEA) of 1994. Launched in 1965 as a part of President Lyndon B. Johnson's famous "War on Poverty," ESEA provides federal funds to districts serving low-income students, among other things. It also offers general grant aid to state education agencies to improve K–12 education. According to a 2009 report by the National Academy of Education, the reauthorization of ESEA in 1994 extended the vision of Goals 2000 by requiring states "to set challenging and rigorous content standards for all students and develop assessments, aligned with the standards, to measure student progress" (Shepard, Hannaway, and Baker, 2009, 2).

The United States continued its standards-based reforms under President George W. Bush through the No Child Left Behind Act (NCLB) of 2001, which was a reauthorization of ESEA under a new name. NCLB called on states to adopt increased testing in reading and math and to report annually proficiency rates for students of color, special education students, English language learners, and students from economically disadvantaged families. The performance of historically marginalized and lower scoring student groups was singled out to highlight and monitor achievement gaps between these groups and their more advantaged peers. NCLB laid out serious consequences for states—and ultimately districts and schools within them—that did not meet annual progress targets. Although state academic standards were intended to help districts, schools, and teachers develop new curricula and instructional practices, the high-stakes testing movement ended up doing just the opposite. Under the threat of being punished for low scores, genuine instruction gave way to test prep. As the National Research Council reported in 2008, "assessment has become the principal driver of most states' standards-based reform efforts" (National Research Council, 2008, 71).

A minority counterargument remains in the policy arena that remains supportive of standardized testing and warns of going too far the other way if schools start abandoning state assessments. Proponents of standards-based testing contend that if the scores are used sensibly, they offer value to inform practitioners and policy makers how well students are performing academically as well as how they are doing over time (Chingos et al., 2015). They make a case for continuing federal testing mandates but without tying them to standards and accountability policies. In other words, don't throw out the baby with the bathwater.

Has Standards-Based Education Worked?

The concept of academic standards is widely honored. The controversy, or at least debate, lies in what those standards are, who decides them, and how progress toward them is assessed. In a nation fixated on testing, standards take on heightened meaning. What is known empirically about the usefulness of standards depends on their implementation. Implementation of standards varies across states, within states, across districts and even within districts (Porter, Polikoff, and Smithson, 2009; Spillane, 2005). Some would argue the most important consideration is how standards appear in the classroom and influence teachers on the front line. Others contend the most important consideration is whether student performance is improving as a result, or whether there are benefits to standardized testing. A 2015 study of the implementation of Common Core found that the willingness and capabilities of teachers are strongly related to how standards are ultimately put into action in schools (Porter, Fusarelli, and Fusarelli, 2015). A 2009 National Academy of Education report echoes these concerns:

> Standards-based education is still the core idea guiding education policy and education reform. . . . As yet, neither state content standards nor state tests reflect the ambitions of standards-based reform rhetoric, and the link between high expectations for all students and capacity building has been almost forgotten. (Shepard, Hannaway, and Baker, 2009, 7)

The late educator Deborah Meier assembled a range of authors to speak to the fundamental question and title of her book, *Will Standards Save Public Education?* (Meier, 2000). Although published two decades ago, many of the book's arguments remain cogent today. One key message from Meier is that standards should not be equated with *standardization*. In other words, a set of standards does not necessarily have to lead to everyone doing the same thing in schools. Students learn differently, at different rates, and using different abilities. Holding students to specific age or grade-level academic standards flies in the face of this truism.

Standards can help guide teachers, schools, and districts; but no set of standards can possibly cover all that one must know to be college or career ready. The standards movement has been set back in recent years as rates of failure to pass high school exit exams have been made public. Too many tests were seen to focus on narrow bits of knowledge that were relevant only for preparing students to take even more esoteric exams in college. Deborah Meier stepped forward again to issue a mandate: "No student should be expected to meet an academic requirement that a cross-section of successful adults in the community cannot" (Kohn, 2019). Alfie Kohn, a longtime critic of standardized testing, added a corollary to Meier's mandate: "Any public officials who talk sanctimoniously about the need to 'raise the bar' and demand 'tougher standards' should be required by law to take these exams themselves . . . and have their scores published in the newspaper" (2019).

FURTHER READING

Chingos, M. M., Dynarski, M., Whitehurst, G. J., and West, M. R. 2015. *The case for annual testing.* Washington, DC: Brookings Institute.

Kohn, A. 2019. "The education conversation we should be having." *Washington Post*, October 3, 2019. Retrieved from https://www.washingtonpost.com/education/2019/10/30/education-conversation-we-should-be-having

Koyama, J. 2015. "When things come undone: The promise of dissembling education policy." *Discourse: Studies in the Cultural Politics of Education*, 36, 548–559.

Meier, D. 2000. *Will standards save public education?* Boston, MA: Beacon Press.

National Commission on Excellence in Education. 1983. *A nation at risk: The imperative for educational reform.* Washington, DC: Government Printing Office. April. https://www2.ed.gov/pubs/NatAtRisk/index.html

National Research Council. 2008. *Common standards for K-12 education?* Considering the Evidence: Summary of a Workshop Series. Washington, DC: National Academies Press.

Porter, R., Fusarelli, L. D., and Fusarelli, B. C. 2015. "Implementing the Common Core: How educators interpret curriculum reform." *Educational Policy*, 29, 111–139.

Porter, A. C., Polikoff, M. S., and Smithson, J. 2009. "Is there a de facto national intended curriculum? Evidence from state content standards." *Educational Evaluation and Policy Analysis*, 31(3), 238–268.

Shepard, L., Hannaway, J., and Baker, E. 2009. *Standards, assessments, and accountability. Education policy white paper.* Washington, DC: National Academy of Education.

Spillane, J. P. 2005. "Standards deviation: How schools misunderstand education policy." (Policy Brief RB-43, June 2005). Philadelphia, PA: The Consortium for Policy Research in Education. https://www.cpre.org/sites/default/files/policybrief/883_rb43.pdf

Q17. ARE THE COMMON CORE STATE STANDARDS A NATIONAL INITIATIVE—AND IF SO, DO THEY AMOUNT TO A NATIONAL CURRICULUM?

Answer: It depends on whom you ask. Supporters of the Common Core State Standards (or simply Common Core) would say that academic standards are up to states to adopt voluntarily and use as guidance for state and local curricula. Founders of the Common Core also contend that the standards were developed not by the federal government but by a range of education stakeholders, including teachers and content area experts. Skeptics will say otherwise, arguing that they are neither common nor are they the states'. Critics contend that states were under pressure to adopt the Common Core to qualify for federal funds; they would also say the development of the standards was heavily influenced by an independent nonprofit organization contracted by the U.S. Department of Education. The tight coupling of the Common Core with a nationwide achievement test raised suspicions among those wary of federal overreach of K–12 public education.

The Facts: The Common Core State Standards were developed in 2009, initiated by the National Governors Association and the Council of Chief State School Officers. The Common Core represents K–12 academic standards in math and English language arts/literacy (sometimes referred to as ELA). The high school ELA standards for reading, writing, speaking and listening, and language were also intended to apply as literacy standards in subjects like social studies and science.

The Common Core was introduced amid significant controversy. Conservatives and liberals alike found reasons to criticize the Common Core, albeit for different reasons (Williams, 2014). For instance, powerful teachers' unions bemoaned its hasty and disorganized rollout and remained wary of more high-stakes tests that would follow them. Republicans decried the heavy federal involvement and financial investment. The public was continually reminded that the standards were developed in grassroots fashion by several stakeholder organizations, including the nation's two largest teachers' unions, the International Reading Association and the National Council of Teachers of Mathematics, and the Council of Chief State School Officers. The reminders didn't seem to change public opinion that it was a federal initiative. The reminders didn't sway critics—including a good portion of the American public—who did not like the idea of the federal government dictating education policy, which has traditionally been shaped and managed at the state level.

The main Common Core website (http://www.corestandards.org/) argues in its *myths vs. facts* page that "The Common Core drafting process relied on teachers and standards experts from across the country. In addition, many state experts came together to create the most thoughtful and transparent process of standard setting." Critics, though, contended that the involvement and input of those parties was perfunctory or limited and that the process was actually dominated by Achieve (a federally contracted education organization), the National Governors Association, and then-U.S. Secretary of Education Arne Duncan (Ravitch, 2016). Suspicions arose that corporate elites had helped underwrite their development. According to Ravitch (2019; 2020), the Bill and Melinda Gates Foundation contributed more than $200 million to underwrite the Common Core. Some viewed such involvement watchful of ulterior motives, while others saw it as generous philanthropists looking to improve American education.

It is understandable why, to many, the Common Core are viewed as a national initiative. Part of the American Recovery and Reinvestment Act of 2009 was the U.S. Department of Education's Race to the Top program. Race to the Top tied $4.35 billion in competitive funding opportunities to the requirement that states adopt internationally benchmarked college and career ready standards and assessments (https://www2.ed.gov/programs/racetothetop/factsheet.html). Although Race to the Top did not specify that the college and career ready standards had to be the Common Core, many states interpreted it as such and for good reason. It turned out that most states initially adopted the Common Core and *all* of the states that were awarded Race to the Top grants were among those that did.

Much distrust of the Common Core was likely because it was tied to a resurgence in high-stakes testing, which many oppose. If you have standards, they are worthless unless you know whether you have met them; and the only way to know is to have a test to see. Such was the level of reasoning that prevailed throughout the entire effort. For instance, a 2015

California poll of representative voters found that opposition to the Common Core was commensurate with, "[i]n particular, opposition to President Obama, opposition to testing, support for current funding levels and local funding control, and two specific mis/negative conceptions about the standards" (Polikoff et al., 2016, 265).

A major point of contention has been whether the Common Core constitutes a national curriculum. A curriculum comprises lessons, academic content, assessments, and learning materials used to deliver instruction on a subject. Thus at first glance, the Common Core doesn't align with the formal definition of a curriculum. However, the Common Core are the standards against which all the components of a curriculum are (theoretically) based. Assessments should be aligned with the standards, lessons should teach to the standards, learning materials should reflect learning goals inherent in the standards. At the very least, the Common Core helps shape the curriculum of those states that adopted it.

By February 2014, 45 states and the District of Columbia had adopted the standards. In 2020, there was some retraction with only 41 states, the District of Columbia, and four territories following the Common Core. Some of the initial adopters pulled out (e.g., Indiana, Oklahoma, and South Carolina) or at least stopped referring to their state standards as Common Core. Implementation has also not been uniform across the states.

The implementation of the Common Core, however, was criticized for being rushed, inconsistent across states, and excessively tied to a battery of federally supported standardized assessments. Teachers found it difficult to implement, especially at first. The standards themselves were substantially more difficult to obtain than prior standards, and while Common Core opponents acknowledged that academic rigor is to be lauded, they complained that its uniform academic expectations for all students were unrealistic and, in some cases, harmful.

Many educators, for example, decried some of the recommendations put forth as arbitrary or short-sighted, such as guidance that reading lessons should be apportioned with less emphasis on literature (Common Core standards call for half of elementary school reading assignments to be nonfiction and by the twelfth grade, this climbs to 70 percent). Other scholars such as Diane Ravitch questioned why a reform this massive would be rolled out on such a large scale without any field test to ensure its effectiveness or work out the inevitable kinks (Ravitch, 2016).

Proponents of the Common Core, however, commended the standards' rigor, breadth, and inclusion of learning standards beyond content knowledge (i.e., cognitive strategies) (Conley, 2011; Goldstein, 2019). In a 2009 presentation to the U.S. House of Representatives' Committee on

Education and Labor, the Executive Director of the Council of Chief State School Officers, Gene Wilhoit, testified that the ambitious learning targets contained in the Common Core guidelines would improve U.S. competitiveness in the world, particularly in science, math, and technology subjects (Wilhoit, 2009). Although, to date, very few studies have addressed the effectiveness of the standards, a 2019 study compared student performance in states that adopted College and Career Ready standards (CCR is a subset of the Common Core designed for high school students) to those that did not between the years 2010 and 2017 (see Barnum, 2019). The initial results show that the influences of CCR standards on academic achievement were very small and, in some cases, negative. In fact, the only statistically significant result was a negative effect for fourth-grade reading scores one year and three years following CCR adoption.

FURTHER READING

Apple, M. W. 2001. "Will standards save public education?" *Educational Policy*, 15(5), 724–29.

Barnum, M. 2019. "Nearly a decade later, did the Common Core work? New research offers clues." *Chalkbeat*, April 29, 2019. Retrieved from https://www.chalkbeat.org/2019/4/29/21121004/nearly-a-decade-later-did-the-common-core-work-new-research-offers-clues

Conley, D. T. 2011. "Building on the common core." *Educational Leadership*, 68(6), 16–20.

Goldstein, D. 2019. "After 10 years of nopes and setbacks, what happened to the Common Core?" *New York Times*, December 6, 2019. Retrieved from https://www.nytimes.com/2019/12/06/us/common-core.html

Hill, H. C. 2001. "Policy is not enough: Language and the interpretation of state standards." *American Educational Research Journal*, 38(2), 289–318.

Paul, C. A. 2016. "Elementary and Secondary Education Act of 1965." *Social Welfare History Project*. Retrieved from http://socialwelfare.library.vcu.edu/programs/education/elementary-and-secondary-education-act-of-1965

Phillips, G. W. 2010. *International benchmarking: State education performance standards*. Washington, DC: American Institutes of Research.

Polikoff, M. S. 2017. "Is Common Core 'working'? And where does Common Core research go from here?" *AERA Open*, 3(1). https://doi.org/10.1177%2F2332858417691749

Polikoff, M. S., Hardaway, T., Marsh, J. A., and Plank, D. N. 2016. "Who is opposed to Common Core and why?" *Educational Researcher*, 45(4), 263–266.

Porter, A. C., Polikoff, M. S., and Smithson, J. 2009. "Is there a de facto national intended curriculum? Evidence from state content standards." *Educational Evaluation and Policy Analysis, 31*(3), 238–268.

Ravitch, D. 2016. *The death and life of the great American school system: How testing and choice are undermining education.* New York: Basic Books.

Ravitch, D. 2019. "The most important article written about Common Core." DianeRavitch.net, December 20, 2019. Retrieved from https://dianeravitch.net/2019/12/20/the-most-important-article-written-about-common-core

Ravitch, D. 2020. *Slaying Goliath: The passionate resistance to privatization and the fight to save America's public schools.* New York: Knopf.

Shanahan, T. 2015. "What teachers should know about Common Core: A guide for the perplexed." *The Reading Teacher, 68,* 583–588.

Spillane, J. P. 2005. "Standards deviation: How schools misunderstand education policy." *CPRE Policy Briefs.* Retrieved from http://repository.upenn.edu/cpre_policybriefs/31

Supovitz, J., Fink, R., and Newman, B. 2016. "From the inside in: Common Core knowledge and communication within schools." *AERA Open, 2*(3).

Wilhoit, G. 2009. *Improving our competitiveness: Common Core Education Standards.* Prepared testimony before the Committee on Education and Labor, U.S. House of Representatives, December 4.

Williams, J. P. 2014. "Who is fighting against Common Core? The push against Common Core is coming from both sides of the political aisle." *U.S. News & World Report,* February 27, 2014. Retrieved from https://www.usnews.com/news/special-reports/a-guide-to-common-core/articles/2014/02/27/who-is-fighting-against-common-core

Q18. HAS TIME THAT STUDENTS SPEND PREPARING FOR AND TAKING STANDARDIZED TESTS INCREASED DRAMATICALLY IN U.S. PUBLIC SCHOOLS?

Answer: Testing, in its various forms, can play an important role in education. It can serve as a diagnostic tool to determine how well students are learning certain concepts and skills. Testing can also help policy makers and administrators gauge how schools are performing in core subject areas over time and for specific subgroups of students. However, "you can't fatten cattle by weighing them," goes the Midwest adage, and numerous educators have emphasized that time spent on testing is time taken away from more interactive and creative methods of teaching and learning. Taking into consideration the time that students spend preparing for and taking exams, the comparably small amount of testing done in other countries with high-performing education systems, the financial motivations of standardized testing companies, and perceptions of many educators, parents, and students, the answer is an emphatic, Yes.

The Facts: Increased standardized testing has reached nearly every school district in the nation since 2000. Almost all of it has been mandated by the federal government, or by state governments that were pressured by federal mandates. Put another way, federal aid disbursements were made conditional upon states adopting testing and accountability programs. It is unlikely, absent the mandated pressure, that many districts would have elected more standardized testing of their own accord. A 2013 analysis conducted by the Organization for Economic Cooperation and Development (OECD) found that the United States had the highest stakes attached to testing among developed countries (OECD, 2013, 151). That is, more than any other nation studied by the OECD, standardized testing in the United States is embedded in systems of significant rewards and punishments.

A New Level of Accountability under No Child Left Behind

A look back at the origins of the U.S. testing movement at the federal level is instructive. In 2001, the federal government passed sweeping legislation that put public schools under the microscope like never before. The No Child Left Behind Act (NCLB) of 2002 ushered in a new wave of high-stakes assessments for schools. NCLB constituted a reauthorization of the federal Elementary and Secondary Education Act (ESEA) of 1965. The ESEA was signed into law by President Lyndon Johnson to provide additional resources to students from economically disadvantaged backgrounds. Although responsibility for public education still remains the domain of state and local governments, these federal investments were, and remain, intended to ensure a minimum level of education quality and equity across the nation.

However, the NCLB required a new and heightened level of accountability for public schools. In exchange for NCLB funding, states were required to develop accountability systems to monitor school performance with standardized tests. The minimum testing requirement was to test students annually during third to eighth grade and once during high school in English language arts and mathematics. Science was also to be tested during fifth to eighth grade, although states were not required to hold schools accountable for these scores unless they opted to do so. Most notably, state accountability systems were mandated to report the outcomes of students' performance at each tested grade level overall and by specific subgroups, including race/ethnicity, poverty status, English language learners, and students with special needs.

Under NCLB, schools, districts, and states that did not meet performance standards were put on watch. When below standard performance was deemed chronic, sanctions were applied. These sanctions took the form of requiring implementation of predetermined reform options, such as firing administrators, removing staff, reconstituting schools, or providing for school choice. More than a decade into its passage, pushback against NCLB generated some flexibility for states that applied for federal "waivers" after 2012.

NCLB's emphasis on statewide assessments prompted a considerable increase in student testing, ostensibly to help prepare students for these exams. In an effort to do better on NCLB mandated exams, many states added supplemental tests to help prepare students on tested subjects. Most districts began administering their own battery of assessments—often referred to as benchmark exams—to see how they were faring in English and math, especially. Many of these exams are sold by testing companies that help administer and score them. The Iowa Test of Basic Skills, California Achievement Test, Stanford Achievement Test, and Measures of Academic Progress Suite are among the most commonly used. The Measures of Academic Progress (MAP) is sponsored by the Northwest Evaluation Association (NWEA), a nonprofit but high revenue-generating testing organization. The MAP is popular, particularly among large, urban school districts, providing both fall and spring tests in core subject areas to assess growth in performance. NWEA reports that their assessments are used by more than 9,500 schools, districts, and education agencies in 145 nations around the world.

In 2019, NWEA began rolling out a new battery of interim tests, which they refer to as "through-year" tests, to be administered three times during the year (Cavanagh, 2019). NWEA stated that these new tests are not intended to replace the twice-a-year administered MAP. NWEA indicated their new computer-adaptive, 45-minute assessments can replace summative year-end assessments, which they (and many others) claim come too late in the school year to benefit instruction. However, testing experts have questioned the validity of using interim assessments to generate a summative annual score (Gewertz, 2015).

In addition to district administered tests, there are also state-level exams in some locations. Currently, 13 states require high school exit exams for graduation, down from roughly half the states in 2002 (Gewertz, 2019). These states include Florida, Indiana, Louisiana, Maryland, Massachusetts, Mississippi, New Jersey, New Mexico, New York, Ohio, Texas, Virginia, and Washington. Some exit exams take the form of end-of-course exams that students must pass to earn a diploma. Twenty-five states require students to take the college entrance exams, SAT or ACT. This number of states has grown considerably over the last decade. These exams are usually taken by eleventh-graders but are accompanied by "pre-exams" (e.g., Preliminary SAT or PSAT) in earlier grades. These tests are typically used to satisfy the high school testing requirement per state accountability policies.

NCLB officially ended in 2015 and was replaced by another major reauthorization of ESEA, this time under the name Every Student Succeeds Act (ESSA) (https://www.ed.gov/esea). ESSA continued much of the general federally required state oversight of education, with a new emphasis on preparing students for college and careers. Annual statewide assessments in math and English language arts in grades three through eight and high school are still mandatory under ESSA, just as they were in the NCLB era. In addition, students must be tested in science once during third to fifth grade, once during sixth to ninth grade, and once during tenth to twelfth grade. All English language learners in grades K–12 are tested annually on English language proficiency assessments. Although ESSA was intended to de-emphasize the heavy testing brought on by NCLB, many believe that ESSA provisions did not go far enough in that regard.

The School Testing Industry

Many educators believe that the testing industry has run amok, creating a counterproductive focus on testing in schools. Testing companies have reaped enormous financial benefits from the high-stakes assessment movement and continue to do so (Davis, 2016). Following the testing requirements of NCLB of 2001, the major testing companies lined up to provide tests and reap profits. Pearson Education, a British owned publishing and assessment company, contracted with the state of Texas for five years for nearly $500 million to create and administer Texas state assessments. Students who failed exams were offered state-funded tutoring provided by Pearson. Pearson has also cornered the national market on GED testing through its GED Testing Service. The Pearson GED.com website indicates they are "the sole provider of the official GED® test" and that they have "helped over 20 million people attain their GED®." Meanwhile, it has been estimated that by the mid-2010s, Americans were annually spending more than $13 billion on test preparation, tutoring, and counseling alone (Kamenetz, 2015).

The introduction of the Common Core State Standards in 2009 also prompted the federal government to fund two large testing consortia—Smarter Balanced Assessment Consortium and Partnership for Assessment of Readiness for College and Careers (PARCC). The idea behind the funding was to develop tests that not only aligned with the new Common Core standards, but that tapped students higher-order thinking skills in a more sophisticated manner. The tests were meant to be fairer and more useful to states, schools, and educators. The federal Race to the Top Assessment program awarded an initial $330 million to the two state testing consortia. These tests were piloted in 2013–2014 and as of 2019 about one-third of states were using either the Smarter Balanced or PARCC assessments (Gewertz, 2019). Anya Kamenetz, an education correspondent with National Public Radio, estimated that $13.1 billion would be spent in 2015 on test preparation, tutoring, and counseling (Kamenetz, 2015).

The Burden of Testing

The Center for American Progress, a liberal think tank based in Washington DC, commissioned a study of testing practices in a pair of urban and suburban districts in each of seven states (Lazarín, 2014). The study found that students "take as many as 20 standardized assessments per year and an average of 10 tests in grades 3–8." The author noted that "the regularity with which testing occurs, especially in these grades, may be causing students, families, and educators to feel burdened by testing" (Lazarín, 2014, 3). The study also found that students spend more time taking district-based standardized tests than state tests. Early grade levels test three times as much on district tests as opposed to state exams, and high school students are tested about twice as often on district exams than on state exams (Lazarín, 2014).

The Center for American Progress study also found that urban schools undertake a disproportionate amount of district testing relative to their suburban peers. In the early grades, the typical urban student in the study sample spent about 50 percent more time on district tests than state tests compared with suburban students. Middle school urban students spent roughly 75 percent more time taking district-based standardized exams than state tests. Urban high school students spend "266 percent more time taking district-level exams than their suburban counterparts" (Lazarín,

2014, 4). The students who likely need and deserve more instructional time are not getting it at the same rate as suburban students, according to the study.

Another study funded by the American Federation of Teachers, the nation's second-largest teachers' union, reported on test-taking patterns in two midsized school districts, one in the Midwest and another in the East. The limited sample notwithstanding, researchers found that students in the heavily tested grades were spending between 20 and 50 hours each year taking exams (Nelson, 2013). One of the districts administered 14 different assessments every year to all students at one grade level. In addition, in high-stakes testing grades, students spent between 60 and 110 hours annually in test preparation. One month of school is equivalent to approximately 110 hours.

The Council of the Great City Schools, which represents the nation's 74 largest urban school districts, analyzed survey and testing calendar data from 66 district members, along with interviews and a review of federal, state, and locally mandated assessments. This analysis found that students took an average of 112 tests between Pre-K and twelfth grade. In addition, "[t]he average amount of testing time devoted to mandated tests among eighth-grade students in the 2014–15 school year was approximately 4.22 days or 2.34 percent of school time" (Hart et al., 2015, 9). Their analysis also revealed that some tests collected redundant information.

Backlash and Opting Out

The year 2013 witnessed the start of a national parent and student Opt Out movement. Weary of excessive testing and in some regard in protest to the new Common Core standards, parents took advantage of test waivers for children in sufficient numbers to get the attention of policy makers. A 2014 *Purple Insights* poll of more than 800 parents and caregivers reported that nearly half believe there is too much standardized testing in schools (Lazarín, 2014, 2).

During the height of the Opt Out movement, even some teachers refused to administer tests, while district leaders likewise issued calls for change in state testing requirements (Strauss, 2015). In a nationally representative survey of more than 3,300 traditional public school teachers, the Center on Education Policy gathered perceptions on a wide range of education topics, including testing. An overwhelming majority of teachers (81 percent) said they thought their students spent too much time taking state- or district-mandated exams (Rentner et al., 2016). The teachers recommended reducing the number and duration of such tests, rather than eliminating them.

The majority of teachers also thought they spent too much time on preparing their students for taking state- and district-wide assessments. Roughly a quarter of teachers (26 percent) indicated they spent *more than a month* a year preparing students for district-mandated tests.

Parents were not far behind teachers in their rejection of the heavy emphasis placed on testing. Driven by parents communicating on social media platforms such as Facebook and Twitter, an Opt Out movement that started in 2012 in Long Island, New York, spread across the state in opposition to the mandated Common Core testing. In 2015, 200,000 eligible public school students (20 percent) were opted-out of the testing by their parents in the state of New York. The same percentage of New York students opted out a year later (Pizmony-Levy and Cosman, 2017). The large number of opt-outs gave New York Governor Andrew Cuomo little choice but to suspend a recently adopted teacher evaluation system that was based on students' test scores (Ravitch, 2020, 97–102).

Concerns about overtesting reached the federal level early in the Opt Out movement. In August 2014, Secretary of Education Arnie Duncan, an ardent assessment and accountability proponent, stated in his back-to-school blog entry, "I believe testing issues today are sucking the oxygen out of the room in a lot of schools" (Duncan, 2014). Soon after, the federal government issued calls for reducing the number of unnecessary tests, creating assessments that measured critical thinking and fewer basic skills, and generally relying less on testing.

In 2015, as part of ESSA, President Barack Obama announced a Testing Action Plan "to restore balance to America's classrooms by ensuring fewer, better, and fairer tests." The intent was to reduce unnecessary and redundant testing, and encourage more innovative ways to assess student learning.

Testing in Private Schools

In public schools, the vast majority of mandated, standardized testing occurs under government auspices. Public schools are asked to take the National Assessment of Educational Progress (NAEP), for one. This test, often referred to as the "nation's report card," is a federally sponsored set of exams in core subject areas, such as math, reading, science, and writing. It is administered to a nationally representative group of schools in fourth, eighth, and twelfth grade and is intended to portray how well U.S. schools are performing in core subjects over time.

Meanwhile, private schools are asked—but not required—to administer the NAEP. In most cases, private schools are also not required to administer state exams; and in states where there is no compulsory testing for private schools, those that elect to administer the exams are under no obligation to publicize or share the results. In addition to college entrance exams like the SAT and ACT, private schools may have their own proprietary admissions exams. Private schools tend to use one of two main admissions tests: the Independent Schools Entrance Exam (ISEE) or the Secondary School Admissions Test (SSAT). Public schools do not typically require admissions tests, save for a handful of city "exam" schools and some magnet schools that specialize in subjects like art, music, or a science-technology-engineering-math (STEM) field.

FURTHER READING

Burch, P. 2009. *Hidden markets: The new education privatization.* New York: Routledge.

Cavanagh, S. 2019. "A future without summative state tests? NWEA touts new product." *EdWeek Market Brief.* October 23, 2019. Retrieved from https://marketbrief.edweek.org/marketplace-k-12/future-without-summative-state-tests-nwea-touts-new-product

Davis, O. 2016. "No test left behind. How Pearson made a killing on the US testing craze." *Talking Points Memo.* Retrieved from https://talkingpointsmemo.com/features/privatization/four

Duncan, A. 2014. "A back-to-school conversation with teachers and school leaders." Homeroom: The official blog of the U.S. Department of Education. August 21, 2014. https://blog.ed.gov/2014/08/a-back-to-school-conversation-with-teachers-and-school-leaders/

Gewertz, C. 2015. "ESSA's flexibility on assessment elicits qualms from testing experts." *Education Week,* December 18, 2015. Retrieved from https://www.edweek.org/ew/articles/2015/12/21/essas-flexibility-on-assessment-elicits-qualms-from.html

Gewertz, C. 2019. "Which states require students to take the SAT or ACT?" *Education Week,* April 9, 2019. Retrieved from https://www.edweek.org/ew/section/multimedia/states-require-students-take-sat-or-act.html

Hart, R., et al. 2015. *Student testing in America's Great City Schools: An inventory and preliminary analysis.* Washington, DC: Council of the Great City Schools.

Kamenetz, A. 2015. *The test: Why our schools are obsessed with standardized testing—But you don't have to be.* New York: Public Affairs.

Lazarín, M. 2014. *Testing overload in America's schools.* Washington, DC: Center for American Progress.

Nelson, H. 2013. *Testing more, teaching less: What America's obsession with student testing costs in money and lost instructional time.* Washington, DC: American Federation of Teachers, AFL-CIO. Retrieved from https://www.aft.org/sites/default/files/news/testingmore2013.pdf

Nichols, S. L., and Berliner, D. C. 2007. *Collateral damage: How high-stakes testing corrupts America's schools.* Cambridge, MA: Harvard Education Press.

OECD. 2013. *PISA 2012 results: What makes schools successful? Resources, policies and practices* (Volume IV). Paris, France: PISA, OECD Publishing. http://dx.doi.org/10.1787/9789264201156-en

Pizmony-Levy, O., and Cosman, B. 2017. *How Americans view the opt out movement.* New York: Teachers College Press. Retrieved from https://academiccommons.columbia.edu/doi/10.7916/D87D36HP/download

Rapoport, A. 2011. "Education Inc.: How private companies are profiting from Texas public schools." *Texas Observer*, September 6, 2011. Retrieved from https://www.texasobserver.org/the-pearson-graduate

Ravitch, D. 2010. *The life and death of the great American school system: How testing and choice are undermining education.* New York: Basic Books.

Ravitch, D. 2020. *Slaying Goliath: The passionate resistance to privatization and the fight to save America's public schools.* New York: Knopf.

Rentner, D. S., Kober, N., Frizzell, M., and Ferguson, M. 2016. *Listen to us: Teacher views and voices.* Center on Education Policy. Washington, DC: The George Washington University.

Strauss, V. 2015. "Confirmed: Standardized testing has taken over our schools. But who's to blame?" *Washington Post*, October 24, 2015. Retrieved from https://www.washingtonpost.com/news/answer-sheet/wp/2015/10/24/confirmed-standardized-testing-has-taken-over-our-schools-but-whos-to-blame

Q19. HAS HIGH-STAKES TESTING IMPROVED SCHOOLS?

Answer: On the whole, high-stakes testing has not been an effective means of improving education, although a few studies have attributed small increases in test scores to high-stakes accountability systems.

The Facts: High-stakes tests are those with significant consequences attached to them; for example, whether a student graduates or advances to the next grade or whether a probationary teacher is let go. Students'

performance on standardized exams may be used as part of the evaluation of teachers or principals, or to sanction or reward schools and districts. Depending on the accountability system, consequences for poor test performance can sometimes mean additional support for schools to help develop capacity and bring needed resources to the organization. More often, however, test-based accountability policies threaten or deliver negative consequences to the schools and those who work in them. Examples of the latter include major reconstitution of the organization (e.g., the conversion of a traditional public school into a charter school) or governance structure (e.g., state takeover in which new administrators are appointed by state boards), or removal of teachers or principals. Over the last decade, there has been a notable shift toward holding schools accountable to growth targets on state assessments in contrast to absolute levels of performance.

The purpose of most high-stakes accountability systems is to improve academic achievement in tested subjects, such as math and reading. Several research efforts have investigated the influence of high-stakes accountability systems on schools, including whether such policies have improved test scores. There is some evidence that low-performing schools respond to test-based accountability with higher test scores.

For example, a 2013 study found that Florida elementary schools that had received an "F" grade based on school test scores in the early 2000s saw small increases in student achievement in math and reading across a three-year period (Rouse et al., 2013). The researchers described the gains as roughly the equivalent of moving from the 50th to the 54th percentile. These are not large gains and, further, could be a result of a statistical phenomenon known as the regression effect, where initial scores that are either very low or high end up nearer the average on a second measurement. In other words, those F-graded schools had only one place to go: up. The researchers reported that the low-scoring schools appeared to pursue several strategies: focusing on low-performing students, increasing time on instruction, organizing the day and learning environment differently, expanding resources for teachers, and reducing control by the school principal. The explanatory power of these factors was limited, however. Roughly 15 percent of the test score gains in reading and 44 percent of the gains in math were accounted for by changes in these strategies, although the study design did not permit causal conclusions or the ability to conclude which among these factors was most salient. Overall, there exists fairly weak evidence that Florida's high-stakes accountability system improved schools.

Playing the Numbers Game

How have students performed over time on state exams that are not considered high stakes? The U.S. Department of Education currently administers the National Assessment for Educational Progress (NAEP) to a representative sample of students and schools across the nation. NAEP's primary areas of assessment are math, reading, science, and writing, with periodic assessments in civics, economics, U.S. history, geography, technology and engineering literacy, and the arts. Because NAEP is not tied to state or local accountability programs, it can be considered a measure of achievement not directly subject to accountability pressures.

A 2007 study analyzed fourth-grade NAEP reading scores over time and found that since the introduction of the high-stakes federal policy of No Child Left Behind (NCLB), growth in the NAEP scores actually became flatter (Fuller et al., 2007). A similar study from 2006 found that NAEP reading scores remained generally unchanged through the NCLB period (2002 to 2014) and NAEP math score gains were consistent with the increasing trajectory prior to NCLB (Lee, 2006). A subsequent analysis in 2011 claimed that NCLB produced increases in fourth-grade math scores and, to a lesser extent, eighth-grade math scores, but no evidence was found that NCLB increased fourth-grade reading achievement (Dee and Jacob, 2011).

Another 2006 study analyzed the relationship between accountability pressure and NAEP performance across 25 states with strong accountability laws (Nichols, Glass, and Berliner, 2006). Judgments of the severity of the states' accountability laws were coalesced into a scale of accountability pressure measure. This measure of pressure was then correlated with each state's average NAEP score in reading and math. The researchers found no relationship between accountability pressure and NAEP achievement in reading and math.

At the very least, NAEP-based comparisons call into question the validity of any NCLB high-stakes test scores that exhibited upward trajectories. Do the tests used in high-stakes accountability systems actually measure general increases in knowledge? Or are they merely narrow measures of performance on the particular tests in question? Although high-stakes approaches may have spurred increases in test scores, the NAEP analysis raises the possibility that in some cases these gains are due to targeted test preparation or, in worst-case scenarios, unethical behavior on behalf of desperate school administrators. Irregularities in the administration of some high-stakes tests have led to dismissal of administrators and even criminal charges in some highly visible instances (Pareene, 2011).

The National Research Council (2011) panel on school accountability has acknowledged the improvement in test scores apparently influenced by accountability policies, but also questioned their capacity to effect broader and more lasting change. Other researchers have expressed similar concerns. A 2013 study, for example, reported that "there is ample evidence that schools respond to accountability pressures in ways that affect measured performance but may not lead, to generalized improvements" (Rouse et al., 2013, 252). Many studies indicate that schools focus on subjects tested and prepare students for tests, while also paying more attention to students whose scores play a significant role in satisfying accountability requirements. Students who fall near or just below the next performance level, particularly the highly prized level christened by NCLB as proficiency, are referred to as the "bubble kids." The kids on the bubble end up getting considerable attention from teachers seeking to reach annual progress targets of students performing at increased levels.

Another unintended consequence of the emphasis on testing is the strategic reshaping of the test-taking pool (Cullen and Reback, 2006). Even prior to NCLB, studies have shown that high-stakes tests prompt schools to "game the system." For instance, researchers from the National Bureau of Economic Research examined student classification data following the enactment of Florida's Comprehensive Assessment Test (FCAT) in 1996. They analyzed more than 4 million students and found gaming of the system by a reshaping of the test pool: ". . . low-performing students and students from low socio-economic backgrounds were significantly and substantively more likely to be reclassified into disability categories exempted from the accountability system" (Figlio and Getzler, 2006, 37).

A separate 2006 analysis of Florida's testing regime found that schools selectively culled low-performing students near the test-taking window by assigning lengthy suspensions (Figlio, 2006). A set of studies published in 2002 and 2005 found that similar gaming behaviors occurred among teachers in the Chicago Public Schools, including increasing test prep activities, expanding student placements in special education, retaining students in grade, and placing less attention on the untested subjects of science and social studies (Jacob, 2002; 2005). Another study found gaming behaviors under Texas' school accountability system, with schools targeting test exemptions among low-performing Hispanic and Black students, as well as overclassifying students as special needs or encouraging their absences on testing days (Cullen and Reback, 2006).

Further Negative Effects of High-Stakes Exams

Among other consequences of high-stakes tests are a strong focus on the tested subjects of math and reading at the expense of subjects that are not or cannot be tested, such as art, social studies, and music (Koretz, 2008; Nichols and Berliner, 2007; Rothstein, Jacobsen, and Wilder, 2008). At the same time, several reports indicate that the teaching of test prep skills to students often takes place at the expense of facilitating higher-order learning and engaging students in more complex problem-solving exercises (Center on Education Policy, 2015; Nichols and Berliner, 2007).

NCLB provisions specifically held schools, districts, and states accountable for having 100 percent of students reach "proficiency" in tested subjects. The definition of "proficiency" was in effect determined by a cut score (or minimum score) on state tests. More recently, school accountability has stressed growth in performance over minimum levels of performance. However, the measurement of which students attain proficiency, and which do not, still applies. As a consequence of this accountability policy, schools and their administrators may place increased attention on those students near (or just below) the proficiency cutoff line (noted above as "kids on the bubble"). It stands to reason, then, that a policy holding schools accountable to attain certain percentages of "proficient" students would lead them to shift energies heavily toward those students nearest the cutoff.

A number of qualitative studies indicate that schools, administrators, and educators focus on students who score near or just below test-score cutoffs that distinguish between proficient and below-proficient performance (Booher-Jennings, 2005; Brown and Clift, 2010; Stecher et al., 2008). Quantitative studies are inconclusive in terms of whether students "on the bubble" are treated differently as a result of high-stakes accountability systems (Lauen and Gaddis, 2016). For instance, some find gains made by students below the cutoff scores or in the middle of the test score distribution (e.g., Krieg, 2008; Neal and Schanzenbach, 2010), and others find no differences in achievement gains (Ladd and Lauen, 2010; Springer, 2008). But the quantitative analyses may miss the point: research has shown that educators and administrators prioritized "bubble" students, regardless of whether it had any distinguishable effects on their test scores. Critics assert that in doing so, schools gave less attention to students not near the proficiency cut-off.

Campbell's Law

The late Donald T. Campbell, noted social psychologist, long ago predicted this type of behavior would result with testing attached to high-stakes consequences. He observed, in what is now known as Campbell's Law: "The more any quantitative social indicator is used for social decision-making, the more subject it will be to corruption pressures and the more apt it will be to distort and corrupt the social processes it is intended to monitor" (Campbell, 1979, 85).

Assessment specialists have always cautioned that important decisions affecting a student's future life opportunities should not be made on the basis of test scores alone, and certainly not based on a single test (American Educational Research Association, American Psychological Association, National Council on Measurement in Education, Joint Committee on Standards for Educational and Psychological Testing, 2014). The higher the stakes attached to any test, the greater the chance the associated pressures will result in test-performance distortions or inaccurate results.

FURTHER READING

American Educational Research Association, American Psychological Association, National Council on Measurement in Education, Joint Committee on Standards for Educational and Psychological Testing (U.S.). 2014. *Standards for educational and psychological testing.* Washington, DC: AERA.

Amrein, A. L., and Berliner, D. C. 2003. "The effects of high-stakes testing on student motivation and learning." *Educational Leadership,* 60(5), 32–37.

Booher-Jennings, J. 2005. "Below the bubble: 'Educational triage' and the Texas accountability system." *American Educational Research Journal,* 42(2), 231–268.

Brown, A. B., and Clift, J. W. 2010. "The unequal effect of adequate yearly progress: Evidence from school visits." *American Educational Research Journal,* 47(4), 774–798.

Campbell, D. T. 1979. "Assessing the impact of planned social change." *Evaluation and Program Planning,* 2(1), 67–90.

Center on Education Policy. 2015. *Knowing the score: The who, what, and why of testing. Test Talk.* Retrieved from http://lwvccpa.org/wp-content/uploads/2015/11/Who-What-and-Why-of-Testing.pdf

Cullen, J. B., and Reback, R. 2006. "Tinkering toward accolades: School gaming under a performance accountability system." *Advances in Applied Microeconomics,* 14(1), 1–34.

Dee, T. S., and Jacob, B. 2011. "The impact of No Child Left Behind on student achievement." *Journal of Policy Analysis and Management,* 30(3), 418–446.

Figlio, D. N. 2006. "Testing, crime and punishment." *Journal of Public Economics*, 90(4–5), 837–851.

Figlio, D. N., and Getzler, L. S. 2006. "Accountability, ability and disability: Gaming the system?" In T. J. Gronberg and D. W. Jansen (Eds.), *Improving school accountability: Check-ups or choice*. Bingley, UK: Emerald Group Publishing Limited, 35–49.

Fuller, B., Wright, J., Gesicki, K., and Kang, E. 2007. "Gauging growth: How to judge No Child Left Behind?" *Educational Researcher*, 36(5), 268–278.

Jacob, B. 2002. "Accountability, incentives and behavior: The impact of high-stakes testing in the Chicago Public Schools." *NBER Working Paper* 8968. Cambridge, MA: National Bureau of Economic Research.

Jacob, B. 2005. "The impact of high-stakes testing on student achievement: Evidence from Chicago." *Journal of Public Economics*, 89(5–6), 761–796.

Koretz, D. 2008. *Measuring up: What educational testing really tells us*. Cambridge, MA: Harvard University Press.

Krieg, J. M. 2008. "Are students left behind? The distributional effects of the No Child Left Behind Act." *Education Finance and Policy*, 3, 250–281.

Ladd, H. F., and Lauen, D. L. 2010. "Status versus growth: The distributional effects of school accountability policies." *Journal of Policy Analysis and Management*, 29, 426–450.

Lauen, D. L., and Gaddis, S. M. 2016. "Accountability pressure, academic standards, and educational triage." *Educational Evaluation and Policy Analysis*, 38(1), 127–147. https://doi.org/10.3102/0162373715598577

Lee, J. 2006. *Tracking achievement gaps and assessing the impact of NCLB on the gaps: An in-depth look into national and state reading and math outcome trends*. Cambridge, MA: The Civil Rights Project at Harvard University.

National Research Council. 2011. *Incentives and test-based accountability in education*. Washington, DC: National Academies Press.

Neal, D., and Schanzenbach, D. W. 2010. "Left behind by design: Proficiency counts and test-based accountability." *The Review of Economics and Statistics*, 92(2), 263–283.

Nichols, S. L., and Berliner, D. C. 2007. *Collateral damage: How high-stakes testing corrupts America's schools*. Cambridge, MA: Harvard Education Press.

Nichols, S. L., Glass, G. V, and Berliner, D. C. 2006. "High-stakes testing and student achievement: Does accountability pressure increase student learning?" *Education Policy Analysis Archives*, 14(1). https://doi.org/10.14507/epaa.v14n1.2006

Pareene, A. 2011. "Paranoid Michelle Rhee blames her 'enemies' for cheating report." *Salon.com*, March 29, 2011. Retrieved from https://www.salon.com/control/2011/03/29/rhee_cheating

Rothstein, R., Jacobsen, R., and Wilder, T. 2008. *Grading education: Getting accountability right*. New York: Teachers College Press.

Rouse, C., Hannaway, J., Goldhaber, D., and Figlio, D. 2013. "Feeling the Florida heat? How low-performing schools respond to voucher and accountability Pressure." *American Economic Journal: Economic Policy*, 5(2), 251–281. Retrieved from http://www.jstor.org/stable/43189334

Ryan, R. M., and Deci, E. L. 2020. "Intrinsic and extrinsic motivation from a self-determination theory perspective: Definitions, theory, practices, and future directions." *Contemporary Educational Psychology*, 30(3), 33–56.

Springer, M. G. 2008. "The influence of an NCLB accountability plan on the distribution of student test score gains." *Economics of Education Review*, 27(5), 556–563.

Stecher, B. M., et al. 2008. *Pain and Gain: Implementing No Child Left Behind in three states, 2004–2006* (Vol. 784). Santa Monica, CA: RAND Corporation.

Q20. IS IT DIFFICULT FOR PUBLIC SCHOOLS TO FIRE BAD TEACHERS?

Answer: The procedures that most schools are required to follow—procedures called due process—are in place to protect good teachers from unfair firings. But these procedures also make firing poor teachers a complex and time-consuming process. Education scholars note, however, that some school administrators are also adept at weeding out underperforming teachers without resorting to outright termination (by issuing negative evaluations of performance, for example).

The Facts: Politicians, school leaders, and educators alike have long bemoaned how hard it is to get rid of a bad teacher. Fingers point in all directions to place blame. Among the allegations are that teachers' unions are overly protective; tenure laws are restrictive and counterproductive; administrators lack the fortitude or time to "counsel out" poor teachers; school boards eschew costly legal battles; and teacher evaluation data are too weak to detect or prove ineffectiveness. Some allegations carry weight; others don't. Ineffective teachers may not be the norm, but they can disrupt the work culture and, worse yet, represent a lost opportunity for students to get a good education. But is it really true that bad teachers are hard to fire?

The number of public school teachers dismissed for poor teaching performance suggests that dismissals do not happen with great regularity. According to a 2010–2011 national survey of school districts, for every 1,000 teachers, only 6 are terminated or not renewed annually for poor performance, including those with tenure (National Center for Education Statistics, 2012). Typically, tenure is granted to teachers who perform satisfactorily for their first three years under contract, although not every state has tenure laws and some use different terminology. For tenured teachers only, the average number of dismissals is much smaller, just above 1 in 1,000.

Termination figures for teachers with all tenure statuses vary somewhat by state. For instance, in three nonunion states—North Carolina, Texas, and Georgia—the average number of teachers in 1,000 who were terminated were 5.4, 5.5, and 6.5, respectively, in 2010–2011. The union states Missouri, Utah, and Massachusetts observed slightly higher numbers: 8.3, 9.3, and 10.5, respectively. While these data are based on teachers who were dismissed due to poor performance ("e.g., failed to perform professional duties and responsibilities, did not meet performance expectations") (U.S. Department of Education, 2011, 21) they do not account for poor performing teachers who left on their own or who were quietly counseled out by administrators. A study published in 2020 found that, among a nationally representative sample of teachers who left teaching between the 2011–2012 and 2012–2013 school years, 88 percent voluntarily quit for reasons other than retirement (Han, 2020). It should be noted here that there is no way of knowing what percentage left because they realized that they were not performing well; it represents a general indicator of attrition for nonretirement reasons.

The fact that the union states in the above example terminated teachers at higher rates than nonunion states rubs against the grain of critiques claiming unions are overprotective of ineffective teachers. A 2020 analysis of a large-scale and nationally representative sample of school districts found a similar pattern; highly unionized districts exhibited more involuntary dismissals than nonunionized districts (Han, 2020). The explanation is consistent with economic theory: because unions demand higher pay for their members, they tend not to put up with bad teachers and risk losing the high salaries they negotiated so hard for. The lower dismissal rates among the nonunion states may also be a result of the lack of labor protections; a teacher who does not have union protection, such as union legal counsel, may be more likely to voluntarily resign than challenge an impending dismissal.

The question of whether it is difficult to fire a bad teacher is posed here, in part, because so many people believe it to be the case; it's become part of the storyline in education. To some degree, the question itself also implies there are many bad teachers out there who have yet to be fired. However, many teachers performing poorly are gently counseled out of the profession by their principals. The notion that public schools have an abundance of incompetent teachers who never leave also conflicts with the high rates of burnout in the teaching profession. Not all of those "burnouts" are excellent teachers frustrated by an intransigent bureaucracy; some are teachers who are frustrated by their own lack of success.

The U.S. Bureau of Labor statistics has reported rates of "layoffs and discharges" by industries for more than 20 years. Consider the rate of layoffs and discharges for the Finance & Insurance industry in 2019, a profession somewhat comparable in required level of education to school teaching. In 2019, the approximate rate of layoffs and discharges was 27 per 1,000 workers for a nine-month period, comparable to the work-year of teachers. This figure, 27 per 1,000, includes both discharges (a euphemism for "firing") and layoffs, a suspension of work for various reasons but likely not involving release from work for reasons of poor performance. If half of the "layoffs and discharges" were for reasons of poor performance, then the firing rate in the finance and insurance industry would be approximately 13 per 1,000. Recall that the annual rates of teacher firings for Missouri, Utah, and Massachusetts were 8.3, 9.3, and 10.5 per 1,000 teachers, respectively. The difference between 13 and 10 per 1,000 hardly justifies the myth that incompetent teachers are never fired while industry ruthlessly weeds out incompetence.

Some ineffective teachers are "laid off," "re-assigned," "counseled," or "unscheduled," but they are rarely "discharged" or "fired." When it does happen, the termination or firing of teachers almost always occurs due to a serious contract violation (e.g., repeatedly being late to work), or inappropriate or illegal behavior. A study published in 2018 examined 136 teacher dismissals between 2011 and 2017 in three school districts in Georgia: Atlanta Public Schools, Fulton County, and DeKalb County (Saultz, 2018). Georgia is among the five "right-to-work" states noted above that prohibit collective bargaining for educators. The study found that roughly 4 percent of teacher dismissals mentioned teacher ineffectiveness, instructional quality, or student learning. The study was limited in scope, but does support the contention that most teacher dismissals are due to professional work issues such as being late to work and violating rules or laws rather than their ineffectiveness as an instructor.

Teacher Evaluation

The small fraction of teachers who are let go each year feeds the narrative that it is hard for public schools to fire bad teachers. Although one would hope that the percentage of so-called bad teachers is small, other evidence suggests that some poor performing teachers may be slipping through the cracks. One source of this slippage may be the way in which teachers are evaluated.

In a 2009 study of teacher evaluation systems, investigators found a mismatch between formal teacher evaluation ratings and evaluators' professional opinions about the distribution of ratings (Weisberg et al., 2009). Very few teachers are identified as "Unsatisfactory" according to formal ratings; and yet, if the administrators in the school are asked to gauge teacher effectiveness, the percentage of unsatisfactory ratings would generally be much higher. This is not all that surprising, given that most teacher evaluation systems are based on one or two classroom observations per year. The Principal Investigator of a Wallace Foundation University Principal Preparation Initiative indicated in 2020 that classroom observations track a narrow set of evaluation criteria and are not designed—nor are they sufficient—for an assessment of holistic performance (Richard Gonzales, personal communication, March 16, 2020).

A 2017 analysis of teacher performance ratings across 24 states that had revised their teacher evaluation programs showed that in the "vast majority" of these states, the percentage of teachers rated unsatisfactory was less than 1 percent (Kraft and Gilmour, 2017). However, this does not mean that the other 99 percent were rated as high-performing. In the study, the distribution of performance ratings varied considerably across states; between roughly 1 and 29 percent rated "below proficient" and 6 to 62 percent rated "above proficient." A 2009 study finds that this continues a pattern reported throughout the country where teacher evaluation systems, as currently constructed, rarely identify teachers as poor performers (Weisberg et al., 2009).

Teachers are sometimes their own toughest critics. In a 2003 Public Agenda survey of a random sample of more than 1,300 public school teachers, 59 percent indicated that "a few" and another 17 percent indicated "more than a few" of their colleagues in their building "fail to do a good job and are simply going through the motions" (Farkas, Johnson, and Duffett, 2003). Nineteen percent said there were no such teachers in their school. These percentages should not be overinterpreted, however. For example, if some of the respondents taught in the same school, they could be thinking of the same "bad apples," so to speak.

What Tenure Is . . . And Is Not

Labor laws, such as teacher tenure, may impede school administrators' efforts to dismiss ineffective teachers. In a 2001 national random sample of 853 public school superintendents and 909 public school principals, 73 percent of superintendents and 69 percent of principals favored "making it much easier for principals to remove bad teachers—even those who have tenure" (Farkas et al., 2001). It is noteworthy that federal labor laws impose many of the same restrictions on all types of employers.

Teacher contracts are treated differently in different states. According to a 2012 report from a conservative-leaning think tank, the vast majority of states either require (32 states) or permit (14 states) collective bargaining of teacher contracts (Winkler, Scull, and Zeehandelaar, 2012). Only Georgia, North Carolina, South Carolina, Texas, and Virginia ban collective bargaining for educators. According to an Education Commission of the States' 2014 analysis, 16 states require districts to consider a teacher's formal performance evaluation prior to granting tenure (Thomsen, 2014). In seven states, if teachers are rated as "ineffective," districts must return tenured or nonprobationary teachers to probationary status, meaning their contract may not be renewed.

Even in states with teacher labor unions, rules governing probationary periods and tenure can differ. For instance, in some union states, newly hired teachers can be dismissed in their first year without cause. After a successful probationary period, typically three years, teachers can earn tenure status, which affords them certain employee protections. Tenure is not automatically granted, however. Depending on the teacher's performance as deemed by the superintendent, novice teachers can simply not be renewed and not considered for tenure. For instance, Connecticut's probationary period is 40 months, or what equates to four years of teaching. After the four years, the teacher can obtain tenure "provided the superintendent offers the teacher a contract to return for the following school year on the basis of effective practice as informed by performance evaluations conducted pursuant to [state statute]" (CT Gen Stat, 2019). However, in practice, nonrenewals after four years seldom occur, most likely because the teacher who has persisted that long has been performing satisfactorily. Novice teachers can be nonrenewed any year leading up to the tenure decision. Being nonrenewed is technically not being fired, but it is a euphemism that has the same effect.

Despite common false impressions, tenure does not mean a job for life, irrespective of performance. Tenure is intended to provide teachers protection from being terminated without good reason. Teachers serve in an intellectual field where a diversity of views is welcomed in the service of facilitating students' education. But sometimes this diversity creates controversy. Tenure serves as a protection for teachers to act with some degree of autonomy for the benefit of their students. It affords teachers some degree of assurance that they cannot be fired capriciously or without good reason when they believe that they are acting in the best interest of their students. Due process and tenure are meant to protect good teachers, not protect bad ones.

Critics of teacher tenure, however, argue that it goes too far to protect teachers. They view tenure as an obstacle to dismissing bad teachers. Although it is difficult, though not impossible, to fire an ineffective tenured teacher, the research indicates that relatively few bad teachers escape scrutiny by their superiors or their colleagues and remain in schools. While there are indeed cases in which ineffective teachers are pulled from the classroom and given district level jobs until they decide to leave or retire, they are the exception.

Due Process, "Just Cause," and Teacher Development

A number of school administrators report that bad teachers can be dismissed and that there is a path to do so, particularly during the beginning teacher's probationary period. During this probationary window, administrators may choose not to renew teachers who they deem to be underperforming or who have not responded adequately to instructional coaching. The task of eliminating poor performing teachers who have passed their probationary period and achieved tenure becomes more difficult. Here is where administrators must carefully follow due process.

Although a universal legal concept, due process is treated differently by states. For instance, state laws governing due process may "differ in the forum prescribed for such hearings, the timeline for completing them, and the kinds of evidence that can be introduced" (Sawchuk, 2014). Connecticut, for example, limits the length of time from when a teacher is given notice to a decision to 85 days. The hearing, which is required, cannot exceed 12 hours in cases of teacher performance.

Perhaps the most complex part of due process is establishing "just cause" for termination in the case of poor performing teachers. "Just cause" is established according to conditions set forth in collective bargaining or teacher contractual agreements. For instance, one condition specifies that the disciplinary action (e.g., dismissal) is reasonably related to the teacher's record—their length of service and overall performance—and if the poor performance is part of a pattern. Veteran teachers who have earned favorable evaluations and otherwise exhibited good conduct are protected from capricious attempts to dismiss them, because their superiors lack just cause for termination. On the other hand, teachers under contract past the probationary period who have undeservedly been give satisfactory ratings may also receive protections from dismissal under the "just cause" requirement.

School administrators, when asked to assess struggling early-career teachers, need to strike a balance between evaluating performance and evaluating potential. Early career teachers are still in the process of cultivating their craft. It can be challenging for supervisors to make the right call. Education scholar David Berliner suggests that it takes five to seven years to develop expertise in teaching (Berliner, 2004). Certain teachers will acquire expertise more quickly; but in any case, reaching expert status goes far beyond the typical tenure probationary periods of three to four years. Administrators charged with evaluating teachers and gauging potential are put in a bind. Suppose that after the first or even second year, a teacher struggles but shows some signs of improvement. Should the administrator cut her losses and seek a replacement for that novice teacher? Or should she invest in that teacher and help her improve? What level of performance after one, two, or even three years is "good enough" to give the teacher another chance at proving herself?

Decisions to renew or not renew during a novice teacher's probationary period are influenced by a broad context of circumstances. Consider remote, rural schools that have difficulty receiving even a handful of competent applicants for certain teaching positions. Even suburban and urban districts have problems filling positions for which there are national teacher shortages, such as teachers of physics, chemistry, world languages, and certain special education areas. The administrator working under those conditions may give more deference to the struggling beginning teacher because the alternative is no teacher at all. At the same time, administrator turnover can interrupt an improvement plan process. Likewise, newly arriving principals cannot control how teachers were evaluated before they arrived. Particular context can make every act of evaluation of a teacher a complex process. As is usually the case, special circumstances matter.

FURTHER READING

Berliner, D. C. 2004. "Expert teachers: Their characteristics, development and accomplishments." *Bulletin of Science, Technology and Society*, 24(3), 200–212.

CT Gen Stat. 10, 166, § 10-151 (2019).
Farkas, S., Johnson, J., and Duffett, A. 2003. *Stand by me: What teachers really think about unions, merit pay and other professional matters, a report from Public Agenda.* New York: Public Agenda.
Farkas, S., Johnson, J., Duffett, A., and Foleno, T. 2001. *Trying to stay ahead of the game: Superintendents and principals talk about school leadership.* New York: Public Agenda.
Han, E. S. 2020. "The myth of unions' overprotection of bad teachers: Evidence from the district–teacher matched data on teacher turnover." *Industrial Relations: A Journal of Economy and Society, 59*(2), 316–352.
Kraft, M. A., and Gilmour, A. F. 2017. "Revisiting the widget effect: Teacher evaluation reforms and the distribution of teacher effectiveness." *Educational Researcher, 46*(5), 234–249.
Menuey, B. P. 2005. "Teachers' perceptions of professional incompetence and barriers to the dismissal process." *Journal of Personnel Evaluation in Education, 18*(4), 309–325.
National Center for Education Statistics. 2012. SASS, *Schools and Staffing Survey (2010–2011).* Washington, DC: U.S. Department of Education, Office of Educational Research and Improvement, National Center for Education Statistics.
Saultz, A. 2018. "What does one do to get fired around here? An analysis of teacher dismissals in Georgia." *American Enterprise Institute.* June 28, 2018. Retrieved from https://www.aei.org/research-products/report/what-does-one-do-to-get-fired-around-here-an-analysis-of-teacher-dismissals-in-georgia
Sawchuk, S. 2014. "Due process laws vary for teachers by state." *Education Week, 34*(5), 1.
Thomsen, J. 2014. *A closer look: Teacher evaluations and tenure decisions.* Denver, CO: Education Commission of the States.
U.S. Department of Education. 2011. *Public School Questionnaire (with District Items). Schools and Staffing Survey, 2011–12 School Year.* Washington, DC: U.S. Department of Education, National Center for Education Statistics. https://nces.ed.gov/surveys/sass/pdf/1112/SASS3Y.pdf
Weisberg, D., Sexton, S., Mulhern, J., and Keeling, D. 2009. *The widget effect: Our national failure to acknowledge and act on differences in teacher effectiveness.* Washington, DC: The New Teacher Project.
Winkler, A. M., Scull, J., and Zeehandelaar, D. 2012. *How strong are U.S. teacher unions? A state-by-state comparison.* Washington, DC: Thomas B. Fordham Institute.

Q21. DO ASSESSMENT SYSTEMS EXIST THAT CAN ACCURATELY CAPTURE THE VALUE-ADDED IMPACT OF TEACHERS ON THEIR STUDENTS' TEST SCORES?

Answer: Value-added measurement (VAM) was an effort to quantify and assess teacher effectiveness in American schools, but it was heavily criticized as flawed by teachers, politicians, and the courts. It is no longer used to the same extent as it was in the 1990s and early 2000s, but it remains a part of the teacher assessment "mix" in a number of states.

The Facts: VAM is a statistical technique that attempts to measure the amount of gain on standardized tests that can be attributed to a specific teacher. In its most primitive form, this could involve administering the test to a teacher's classroom on the first day of the school year and the last and then calculating the difference: Last-Day-Average – First-Day-Average. Such a simple calculation raises many questions, however, and critics contended that it had numerous shortcomings that made it a poor tool for determining how much achievement a single teacher caused:

1. There are no standardized tests for the subjects that many teachers teach (e.g., art, music, physical education, social studies, and the like).
2. The vast majority of students are taught by more than one teacher in any given year. Which teacher is responsible for the score gain in reading? Did the science teacher also contribute to some students' math scores?
3. What would happen to the VAM score if 5 of a teacher's 25 students moved to another school during the school year? Would eliminating those students' test scores from the First-Day-Average take care of the problem?
4. Teacher A has a class of students with special needs and teacher B teaches students identified as "gifted and talented." Is it fair or appropriate to compare their VAM scores?

In spite of these obvious limitations, such techniques have occasionally been employed by administrators to assess teacher faculty. In the 1980s, researchers were able to find a handful of school districts that attempted to distribute financial rewards to teachers based on primitive VAM calculations. See, for example, studies published in 1986 (Florio, 1986; Glass & Ellwein, 1986) and 1988 (Ellwein, Glass, & Smith, 1988). In a 1990 study of a half dozen sites that employed the primitive VAM measure (Last-Day-Average–First-Day-Average) to reward teachers, five common characteristics of VAM programs emerged (Glass, 1990). The researcher found that using student achievement data to evaluate teachers . . .

- is nearly always undertaken at the level of a school (either all or none of the teachers in a school are rewarded equally) rather than at the level of individual teachers since (1) no authoritative tests exist in most areas of the secondary school curriculum, nor for most special roles played by elementary teachers; and (2) teachers reject the notion that they should compete with their colleagues for raises, privileges and perquisites;
- is always combined with other criteria (such as absenteeism or extra work) which prove to be the real discriminators between who is rewarded and who is not;
- is susceptible to intentional distortion and manipulation; moreover teachers and others believe that no type of test nor any manner of statistical analysis can equate the difficulty of the teacher's task in the wide variety of circumstances in which they work;
- elevates tests themselves to the level of curriculum goals, obscuring the distinction between learning and performing on tests;
- is often a symbolic administrative act undertaken to reassure the lay public that student learning is valued and assiduously sought after. (Glass, 1990, 240)

These early attempts to attach serious accountability consequences to teachers' students' test scores might have signaled the permanent demise of VAM. But such was not the case. In 1994, VAM was resurrected.

In 1992, the Tennessee legislature enacted a law that required each school district to determine the value added by each teacher to that teachers' class of students. Value was to be assessed by administration of a new assessment exam. Precisely how one should determine how much value was added by a particular teacher was not addressed in the act. The state tried to address that uncertainty through what came to be known as the Sanders and Horn (1994) method.

This method was unveiled by statistician William L. Sanders and his assistant Sandra Horn in a 1994 paper in the *Journal of Personnel Evaluation in Education* with the title "The Tennessee Value-Added Assessment System (TVAAS): Mixed-Model Methodology in Educational Assessment." Sanders was a statistician with the responsibility for the Statistical and Computing Services Unit within the Agricultural Experiment Station at the University of Tennessee, Knoxville.

Sanders called his new VAM method the Tennessee Value-Added Assessment System (or TVAAS). The method was immediately embraced by several prominent Tennessee politicians. Senator Lamar Alexander (Republican) of Tennessee was a national figure having served as president of the University of Tennessee before accepting appointment by George H. W. Bush to the post of Secretary of Education from 1991 to 1993. Alexander was an immediate backer of the TVAAS. However, TVAAS lacked backers among many statisticians who had spent their careers studying educational measurement.

A group of a couple dozen statisticians and educators from around the world began discussing TVAAS in September of 1994 on an internet discussion group called EDPOLYAN (Glass, 2020). Sanders' method was easily recognized to be a simple mixed linear regression model familiar to statisticians in all fields. Use was made of a string of earlier class averages for a teacher to correct for the fact that students begin a school year with very different levels of achievement and learn at very different rates. Over a period of months, the discussants on EDPOLYAN expressed their doubts that the TVAAS could accomplish what it claimed it could do. A couple contributors took the model and applied it to some data close at hand and revealed one of the most serious flaws in the technique: it produced unreliable results. A teacher whose VAM score ranked her as one of the top teachers in the district in Year 1 suddenly earned a VAM score near the bottom of the district in Year 2—same teacher, same subject, different students, wildly different VAM scores. Sanders entered the discussion at one point to defend his method, but quickly withdrew. The contributors to EDPOLYAN felt that they had put TVAAS to rest and that no device so lacking in reliability and validity would ever be imposed on the nation's teaching force. They underestimated the political appeal of VAM, however.

Multiple states and school districts adopted the TVAAS, rechristened in some instances to give the approach a sense of local relevance: TxVAAS in Texas, the PVAAS in Pennsylvania. In addition, the generically named EVAAS was introduced in states like Ohio, North Carolina, and South Carolina and in many other districts throughout the nation. The use of VAM thus became more common—but it was not widely adopted nationwide due to continued pushback from teachers and research-based arguments concerning its capacity to accurately measure teacher performance. VAM resurfaced again amid a major shift in teacher evaluation policy that occurred around 2009—a shift prompted by major federal interest in using test scores to evaluate teachers. The Obama administration under Secretary of Education Arnie Duncan sought to put its own stamp on Bush administration policy by enhancing No Child Left Behind with a competitive grant program called Race to the Top (RTTT). RTTT was funded at $4.35 billion as part of the 2009 American Recovery and Reinvestment Act.

RTTT favored the use of standardized test scores to reward and sanction teachers and schools. One of the stipulations of the RTTT grant was that states had to implement a merit pay system based, in significant part, on student achievement scores. States were also encouraged to base other personnel decisions (e.g., retention, tenure, termination) on student growth data. For example, in four states—Delaware, Louisiana, Rhode Island, and Tennessee—some teachers seeking to update their licenses had to meet certain criteria for their students' test scores. VAM was being pushed heavily by corporations like Pearson Education, a major standardized test company, and SAS Institute that had acquired the rights to the use of TVAAS.

VAM accountability was touted as the new wave that would weed out incompetent educators, reward great teachers, and move the nation's schools to the highest levels of excellence. But critics of VAM continued to assert that nothing had been done to correct the shortcomings identified by the discussants at EDPOLYAN some 20 years earlier.

In Colorado, a state senator and former Teach for America teacher, Michael Johnson, introduced SB 191, which was quickly passed into law in 2010. The Colorado law stipulated that 50 percent of a teacher's job rating must be based on the teacher's students' growth in standardized test scores. Six years later, the Colorado version of VAM was declared a failure by critics. In the Chicago teacher strike of 2010, VAM was among two core issues (the other being teacher seniority) causing teachers to leave the classroom to protest. Protests of evaluating teachers based on students' test scores erupted from Washington state to Rhode Island in 2013.

Critics contend that the unreliability of VAM as a measurement instrument was apparent wherever it was applied. A 2012 analysis reported that teachers' value as measured by VAMs jumped wildly from high to low to average from year to year with no apparent change in their teaching or their students' learning (Darling-Hammond et al., 2012). A 2008 study of five school districts across the country found significant unreliability of VAM rankings of teachers (Sass, 2008). When the researcher looked at teachers ranked in the bottom 20 percent on VAM measures for one year, he found only about a third of them were similarly in the bottom 20 percent the next year. Moreover, another 30 percent had advanced to near the middle of the group of teachers on VAM scores the following year. Of teachers whose VAM scores put them in the top 20 percent in Year 1, only about one-fourth were in the top 20 percent in Year 2, and another

20 percent had dropped below the group average. An instrument without reliability (i.e., consistency from time to time) cannot have validity (i.e., fidelity to its intended target). An instrument must measure something consistently before it can be said to measure that which it purports to measure.

In 2009, the Bill and Melinda Gates Foundation contributed more than $200 million to a program to test the efficacy of VAM in improving teaching and learning. Joined with tax-payer funds, $597 million were spent between 2009 and 2016 in three school districts (Hillsborough County, Florida; Memphis, Tennessee; Pittsburgh, Pennsylvania) and in four charter school chains to test VAM as a means of improving staffing decisions. The Gates Foundation funded the RAND Corporation and the American Institutes for Research to evaluate the program. Their 2019 research report concluded that with minor exceptions, the initiative did not increase student achievement, graduation rates, or change the quality of teachers (Stecher et al., 2019). A 2014 study examined a subset of more than 300 teachers involved in the same program (Polikoff and Porter, 2014). In doing so, researchers looked at how VAM scores correlated with observational measures of teacher quality. One would assume that if a teacher scores high on a teacher quality measure, she would also do well in terms of VAM, and vice versa. However, that was not the case according to the researchers, who found only small relationships between the two.

Division 15 of the American Psychological Association condemned the use of VAM in a policy brief released in January 2020 (Lavigne and Good, 2020). The report's authors concluded:

1. VAM scores do not adequately compare teachers. VAM scores are unable to account for teachers' disparate contexts and all of the factors that explain student achievement outcomes.
2. A teacher's effectiveness often varies. Thus, it is difficult to achieve appropriate reliability to justify its use in high-stakes teacher evaluation. Even if abundant data were available (e.g., 10 years), decisions based upon student achievement would be wrong 12 percent of the time.
3. Many teachers do not have VAM scores. Typically, nearly a third of teachers do not have VAM scores. Thus, assigning a VAM score to these teachers based upon the average score of other teachers (a school-level value-added score) is unfair.
4. VAM scores do not help teachers improve their instruction. This is, in part, because teachers' VAM scores are weakly—and sometimes not at all—related to what teachers actually do in classrooms (e.g., observational data). Furthermore, VAM scores do not identify for teachers areas

in need of improvement (e.g., concepts that were particularly difficult, student misconceptions).
5. The use of individual value-added scores discourages collegial exchange and the sharing of ideas and resources across the school. (Lavigne and Good, 2020, 3)

VAM was also criticized for serious and unexpected negative side effects. With VAMs, teachers are pushed to show large student gains—the higher the gains, the better their evaluation scores. It means that many teachers are likely to abandon their collaborative efforts of helping students of all classrooms succeed, in order to increase the chances of their own classrooms' success. It means that teachers who seek a bonus, or fear getting fired, must plot to get the most affluent students because, as history shows, these are the students with winning records. In a 2012 study of Houston's Independent School District, which had a history of merit pay, teachers talked about the "money kids," the kids who get them the big bonuses (Amrein-Beardsley and Collins, 2012). These were middle class or wealthy children with low average scores from the year before. Because they came from well-resourced families and had low scores the year before, it was expected they would grow the most. The way that the scoring system placed emphasis on "value-added" students who would not generally score well or show marked improvement—such as English language learners, students with special needs, and gifted and talented students—were to be avoided. The latter are to be avoided because most tests do not have enough "ceiling" in them to track the gains made by students who are well ahead of their grade level. They may actually gain a lot, of course, but it will not show on the tests because gifted children are often performing well above what is measured at their particular grade. Therefore, teachers seeking bonuses learned to avoid having them in their class.

Critics of VAM say that its use revealed a dark side of the pressures facing some school districts. A 2007 study found that under the pressure of losing one's employment or being censured in the local media, some teachers and administrators cheated on test administration and reporting (Nichols and Berliner, 2007). A child or two might be conveniently sent to the library or placed in time-out during the end of year test taking. A time limit might be misread and students given an extra 15 minutes to finish the exam. A 1990 publication revealed one of the more egregious instances in a Texas school district where administrators were promised more than $10,000 if their school met VAM goals, as some administrators were caught changing marks on answer sheets in their private offices before sheets were sent off for machine scoring (Glass, 1990).

Discontent of teachers and their unions soon changed into lawsuits asserting that VAM was being used as the basis for decisions about compensation and employment. Among the several lawsuits, the one filed against the Houston Independent School District (HISD) was the most prominent. VAM scores were being employed to evaluate HISD teachers in more consequential ways than elsewhere in the country. In a single year prior to 2010, more than 200 teachers were fired based mostly on their VAM scores. In 2014, the Houston Federation of Teachers filed suit against the HISD. On October 10, 2017, the suit was dismissed in light of a settlement agreed to by the HFT and the HISD. The court's decision on the question of the use of EVAAS was a devastating blow to the fortunes of VAM backers everywhere: "HISD agrees that it will not in the future use value-added scores, including but not limited to EVAAS scores, as a basis to terminate the employment of a term or probationary contract teacher during the term of that teacher's contract, or to terminate a continuing contract teacher at any time, so long as the value-added score assigned to the teacher remains unverifiable" (*Santos et al. v. HISD*, 2017). Houston dropped its VAM program after the settlement was announced.

Judges in New Mexico issued an injunction in response to a suit that forbade any school district and the state from using VAM as a basis for any high-stakes decision, such as salary increases or termination. In 2019, New Mexico Governor Michelle Lujan Grisham signed an executive order eliminating the state's VAM-based teacher evaluation system.

Other states, however, continue to incorporate VAM to varying degrees into their teacher assessments. The passage of the federal Every Student Succeeds Act in 2016 eliminated federal requirements for teacher evaluation systems in school districts to be closely linked to student test scores. But the resulting flexibility given to states in erecting new teacher assessment systems created an environment in which assessment tools vary considerably from state to state. "If I were to use two words to describe the landscape right now in regard to teacher accountability: messy and complicated," said education scholar Kimberly Kappler Hewitt. "No two states are doing the same thing right now" (Will, 2016).

FURTHER READING

Amrein-Beardsley, A. 2014. "Putting growth and value-added models on the map: A national overview." *Teachers College Record*, 16(1). Retrieved from http://www.tcrecord.org/Content.asp?ContentId=17291

Amrein-Beardsley, A., and Collins, C. 2012. "The SAS Education Value-Added Assessment System in the Houston Independent School District (HISD)." *Education Policy Analysis Archives, 20*(12). Retrieved from http://epaa.asu.edu/ojs/article/view/1096

Darling-Hammond, L., Amrein-Beardsly, A., Haertel, E., and Rothstein, J. 2012. "Evaluating teacher evaluation." *Phi Delta Kappan, 93*(6), 8–15.

Ellwein, M. C., Glass, G. V, and Smith, M. L. 1988. "Standards of competence: Propositions on the nature of testing reforms." *Educational Researcher, 17*(8), 4–9.

Florio, D. H. 1986. "Student tests for teacher evaluation: A critique." *Educational Evaluation and Policy Analysis, 8,* 45–60.

Glass, G. V. 1990. "Using student test scores to evaluate teachers." In J. Millman and L. Darling-Hammond (Eds.), *The new handbook of teacher evaluation: Assessing elementary and secondary school teachers.* Thousand Oaks, CA: SAGE Publications, 229–240.

Glass, G. V. 2020. "An archaeological dig for VAM." *Education in Two Worlds.* Retrieved from https://ed2worlds.blogspot.com/2020/04/an-archaeological-dig-for-vam.html

Glass, G. V, and Ellwein, M. C. 1986. "Reform by raising test standards." *Evaluation Comment, 10,* 1–6.

Harris, D. N. 2011. *Value-added measures in education: What every educator needs to know.* Cambridge, MA: Harvard Education Press.

Lavigne, A. L., and Good, T. L. 2020. "Addressing teacher evaluation appropriately." APA Division 15 Policy Brief Series. Volume 1, No. 2. Retrieved from https://apadiv15.org/wp-content/uploads/2020/01/Addressing-Teacher-Evaluation-Appropriately.pdf

Nichols, S. L., and Berliner, D. C. 2007. *Collateral damage: How high-stakes testing corrupts America's schools.* Cambridge, MA: Harvard Education Press.

Polikoff, M. S., and Porter, A. C. 2014. "Instructional alignment as a measure of teaching quality." *Educational Evaluation and Policy Analysis, 36*(4), 399–416.

Sanders, W. L., and Horn, S. P. 1994. "The Tennessee Value-Added Assessment System (TVAAS): Mixed-model methodology in educational assessment." *Journal of Personnel Evaluation in Education, 8,* 299–311.

Santos et al. v. HISD, 251 F. Supp. 3d 1168 (S.D. Tex. 2017).

Sass, T. R. 2008. "The stability of value-added measures of teacher quality and implications for teacher compensation policy." Policy Brief 4. Washington, DC: The Urban Institute, National Center for Analysis of Longitudinal Data in Education Research.

Stecher, B. M. et al. 2019. "Intensive partnerships for effective teaching enhanced how teachers are evaluated but had little effect on student outcomes." Santa Monica, CA: RAND Corporation. Retrieved from https://www.rand.org/pubs/research_briefs/RB10009-1.html

Will, M. 2016. "Assessing Quality of Teaching Staff Still Complex Despite ESSA's Leeway." *Education Week,* December 30, 2016. Retrieved from https://www.edweek.org/ew/articles/2017/01/04/assessing-quality-of-teaching-staff-still-complex.html?intc=EW-QC17-TOC&_ga=1.138540723.1051944855.1481128421

Q22. IS THE UNITED STATES LAGGING BEHIND OTHER NATIONS IN K–12 EDUCATION?

Answer: On international tests in reading, science, and math, several countries score better than U.S. students, on average. The conclusion that many in the media and policy arena—to say nothing of the general public—have reached about those scores is that the United States has an inferior education system in comparison to its socioeconomic peers around the world. Other scholars, however, find both the tests and score comparisons to be problematic and of limited utility in judging the quality of American education.

The Facts: International test comparisons show the United States at about the middle of the pack among industrialized nations in math and reading. The results receive considerable media attention, casting the U.S. education system in a negative light. The critical media slants have gone on for over two decades at least (e.g., Goldstein, 2019; Hanushek, 2011; Heim, 2016; Norris, 2004; Raspberry, 1998; Richards, 2020). In many instances, the results have also been seized on by politicians and policy makers to advance their preferred education reform agendas. The test comparisons have unleashed new policy priorities to hold our schools accountable to "world-class" standards through "international benchmarking." But some education experts contend that too much weight is given to these comparisons, given the many socioeconomic differences between nations.

The Testing Olympics

The two most prominent international student achievement surveys are the Programme for International Student Assessment (PISA) and Trends in Mathematics and Science Study (TIMSS). PISA administers exams in reading, science, and math to samples of 15-year-olds every three years. In 2018, China (Beijing, Shanghai, Jiangsu, Zhejiang), Singapore, Macau, Hong Kong, and Chinese Taipei were the top five scoring countries in math. The United States was ranked 36th in math out of the 79 countries and regions that take the PISA. Incidentally, the U.S. Department of Education considers the ranking to be 30th, due to the fact the average scores of other nations immediately above and below the United States are not statistically distinguishable (https://tinyurl.com/wsus58r). The rankings in science show the same or similar countries as math scoring in the top 10— mostly Asian, with the exception of Finland, Estonia, and Canada. In reading, the United States fared better, coming in at 13th. U.S. students scored similar to their peers in Australia, Germany, New Zealand, Sweden, and the United Kingdom in at least two of the three subjects of reading, science, and math.

The TIMSS has been around since 1995 and is administered every four years to samples of fourth- and eighth-graders to assess performance in math and science. The 2015 TIMSS results show that Asian nations score at the top, which has been the case for the past 20 years. Singapore, Hong Kong SAR, Korea, Chinese Taipei, and Japan are the highest scoring nations in mathematics (timss2015.org), while the United States placed at 14th among 49 nations (fourth grade) and 10th among 39 nations (eighth grade). Science scores paralleled math for basically all countries.

International Comparisons: Fair? Useful?

Much is made of the performance of Singapore on PISA tests. In 2015, Singapore students scored the highest in the world on PISA tests of math, science, and reading. Singapore is a sovereign city-state with the highest per capita rate of millionaires of any geopolitical unit in the world. What precisely is the point of comparing Singapore to the United States when evaluating systems of schooling? In 1996, a consortium of wealthy school districts on the north shore of Lake Michigan got together and administered the TIMSS tests in math and science to their 15-year-olds. They scored at a level statistically equal to Singapore and above all other nations. None of the educators who rushed to Finland and Singapore to discover the secrets of superior education took a trip to Chicago in search of education excellence.

The rankings produced by these international tests are problematic in multiple ways. Countries are ranked according to their average scores. Average scores represent a measure of central tendency, but do not capture the variability occurring around it. Some countries exhibit more homogeneous test scores than others, and this homogeneity is likely a function of (a lack of) diversity across race and class. Moreover, outside the very top and bottom ends of the distribution, the differences in average scores are often too small to warrant reliable distinctions in performance. What about the tests themselves? Critics contend that differences in language and culture make attempts to equate test difficulty questionable, at best. The reading tests are highly problematic in this regard, with the virtual impossibility of equating the texts used across languages. Consider a translation of the PISA reading test. A question for American students depended on knowing that an antonym for "pessimistic" was "sanguine." However, in Finnish, no antonym of that type is available, so the same question in Finnish was comparable to "pessimistic versus optimistic" in English.

Detractors say that it is not just translation and measuring system differences that render these international tests of dubious value. In one of the earliest international assessments of reading in the 1970s—the International Association for the Evaluation of Educational Achievement Reading Literacy Study—the nation at the top of the test score distribution was Italy. One might wonder, why Italy? Administration of the tests depended on cooperation of volunteer agencies and persons around the world following directions. Samples of students had to be drawn to represent the entire nation. Further investigation uncovered some irregularities in the sampling of students to take the test in Italy as well as a few other nations. The 2015 administration of the PIRLS (Progress in International Reading Literacy Study) reading test produced a winner far above even the second-place nation: the city of Moscow, Russia. Russia is not known for its approaches to teaching literacy. Even moderately skeptical persons will not ask how the United States can conduct schooling more like Russia. They will instead ask, "How exactly did Moscow administer that test?"

It is not just reading tests that present problems for comparing achievement of school children in many nations. Science involves measurement; measurement scales differ in different nations. Three nations do not employ the metric system: Liberia, Myanmar, and the United States of America. Both Liberia and Myanmar are making moves toward adopting the metric system. Other irregularities in administration of the tests render the results and rankings suspect. Some countries were allowed to use calculators for the math and science tests while others were not. TIMSS administration was aimed at the next-to-last year of high school. But students at that level in some nations average age 19, while in other nations the average age is less than 17.

U.S. student heterogeneity also influences average scores on international tests. Relative to many other industrialized nations, the United States is highly diverse in terms of race, ethnicity, wealth, religion, culture, and language. More diversity in the United States does not mean U.S. students are not as smart as those in other countries; it means the United States has relatively more students falling in the nondominant class. The dominant class will score well on tests because they have possessed advantages in life and in school that nondominant classes do not.

The overseers of PISA, the Organization for Economic Cooperation and Development (OECD), acknowledged in a 2010 report the influence of equity on their exams (OECD, 2010); however, this point is not always taken into account in international comparisons of education systems. Finland's recent performance has them lauded as among the best educational systems in the world. But how is the country of Finland different than, say, the United States? Finland has an extraordinarily low childhood poverty rate relative to the United States. According to the National Center for Children in Poverty, 1 in 5 U.S. children live below the federal poverty line (Koball and Jiang, 2018). The federal poverty line is a conservative figure, with a 2008 study showing families need at least twice that amount to cover basic expenses (Cauthen and Fass, 2008). Using an adjusted poverty threshold, the percentage of children balloons to 43 percent. Finland also pays its teachers higher salaries, has more recess and play time, and far less homework and testing.

In countless empirical studies that explain differences in student achievement, poverty is the strongest predictor of performance (Berliner, 2013). Despite its great wealth and economic prosperity, the United States is one of the more economically and racially stratified nations in the world. It is not immune to poverty's pernicious influences. The OECD estimates of relative childhood poverty place the United States well below average, and countries such as Denmark, Finland, Norway, Sweden, and Korea (all high scoring on international tests) at the top in terms of lowest in childhood poverty. The United States ranked 32nd out of 43 countries in childhood poverty.

Other observers blame the sub-par U.S. rankings on schools not being sufficiently rigorous. Others claim that the United States ranks poorly, particularly in math, because of sorting students into classes by ability; lower tracked students are not taught all that is tested. The primary reason for where the United States ranks as it does, however, is predicated by the socioeconomic diversity of the test takers. The scholar who delivered a lecture at the 2011 annual conference of the Scottish Educational Research Association (SERA), recalls a warning from a comparative education scholar from decades ago that still applies today: "In studying foreign systems of education we should not forget that the things outside the schools matter even more than the things inside the schools . . . (Sadler 1990, 50)" (Alexander, 2012, 5).

One notable critique of PISA and TIMSS was advanced by Professor Yong Zhao, Foundation Distinguished Professor at the University of Kansas, in 2014. Zhao, an American citizen raised in China, is the author of *Who's Afraid of the Big Bad Dragon: Why China has the Best (and Worst) Education System in the World* (2014). With an intimate knowledge of the Chinese school system and a PhD in Education from a U.S. university, Zhao is well situated to address transnational education policy issues. Zhao blames PISA and TIMSS for creating much of the U.S. admiration of foreign education systems.

Zhao has criticized the international assessments for technical problems that render their findings questionable bases for education policy. In addition, he has declared that despite the assertions of the OECD, "the claim that PISA measures knowledge and skills essential for the modern society or the future world is not based on any empirical evidence" (Zhao, 2019). This claim is made repeatedly by the OECD, the sponsors of PISA. Critics, though, contend that the backing for such claims is drawn from the highly speculative work of a small number of economists, whose work has been rejected by the bulk of their colleagues. A 2010 report published by the OECD made the claim that "having all OECD countries boost their average PISA scores by 25 points over the next 20 years . . . implies an aggregate gain of OECD GDP of USD 115 trillion over the lifetime of the generation born in 2010" (Hanushek and Woessmann, 2010, 6). Such speculative assertions have been rebutted by economic scholars in several studies (Kamens, 2015; Klees, 2016; Komatsu and Rappleye, 2017; Stromquist, 2016).

FURTHER READING

Alexander, R. J. 2012. "Moral panic, miracle cures and educational policy: What can we really learn from international comparison?" *Scottish Educational Review*, 44(1), 4–21.

Berliner, D. 2013. "Effects of inequality and poverty vs. teachers and schooling on America's youth." *Teachers College Record*, 115(12), 1–26.

Cauthen, N. K., and Fass, S. 2008. *Measuring poverty in the United States*. New York: National Center for Children in Poverty.

Glass, G. V. 2012. Among the many things wrong with international achievement comparisons. *Education in Two Worlds*. February 17, 2012.

Retrieved from http://ed2worlds.blogspot.com/2012/02/among-many-things-wrong-with.html

Goldstein, D. 2019. "'It just isn't working': PISA test scores cast doubt on U.S. education efforts." *New York Times*, December 3, 2019.

Hanushek, E. 2011. "Why can't U.S. students compete with the rest of the world?" *Newsweek*, August 28, 2011.

Hanushek, E. A., and Woessmann, L. 2010. *The high cost of low educational performance: The long-run economic impact of improving PISA outcomes.* Organization for Economic Cooperation and Development, Programme for International Student Assessment. Retrieved from http://www.oecd.org/pisa/44417824.pdf

Heim, J. 2016. "On the world stage, U.S. students fall behind." *Washington Post*, December 6, 2016.

Kamens, D. H. 2015. "A maturing global testing regime meets the world economy: Test scores and economic growth, 1960–2012." *Comparative Education Review*, 59(3), 420–446.

Klees, S. J. 2016. "Human capital and rates of return: Brilliant ideas or ideological dead ends?" *Comparative Education Review*, 60(4), 644–672.

Koball, H., and Jiang, Y. 2018. *Basic facts about low-income children: Children under 9 years, 2016*. National Center for Children in Poverty. New York, NY: Bank Street Graduate School of Education.

Komatsu, H., and Rappleye, J. 2017. "A new global policy regime founded on invalid statistics? Hanushek, Woessmann, PISA, and economic growth." *Comparative Education*, 53(2), 166–191.

Norris, F. 2004. "U.S. students fare badly in international survey of math skills," *New York Times*, December 7, 2004. Retrieved from https://www.nytimes.com/2004/12/07/us/us-students-fare-badly-in-international-survey-of-math-skills.html

OECD. 2010. *PISA 2009 Results: Executive summary*. Organization for Economic Cooperation and Development, Programme for International Student Assessment. Paris: OECD. Retrieved from http://www.oecd.org/pisa/pisaproducts/46619703.pdf

Raspberry, W. 1998. "American 12th-graders scored at the very bottom of the rankings." *Washington Post*, March 12, 1998.

Richards, E. 2020. "Math scores stink in America. Other countries teach it differently—and see higher achievement." *USA Today*, February 28, 2020.

Stromquist, N. P. 2016. "Using regression analysis to predict countries' economic growth: Illusion and fact in education policy." *Real-World Economics Review*, 76, 65–74.

UNICEF. 2017. *Building the future: Children and the sustainable development goals in rich countries*. Innocenti Report Card no. 14, UNICEF Office of Research—Innocenti, Florence.

Zhao, Y. 2014. *Who's Afraid of the Big Bad Dragon: Why China has the Best (and Worst) Education System in the World*. San Francisco, CA: Jossey-Bass.

Zhao, Y. 2019. *The PISA illusion*. National Education Policy Center. Retrieved from https://nepc.colorado.edu/blog/pisa-illusion

Q23. HOW ARE THE POLITICAL INTERESTS THAT SHAPE EDUCATION POLICY ORGANIZED?

Answer: For more than 40 years, conservative political interests seeking to shape the education policies of the various states have operated through an organization known as the American Legislative Exchange Council (ALEC). Liberal interests have long sought to further their interests through two teacher unions, the American Federation of Teachers (AFT) and the National Education Association (NEA), and their many state affiliates. More recently, the Network for Public Education (NPE) has taken an aggressive approach to influencing education politics and policy with the goal of strengthening and defending the public education system.

The Facts: The modern reader may find it difficult to believe that prior to the middle of the twentieth century, neither state authorities nor the federal government played large roles in the determination of policy for K–12 public education. The Tenth Amendment to the U.S. Constitution specifies that all powers not explicitly reserved for the federal government are delegated to the individual states. Consequently, the creation, function, and support of education, all topics not specified in the Constitution, were left to the states. The states in turn, with few exceptions, handed that responsibility down to townships, cities, and counties.

This state of affairs continued into the twentieth century. With the exception of small amounts of federal monies allocated to states for vocational education in the Smith–Hughes National Vocational Education Act of 1917, federal involvement in funding K–12 education was virtually nonexistent until 1957, when the Russians circled the Earth with Sputnik, the world's first space satellite. Alarmed by what appeared to be the nation's slow progress in science and technology, Congress passed the National

Defense Education Act (NDEA) in 1958. Sizeable amounts of NDEA monies were directed toward the development of elementary and secondary school science curricula. By 1960, the tradition of noninvolvement had been broken. Alarmed by rising levels of poverty and unable to ignore the circumstances of racial minorities in K–12 public schools, the Johnson Administration drove the Elementary and Secondary Education Act (ESEA) through Congress in 1965. In the first year, $1 billion was earmarked for ESEA Title I funding, also referred to as Compensatory Education. The dam had been broken; money flooded from Washington, DC, to the states to the public schools, and education policy became a much more prominent issue at both the state and federal levels.

The Powell Memorandum and Corporate Influence

Prior to the early 1970s, conservative political interests sought little influence on Congress and the executive branch of federal government. With a few notable exceptions, big corporations generally viewed business and government as separate entities. In 1971, however, a 60-year-old corporate lawyer from Virginia, named Lewis F. Powell, was commissioned by the U.S. Chamber of Commerce to write a confidential memo entitled "Attack on the American Free Enterprise System" (Powell, 1971). Powell's memorandum was an anti-Communist and anti-progressive government blueprint for big business interests to exert control over government at every level. It also attacked American universities as hotbeds of anti-business and pro-socialist influence. The Powell Memorandum, as it has come to be called, asserted that:

> Business must learn the lesson . . . that political power is necessary; that such power must be assiduously cultivated; and that when necessary, it must be used aggressively and with determination—without embarrassment and without the reluctance which has been so characteristic of American business. (Powell, 1971)

Powell was appointed to the U.S. Supreme Court in 1972 by President Richard Nixon, where he served until 1987.

The ultimate influence of the Powell Memorandum on American business and politics continues to be debated. Not surprisingly, perspectives tend to fall along partisan lines, with those on the left claiming it was the main inspiration behind a corporate takeover of democracy, while those on the right deemphasizing its impact and role in historical context. Whatever the true level of influence, the American corporate world behaved in a manner that generally paralleled Powell's advice. For instance, the Powell Memorandum called for corporations to become assiduously involved in law making and for the creation of think tanks that would generate research studies and arguments that would sway legislators to provide greater support to the interests of business. In 1960, there were virtually no corporate lobbyists registered in the nation's capital. By the year 2007, there were 15,000. Prominent think tanks were established in the 1970s and 1980s along with other powerful organizations that have become influential participants in discussions of America's education system (Smith, 2012). In the mid-1990s, conservative think tanks outnumbered liberal ones by roughly a 2 to 1 margin and outspent them by a ratio of more than 3 to 1 (Rich, 2001).

To this day, conservative political interests rely on the research produced in freestanding think tanks supported by corporate funding. Among the leading conservative think tanks are the Heritage Foundation, Cato Institute, American Enterprise Institute, Goldwater Institute, Heartland Institute, State Policy Network, Mackinac Center for Public Policy, Manhattan Institute for Policy Research, and Thomas B. Fordham Institution. They are all supported by corporate interests.

Much less frequently, a conservative think tank will find a home in a U.S. university setting—for example, the Center on Reinventing Public Education at the University of Washington, the Hoover Institution at Stanford University, and the Department of Education Reform at the University of Arkansas. Most of their funding comes from corporate-based foundations.

Liberal think tanks are far less common, far less well funded, and exercise far less influence on education policy. Among the most prominent on education issues are the Economic Policy Institute, Center for American Progress, National Education Policy Center, and Education Trust. They are funded from a variety of sources, including private foundations, individual donations, labor unions, and universities. Universities themselves, which are predominantly left-leaning, also influence education policy, although they are far less organized to do so.

The Rise of ALEC

Arguably, one of the most influential politically conservative entities has proven to be ALEC (Underwood and Mead, 2012). Formed in 1973, just two years after the circulation of the Powell Memorandum, ALEC gradually emerged over the space of several decades as the most powerful influence on education policy in the United States. ALEC claims that "the mission of ALEC's Education Task Force is to promote excellence in the nation's educational system, to advance reforms through parental choice, to support efficiency, accountability, and transparency in all educational institutions, and to ensure America's youth are given the opportunity to succeed." In 2020, ALEC assumed the following position with respect to schooling and privatization of K–12 public education on its website:

> . . . it's time to let parents take back control over their children's educations by allowing them to apply competitive pressure to schools and educational providers. Innovative, parent-empowering choices such as charter schools, voucher programs, tax credit scholarships, homeschool, and education savings accounts allow each child the opportunity to reach his or her potential. (American Legislative Exchange Council, n.d.)

ALEC's membership comprises approximately 2,000 state legislators and 300 corporations and foundations. ALEC's legislative members—virtually all of them Republicans—pay dues of $100 for two years, but more than 98 percent of ALEC's funding comes from other sources. Corporate members pay dues that range from $7,000 to $25,000, and additional fees to participate on task forces. ALEC's website says that no single donor provides more than 5 percent of ALEC's revenues.

ALEC's aggressive support for conservative, pro-business, anti-regulatory policy goals have led it to adopt controversial positions on everything from climate change (opposing various proposals to reduce emissions of greenhouse gases) to "stand your ground" laws (urging adoption of such laws across the country). This has led a number of companies to end their ties with the organization in the 2010s, including such corporate giants as Coca-Cola, Kraft Foods, Google, Walgreens, Microsoft, Visa, General Motors, McDonalds, and PepsiCo. In 2011, the Center for Media and Democracy (CMD), a left-leaning watchdog organization, began a series of exposes critical of ALEC's practices and has since kept close tabs on the organization and its supporters. According to CMD's *SourceWatch*, as of May 2019, at least 114 companies and 19 private nonprofits had publicly cut ties with ALEC (SourceWatch, 2020). Subsequently, however, a small number have rejoined.

ALEC is registered with the Internal Revenue Service as a "non-profit charity"; thus, it pays no taxes and is not required to disclose its contributors nor the legislators who are the recipients of its largesse. Of the 1,000 model bills that ALEC causes to be introduced each year, about 10 to 20 percent actually become law. In 2012, 100 bills written by ALEC were passed into law. A 2013 report from CMD found at least 139 ALEC-inspired education bills or budget directives were introduced in 43 states and the District of Columbia in the first half of 2013—and 31 were eventually signed into law (Center for Media and Democracy, 2019). In North Carolina alone, a flurry of ALEC-influenced education policies was introduced in 2013, including a school voucher program, a teacher pay for performance plan that replaced teacher tenure, and termination of master's degree salary increases for teachers (Center for Media and Democracy, 2013). These bills reflect model legislation generated by ALEC, such as their Parental Choice Scholarship Program Act (Anderson and Donchik, 2016).

A prominent corporate member of ALEC is the Pearson Foundation. The Pearson Foundation is the nonprofit arm of Pearson Ltd, headquartered in London, England, with U.S. operations based in Iowa. Pearson has quietly grown into possibly the most powerful education corporation in America. Pearson has made hundreds of millions of dollars creating tests for states. It has managed to acquire the complete operation of the GED test and publishes books and tutorials to prepare students to take the test. It also provides online courses to schools and colleges throughout the world.

Progressive and Liberal Interests in Education

Progressive and liberal influence over education policy is less powerful than conservative, corporate influence. Nevertheless, progressive think tanks such as the Brookings Institution and the Center for American Progress, and more liberal organizations such as the Economic Policy Institute and the National Center for Education Policy do have some impact. At the very least, liberal organizations and policy makers rely on studies generated by these organizations, similar to their conservative counterparts, who rely on right-wing institutes.

Well-funded teacher labor unions have had a more direct impact on the education policy arena. Founded in 1857, the National Education Association (NEA) is the largest union in the United States. But its size belies its influence. With approximately 3 million members, the NEA exercises influence primarily through its state and local affiliates. The NEA was formed during that period in American history when trades and occupations were attempting to redefine themselves as professions. Lawyers, doctors, and engineers did not start life as prestigious professions, they had to cultivate the image and secure its privileges. The same was true with schoolteachers. Organizations that define qualifications for membership and enforce them help achieve these ends. The actions of the NEA and its affiliates have never aligned with those of the nation's labor unions. Consequently, its influence in the political arena has been modest.

The more aggressive representative of liberal interests in public education is the American Federation of Teachers (AFT). Founded in 1916, the AFT now has 3,000 local chapters, and approximately 1.6 million members. In a sense, the AFT competes with the NEA for members. The AFT tends to be more prominent in urban settings, whereas the NEA is more popular in suburban and rural communities and in the Western United States. AFT chapters have repeatedly called for work stoppages and strikes that have shut down the schools of a large city.

A latter-day creation of liberal political interests is the Network for Public Education (NPE), Founded in 2017, the NPE has 400,000 followers. Taking advantage of the communication and outreach possibilities of digital media, the NPE represents a nascent political movement seeking to further the interests of K–12 public schools and stop the advance of the privatization of America's education system.

FURTHER READING

American Legislative Exchange Council, n.d. "Education." ALEC. Retrieved from https://www.alec.org/issue/education

Anderson, G. L., and Donchik, L. M. 2016. "Privatizing schooling and policy making: The American Legislative Exchange Council and new political and discursive strategies of education governance." *Educational Policy*, 30(2), 322–364.

Center for Media and Democracy. 2013. *ALEC at 40: Turning back the clock on prosperity and progress*. Retrieved from http://www.alecexposed.org/wiki/What_is_ALEC%3F

Center for Media and Democracy. 2019. *ALEC in Texas: Uncovering the influence of the American Legislative Exchange Council (ALEC) in the Texas Legislature*. Retrieved from http://www.commoncause.org/wp-content/uploads/2019/08/ALEC-Report-Texas_FINAL_WEB.pdf

Dolny, M. 2008. *The incredible shrinking think tank*. Fairness and Accuracy in Reporting (FAIR). Retrieved from http://fair.org/extra-online-articles/The-Incredible-Shrinking-Think-Tank

Ingram, D., and Crowley, J. 2012. *Gates Foundation cuts ties to U.S. conservative group*. Reuters, April 10, 2012. Retrieved from https://www.reuters.com/article/us-usa-gates/gates-foundation-cuts-ties-to-u-s-conservative-group-idUSBRE83918720120410

Powell, L. F. 1971. *Attack on the American free enterprise system*. Memorandum to the U.S. Chamber of Commerce. Retrieved from https://scholarlycommons.law.wlu.edu/powellmemo

Rich, A. 2001. "U.S. think tanks and the intersection of ideology, advocacy, and influence." *Nira Review*, 8(1), 54–59.

Smith, H. 2012. *Who Stole the American Dream?* New York: Random House.

SourceWatch. 2020. "Corporations That Have Cut Ties to ALEC." Center for Media and Democracy. Retrieved from https://www.sourcewatch.org/index.php/Corporations_that_Have_Cut_Ties_to_ALEC

Underwood, J., and Mead, J. F. 2012. "A smart ALEC threatens public education." *Phi Delta Kappan*, 93(6), 51–55.

5

Teaching and Learning

Teachers, school administrators, psychologists, and education researchers have investigated how children learn and the best ways to teach for more than 100 years. Many of the answers that they have discovered are cast in technical form: Is mere contingency superior to reinforcement for long-term retention? Are deep structure grammatical formulations innate or must they be taught? Although professional educators need to know the answers to these questions, the public's questions about teaching and learning are more pragmatic. Does school start too early in the morning? Is all of this homework necessary? How can a teacher cope when four different native languages are represented in the classroom? How can I get my own work done when my nine-year-old's school has switched to an online class model as a result of the COVID-19 pandemic?

Q24. DO LATER SCHOOL START TIMES MAKE A DIFFERENCE IN CHILDREN'S LEARNING?

Answer: Unequivocally, yes, particularly for older adolescents. Moving school start times to later in the morning is supported by research from some of the most prominent child health and wellness organizations. For the most part, their recommendations go unheeded.

The Facts: Teenagers are biologically programmed to stay up late and awake late. According to a 2007 review of adolescent sleep behavior, compared with their first decade of life, older adolescents become sleepy much later in the evening and are naturally prone to rising much later in the morning (Crowley, Acebo, and Carskadon, 2007). Another study from 2011 found that melatonin levels for teens peak at roughly 7:00 a.m., while adult levels peak around 4:00 a.m.; therefore, waking a teenager at 7:00 a.m. is comparable to waking an adult at 4:00 a.m. (Carrell, Maghakian, and West, 2011). Melatonin is a natural hormone that plays an important role in the body's sleep-wake cycle. In the evening when it becomes dark, the body increases its production to help induce healthy sleep. The research in this area has been proven time and again in several different studies.

However, current practice in many American high schools is to begin classes early—typically between 7:00 and 7:30 a.m. Many teens must wake at the crack of dawn or even earlier to get to school on time. Middle schools generally start 45 minutes to an hour later than high schools, allowing time for the buses that served the high school students to regroup and service the middle school routes. Elementary schools start the latest, even though many parents often have no trouble waking their little ones in the morning. Older teenagers, held hostage by their own circadian rhythms and nightly homework routines, tend to go to bed very late and, in fact, typically struggle to fall asleep before 11:00 p.m., according to a 2007 research review (Crowley, Acebo, and Carskadon, 2007). As a result, most high school and even many middle school students come to school sleep deprived and not optimally prepared to learn.

The Effects of Earlier School Start Times

Centers for Disease Control and Prevention (CDC) collected data on sleep habits from a nationally representative sample of more than 50,000 public and private school students. The investigators relied on four separate administrations of the Youth Risk Behavior Survey (2009, 2011, 2013, and 2015). They found that, overall, two-thirds of school-age children are getting inadequate sleep prior to school—defined as sleeping seven or fewer hours (Wheaton et al., 2016). Among high school students, the data were even worse; nearly 73 percent of students reported sleeping at these levels, or what the CDC refers to as "short sleep duration."

A meta-analysis is a quantitative synthesis of research that is often done when there is an appreciable amount of quantitative research available on a topic of significant interest. For instance, the earliest meta-analysis was done in 1977 on 375 controlled studies that evaluated the efficacy of psychotherapy and counseling (Smith and Glass, 1977). A 2017 meta-analytic review of 61 sleep studies reported that children not sleeping at recommended levels on a regular basis are more prone to exhibit problems with attention, behavior, and learning (Lowe, Safati, and Hall, 2017). Lack of quality sleep also raises the risk of experiencing other health problems, such as obesity, depression, hypertension, and diabetes, as well as motor vehicle accidents and injuries.

Accordingly, evidence from a number of studies done between 2002 and 2016 strongly suggests that an extended sleep opportunity leads to improved overall conditions for student learning. Getting sufficient hours of sleep has been shown to lead to lower levels of self-reported day time sleepiness (e.g., Dexter et al., 2003; Htwe et al., 2008), improved school attendance rates (Wahlstrom, 2002), better health and mental states (Minges and Redeker, 2016), and reduced risk of car accidents (Vorona et al., 2011).

Several studies have examined the effects of earlier school start times (e.g., Danner and Phillips, 2008; Edwards, 2012; Thacher and Onyper, 2016; Wahlstrom et al., 2014; Wolfson et al., 2007). Those investigations were conducted across a range of settings, sample sizes, and research designs. Many of those studies used quantitative methods. A 2017 meta-analysis of 20 studies examining the effects of school start time on student sleep duration showed that although more rigorous, longitudinal research is needed, later start times lead to increased student sleep times and its associated benefits (Bowers and Moyer, 2017). Another, separate 2016 meta-analysis was conducted on experimental research on delayed school start times and adolescent sleep. The literature search turned up six studies that met the qualifications for a valid experimental design, which is considered the most robust design for detecting causal effects. Across the six studies, when school start times were delayed between 25 and 60 minutes, the resultant average sleep time increased between 25 and 77 minutes per school night. The findings also showed reduced sleepiness among students and less evidence of depressive thoughts, caffeine use, and tardiness (Minges and Redeker, 2016). Yet another 2016 meta-analysis of 18 studies showed that later high school start times were associated with greater weekday sleep among high school students, reduced car accidents, and reduced daytime sleepiness (Morgenthaler et al., 2016). Effects on academic achievement and other behaviors were less apparent in this review.

More Sleep = More Savings?

The lack of robust evidence on the effects of delayed start times on academic achievement notwithstanding, common sense would say that children who are more alert are better equipped to learn. Ask any 16-year-old how alert they are in their 7:10 a.m. Algebra II class, and most will give you the honest answer: "I'm hardly awake yet." Two prominent economists who study education policy reviewed the research on school start times and found it to be one of the more cost-beneficial organizational school reforms available (Jacob and Rockoff, 2011). They equated early school start times for disadvantaged students as having the same (negative) effect of a highly ineffective teacher. Not only did the economists claim that "starting school even an hour later can boost performance at low cost" (Jacob and Rockoff, 2011, 5), they further estimated that "moving start times one hour later would result in roughly $17,500 in increased future earnings per student in present value" (10).

In response to a growing concern with early school start times, the American Academy of Sleep Medicine (AASM) released back-to-back position statements in their flagship *Journal of Clinical Sleep Medicine*. The first statement offered consensus recommendations for sleep duration for children and adults of varying ages. The recommendations were developed following a 2016 comprehensive review of 864 published research articles on sleep (Paruthi et al., 2016). The AASM reported that older adolescents between 13 and 18 years of age should get between 8 and 10 hours sleep on a regular basis. (The American Academy of Pediatrics offers a very similar recommendation, suggesting teenagers 14 to 17 years old get 8.5 to 9.5 hours of sleep nightly.) Likewise, children between 6 and 12 years old should be getting 9 to 12 hours per night for optimal health. In 2017, AASM published a second position statement, this time directly addressing school start times. The AASM recommended delaying middle school and high school start times to 8:30 a.m. or later to promote optimal student health and performance. They cautioned that "[e]arly middle school and high school start times work contrary to adolescent circadian physiology and truncate students' sleep opportunity, resulting in chronic sleep loss" (Watson et al., 2017, 623–624).

Obstacles to Change

The research evidence is slowly beginning to influence policy. Several districts across the country have voluntarily moved start times later, including large districts such as Seattle, Washington, and Fairfax County, Virginia. In addition, California has passed a statewide initiative that could have significant influence nationwide. By July 1, 2021, all California high schools will be barred from starting before 8:30 a.m. and middle schools will have to wait until at least 8:00 a.m. before starting classes. Many are waiting to see how the California mandate will play out. Education policy implementation can be a rocky road and requires attention to not only technical challenges, such as altering school start times, bus schedules, and the like, but also to the many adaptive changes required of those who implement it.

So why haven't even more districts or states been receptive to pushing start times later, especially given the strong research evidence on its benefits for children? Legislative bills proposing later school start times have failed in Maine, Minnesota, and Rhode Island. Two years after introducing a 9:15 a.m. start time, Youngstown City School District in Ohio reversed its decision due to problems with the change. The two most common reasons given for not starting school later in the morning relate to disruptions of bus schedules and after-school activities.

Most school districts contract with a single company for busing. Separate bus runs are typically made for elementary, middle, and high schools. Because the same buses are used, school start times for elementary, middle, and high schools are staggered to save costs; it would be far more expensive to run triple the number of buses simultaneously. One solution might be to reverse the order of bus runs (high school, middle school, and then elementary school) and, in turn, the respective school start times. This leads to another common complaint: disruptions to after-school activities. This argument is not without merit. Parents of elementary school-age students, for example, may be accustomed to having their children come home fairly late in the afternoon, when a parent or older sibling may be able to make it home in time for their return. Changing elementary schools to the early start times also puts very young children—such as Kindergartners—waiting at bus stops in the morning darkness.

Parents, students, and others with a stake in after-school extracurricular activities have some legitimate, although not insurmountable, concerns with changing school start times. For instance, how could athletic teams share gyms or practice fields within a shortened after-school timeframe? Or, do later high school end times mean limiting employment opportunities for working teens who depend on such income? According to a 2014 study published in the journal *Pediatrics*, the vast majority of school districts that have made the change to later start times for high school and middle school students appear to have found ways to deal with such concerns (Adolescent Sleep Working Group, 2014).

FURTHER READING

Adolescent Sleep Working Group. 2014. "School start times for adolescents." *Pediatrics, 134*(3), 642–649.

American Medical Association. 2016. "AMA supports delayed school start times to improve adolescent wellness." AMA Press Release, June 14, 2016. Retrieved from https://www.ama-assn.org/press-center/press-releases/ama-supports-delayed-school-start-times-improve-adolescent-wellness

Bowers, J. M., and Moyer, A. 2017. "Effects of school start time on students' sleep duration, daytime sleepiness, and attendance: A meta-analysis." *Sleep Health*, 3(6), 423–431.

Carrell, S. E., Maghakian, T., and West, J. E. 2011. "A's from Zzzz's? The causal effect of school start time on the academic achievement of adolescents." *American Economic Journal: Economic Policy*, 3(3), 62–81.

Crowley, S. J., Acebo, C., and Carskadon, M. A. 2007. "Sleep, circadian rhythms, and delayed phase in adolescence." *Sleep Medicine*, 8(6), 602–612.

Danner, F., and Phillips, B. 2008. "Adolescent sleep, school start times, and teen motor vehicle crashes." *Journal of Clinical Sleep Medicine*, 4(06), 533–535.

Dexter, D., Bijwadia, J., Schilling, D., and Applebaugh, G. 2003. "Sleep, sleepiness and school start times: A preliminary study." *Wisconsin Medical Journal*, 102(1), 44–44.

Edwards, F. 2012. "Early to rise? The effect of daily start times on academic performance." *Economics of Education Review*, 31(6), 970–983.

Htwe, Z. W., Cuzzone, D., O'Malley, M. B., and O'Malley, E. B. 2008. "Sleep patterns of high school students before and after delayed school start time." *Sleep*, 31, A74–A75.

Jacob, B. A., and Rockoff, J. E. 2011. *Organizing schools to improve student achievement: Start times, grade configurations, and teacher assignments.* Washington, DC: Brookings Institution, Hamilton Project.

Lowe, C. J., Safati, A., and Hall, P. A. 2017. "The neurocognitive consequences of sleep restriction: A meta-analytic review." *Neuroscience & Biobehavioral Reviews*, 80, 586–604.

Minges, K. E., and Redeker, N. S. 2016. "Delayed school start times and adolescent sleep: A systematic review of the experimental evidence." *Sleep Medicine Reviews*, 28, 86–95.

Morgenthaler, T. I., et al. 2016. "High school start times and the impact on high school students: What we know, and what we hope to learn." *Journal of Clinical Sleep Medicine*, 12(12), 1681–1689.

Paruthi, S., et al. 2016. "Consensus statement of the American Academy of Sleep Medicine on the recommended amount of sleep for healthy children: Methodology and discussion." *Journal of Clinical Sleep Medicine*, 12(11), 1549–1561.

Smith, M. L., and Glass, G. V. 1977. "Meta-analysis of psychotherapy outcome studies." *American Psychologist, 32*(9), 752.

Thacher, P. V., and Onyper, S. V. 2016. "Longitudinal outcomes of start time delay on sleep, behavior, and achievement in high school." *Sleep, 39*(2), 271–281.

Vorona, R. D., et al. 2011. "Dissimilar teen crash rates in two neighboring southeastern Virginia cities with different high school start times." *Journal of Clinical Sleep Medicine, 7*(02), 145–151.

Wahlstrom, K. L. 2002. "Accommodating the sleep patterns of adolescents within current educational structures." In M. A. Carskadon (Ed.), *Adolescent sleep patterns: Biological, social, and psychological influences.* New York: Cambridge University Press, 172–197.

Wahlstrom, K., et al. 2014. *Examining the impact of later school start times on the health and academic performance of high school students: A multi-site study.* Center for Applied Research and Educational Improvement. St Paul, MN: University of Minnesota.

Watson, N. F., et al. 2017. "Delaying middle school and high school start times promotes student health and performance." *Journal of Clinical Sleep Medicine, 13*(04), 623–625.

Wheaton, A. G., Olsen, E. O., Miller, G. F., and Croft J. B. 2016. "Sleep duration and injury-related risk behaviors among high school students—United States, 2007–2013." *Morbidity and Mortality Weekly Report, 65*, 337–341.

Wolfson, A. R., Spaulding, N. L., Dandrow, C., and Baroni, E. M. 2007. "Middle school start times: The importance of a good night's sleep for young adolescents." *Behavioral Sleep Medicine, 5*(3), 194–209.

Q25. IS BILINGUAL EDUCATION EFFECTIVE?

Answer: In the United States, bilingual education is designed primarily for students whose first language is not English, and it involves teaching academic content in two languages. The amount of a student's first language that is used depends on program type. Predominant programs in the United States include transitional bilingual programs, developmental or late-exit bilingual programs, and two-way or dual bilingual immersion programs. There are always slight variations in implementation of each program. Research shows that bilingual programs positively influence several student outcomes, including oral and written development, English proficiency, cognitive skills, and academic performance. Bilingual programs work well when they are supported by well-trained educators and a school culture that embraces biliteracy and biculturalism. Moreover, some accommodations for students whose native language is not English are mandated by the Supreme Court ruling in *Lau v. Nichols* (1974).

The Facts: In the United States, many of the descriptors that reference students whose first language is not English are deficit-oriented and focus on the singular purpose of acquiring English (e.g., limited English proficient, English as a second language, English language learner). The term *emergent bilingual* is suggested by Dr. Ofelia García, a member of the U.S. National Academy of Education and bilingual education scholar (García, 2009). Emergent bilingual (or simply EB) denotes students who are becoming bilingual through learning another language. The term more accurately captures the developmental nature of becoming and being bilingual.

Beginning with the advent of the U.S. common school in the nineteenth century, bilingual education has been controversial. Public support for bilingual education programs has waxed and waned in response to cultural, political, and economic changes and trends in the United States.

Bilingual Programs and Purposes

The term "bilingual education" captures a range of school programs in which two languages are used to teach academic content. Programs implement bilingual education differently depending on the intended purpose. *Transitional* bilingual programs have the expressed purpose of transitioning the student, as soon as possible, to English-only classrooms. Students in transitional programs receive bilingual language services with the goal of transitioning to an English-immersion environment. *Maintenance* (or developmental or late-exit) bilingual education programs attempt to maintain the student's native language—even when students have been reclassified as fluent-English-proficient, they are provided academic instruction in the native language and their native language literacy skills continue to be fostered. *Dual language immersion bilingual* programs aim to develop bilingualism and biliteracy in students' native language and an additional language; as described in more detail below, dual language programs include two groups of students—students from the language majority population and students from a language minority population.

Most states require public schools to provide bilingual education in schools that enroll a specified minimum number of EB students who speak the same home or primary language. This number is commonly 20 students or more per grade level, although there is no rationale for this threshold; it is arbitrary. All schools, however, are federally mandated to provide language services to all EBs per the seminal Supreme Court case, *Lau v. Nichols* (1974). The unanimous *Lau* ruling declared that the failure to offer supplemental language instruction in public schools for students with severely limited English proficiency violated the Civil Rights Act of 1964. Subsequent court cases have since weakened the strength of *Lau* and set a low bar for what language services need to be provided. While *Lau* did not go so far as to mandate bilingual education, decades of research demonstrates this approach is most beneficial to EB students.

Strong Research Base

Research consistently shows the academic, cognitive, and social benefits of bilingualism. A 2010 systematic review and meta-analysis of 63 studies showed that bilingualism is positively correlated with a number of cognitive outcomes, such as greater working memory, attentional control, and abstract and symbolic representation skills (Adesope et al., 2010). The magnitude of the correlations ranged from small to large. Empirical evidence also demonstrates the effectiveness of bilingual education on oral and written language development, English proficiency, and academic course-taking patterns.

Two rigorous meta-analyses, one done in 1997 and the other in 2005, of studies that compared bilingual education to English-only programming show that students learning English enrolled in bilingual programs significantly outperformed their counterparts who attended English-only programs (Greene, 1997; Slavin and Cheung, 2005). The differences in average performance showed effect sizes on the order of .18 to .33 per year in all academic subject areas. Effect sizes are a tool used to report and interpret effectiveness of one program versus another. As a general statement, an effect size of 1.0 corresponds to approximately one school year's progress on a standardized test of basic skills. A 2015 research article summarized the findings from the two meta-analyses, noting that in studies that employed experimental designs or were done in the United States, the differences were consistently on the higher end of the range from .18 to .33 (Valentino and Reardon, 2015).

More recently, a 2014 study summarized the research on the cognitive development of young emerging bilingual children. Despite some inconsistencies in findings with respect to specific child outcomes (e.g., working memory), the researchers found:

> a relatively consistent pattern of results emerged in certain areas of cognitive development that include executive control, brain

function, and theory of mind. First, across studies, non-verbal executive control skills and theory of mind abilities were changed by the experience of speaking or being exposed to two languages, and typically bilingual children showed more advanced skills than their monolingual peers. (Barac et al., 2014, 711)

As another example, a 2018 publication reviewed the research on the effects of bilingual education on young children's language and literacy levels and academic achievement, with an additional focus on students from high poverty backgrounds. The study found no evidence that bilingual education harmed students and instead discovered considerable evidence that bilingual education resulted in benefits across multiple domains (Bialystok, 2018).

Monolingual Programs

Despite the robust body of research demonstrating the benefits of bilingual education, schools across the United States more commonly implement remedial programs that rely on a monolingual English approach to teaching EBs. The two most common monolingual (or English-only) approaches are *English immersion* and *sheltered English* instruction. English-only programs have the goal of getting language minority students to become proficient in English while also learning academic content in English; they do not have the goal of further developing or maintaining students' native language. *English immersion* represents the purposeful placement of EBs in regular classrooms with the goal of assimilation and English monolingualism. The English submersion approach does not provide support to the EB student in their first language. In fact, very little support in English is even provided. Sheltered programs require teachers to use English as a Second Language (ESL) techniques. Regular classroom teachers can become trained to use ESL techniques. Most teachers who use ESL are monolingual English speakers and not trained bilingual education teachers. As is the case with English submersion instruction, sheltered English instruction does not use the EB's first language. The research evidence shows English-only programs for EB students are far inferior to bilingual education programs in both English language acquisition and content area learning.

As one of the many implications of *Lau* (1974), EB students who are not in bilingual programs are to be supported by ESL services. ESL instruction is predominantly in English with little to no use of the child's first language. ESL instruction typically follows a pull-out model, in which students are pulled out of the regular classroom to receive support. Pull-out models can offer some instructional advantages, but they come at the cost of separating students from their peers and depriving them of the classroom context that would assist in their learning. English-only instruction is also considered a "subtractive" form of schooling because it deprives the child continued development in the EB's first language. (The opposite of subtractive would be an "additive" approach to schooling, an approach that is more consistent with developmental and maintenance bilingual education programs.) Because of the major shortage of trained ESL and bilingual teachers, many districts are forced to hire nonspecialists—some not even trained in education—to tutor EB students in or outside of the regular classroom. Most large and medium-sized urban districts must accommodate dozens of languages, not just Spanish. More than 175 languages are represented in New York City Public Schools, for instance. ESL is the de facto service for EBs who are speakers of low-incidence languages.

Why Aren't Bilingual Education Programs More Prominent?

A national study done in 2002 shows that, overall, well-resourced bilingual education programs implemented with fidelity are most effective for EBs due to the cognitive and cultural competency benefits of bilingualism (Thomas and Collier, 2002). However, despite this body of literature, language learning programs in the United States are more likely to rely on monolingual approaches.

Bilingual education has long been a controversial topic in the United States. However, two separate books published in 2000 argue that, after some progress in the 1960s and 1970s toward more equitably supporting EB students in public schools, the 1980s and 1990s witnessed an increasingly nationalistic, anti-immigrant shift in ideology and public discourse (González and Melis, 2000; Schmidt, 2000). Simultaneously, there were legal challenges that eroded support for bilingual education [see, for example, *Otero v. Mesa County Valley School District* (1980); *Keys v. School District No. 1* (1983); *Castañeda v. Pickard* (1981); and *Gomez v. Illinois Board of Education* (1987)]. This broader shift included a backlash against bilingual education programs designed to maintain heritage language and manifested in a resurgence of English-only approaches to educating EB students. A 2013 book revealed that such backlash is perhaps best evidenced by billionaire Ron Unz's "English for the Children" campaign, which served to pass English-only initiatives in states serving large numbers of EB students (Haver, 2013). California's Proposition 227 (1997),

Arizona's Proposition 203 (2000), and Massachusetts Question 2 (2002) were each passed in their respective ballot initiatives, effectively banning bilingual education in those states. A 2008 study reported that bilingual programs were replaced by English-immersion programs, which allowed for an abbreviated transition period typically not to exceed one year (Johnson, 2008).

At the federal level, policy impacting EB students changed substantially with the passage of the No Child Left Behind (NCLB) Act in 2001. In the wake of NCLB, federal funding programs designed to support EBs were rewritten entirely. For example, Title VII and the Bilingual Education Act (BEA) were eliminated and replaced with Title III Language Instruction for Limited English Proficient and immigrant students. The word "bilingual" was removed entirely from the legislation and offices formerly associated with Title VII. According to a 2005 conference research paper that analyzed U.S. language policy reported in the press, the focus of Title III following NCLB was solely on English, and the need to learn English quickly and effectively in order to partake in English assessments after three years of instruction (Wright, 2005). That same study reported that the English-only initiatives pushed by Unz in California, Massachusetts, and Arizona had an impact on the federal education law (Wright, 2005).

English-only proponents relied on data demonstrating EB students were far below expectations. Average test scores for EB students were low, many students were held back to repeat a grade, and dropout rates were high during this period when bilingual education was taking the blame. However, poor student outcomes should not have been laid at the door of bilingual programs. For one thing, a 1997 report showed that the majority of EB children in California were not even in bilingual education programs—and that among those that were, at least a third did not have a credentialed bilingual education teacher (Gándara, 1997). Thus, it was not that bilingual education was inherently flawed but rather that it was being poorly or ineffectively implemented. In schools where there were well-trained bilingual education teachers, school leaders knowledgeable of bilingual education, and adequate ancillary supports, bilingual education was and continues to be effective.

Like many other scholars who have studied the intersection of bilingual education and American politics, multicultural education scholar Sonia Nieto believes that negative views of bilingual education are a response more to highly politicized questions about preserving "the American ethnic identity and the whitewashing cultural melting pot than to empirical facts" (Nieto, 2009, 68). A 2003 historical analysis of bilingual education found that changing political, social, and economic forces at local, state, and federal levels have all shaped perceptions of language diversity in the U.S. education system, led strongly by "symbolic politics of language, creating resentment of special treatment for minority groups" (Ovando, 2003, 2). In turn, similar studies find this symbolic politics of language has tended to—explicitly or implicitly—dominate policy decisions on how to educate language-minority students (Ovando and McLaren, 2000; Ovando and Wiley, 2003). These and other scholars have found rather than being informed by empirical research, language policy in the United States is often informed by subtractive values propagated through sociopolitical and socioeconomic forces seeking to maintain White, monolingual English hegemony.

Indeed, around 20 years after they were first introduced, the data demonstrates that the English-immersion laws in California, Arizona, and Massachusetts are not meeting the needs of the diverse EB population. An increased recognition of the value of bilingualism and research evidence on the academic benefits of dual language programs have led to the repeal of the California and Massachusetts English-only laws in 2016 and 2017, respectively. A 2019 *Education Week* news article reports that Arizona is also moving forward with its own reversal (Mitchell, 2019).

The Emergence of Dual Language Programs

Dual language or two-way immersion bilingual programs have witnessed rapid proliferation since the first decade of this century, with estimates as high as 2,500 programs nationwide as of 2017 (Arias, 2018). Dual language programs serve a variety of grade configurations (e.g., K–3, K–6), but usually begin in kindergarten. They can operate schoolwide or as a program within a school (Howard et al., 2018). Dual-language classrooms provide academic instruction in two languages to both native English speakers and EB students sharing a common first language. The most common language pairings are English–Spanish, followed by English–Mandarin Chinese. Professor Mileidis Gort, an expert in biliteracy education, contends that the success of acquiring two languages depends critically on the learning environment, which means that EB students "need to interact and be engaged with people who speak both languages on a regular basis" (Gort, 2019).

The increase in dual language programs is due in good part to strong and ever-increasing evidence of their far-reaching benefits. Studies done in 2013, 2015, and 2017 convincingly show that EB students in dual language programs consistently outperform their peers in English-only or transitional bilingual programs (Marian, Shook, and Schroeder, 2013; Steele et al., 2017; Valentino and Reardon, 2015). A 2013 study found that dual language programs not only help monolingual students become proficient in two languages, they also enhance cognition and general academic performance (Esposito and Baker-Ward, 2013). Another advantage of dual language programs is that they are less segregated by race, ethnicity, or social class than transitional or maintenance bilingual education programs, a fact revealed by a 2017 analysis (Steele et al., 2017). Dual language programs thus integrate students in ways that promote cross-cultural understanding.

The proliferation of dual language programs is also likely due to increased demand from monolingual English-speaking families who recognize the value of bilingualism. They may value any number of perceived benefits, which range from academic advancements, cognitive developments, exposure to diverse peers in the classroom, and of course the acquisition of a second language—the latter offering a unique currency that could lead to enhanced life opportunities.

Looking to the Future

It remains a contradiction that at the same time that proficiency in foreign language is valued in English-speaking students in schools, those same foreign languages are devalued in students whose first language is not English. Admissions requirements at prestigious colleges demand at least four years of a foreign language and, by and large, high schools provide the opportunities through foreign language courses. As of 2020, 40 states have endorsed a policy to recognize graduating seniors who are fluent in two or more languages with the Seal of Biliteracy. At the same time, a majority of EB students are not enrolled in bilingual education programs, cutting short their ability to further develop or even maintain their native language. In today's global society, being proficient in more than one language is an asset, not a liability.

FURTHER READING

Adesope, O. O., Lavin, T., Thompson, T., and Ungerleider, C. 2010. "A systematic review and meta-analysis of the cognitive correlates of bilingualism." *Review of Educational Research*, 80(2), 207–45.

Arias, M. B. 2018. Preface. In M. B. Arias and M. Fee (Eds.), *Profiles of dual language education in the 21st century*. Bristol, UK: Multilingual Matters.

Barac, R., Bialystok, E., Castro, D. C., and Sanchez, M. 2014. "The cognitive development of young dual language learners: A critical review." *Early Childhood Research Quarterly*, 29(4), 699–714.

Bialystok, E. 2018. "Bilingual education for young children: Review of the effects and consequences." *International Journal of Bilingual Education and Bilingualism*, 21(6), 666–679.

Douglas, W. O., and Supreme Court of the United States. 1973. U.S. Reports: *Lau v. Nichols*, 414 U.S. 563. [Periodical] Retrieved from the Library of Congress, https://www.loc.gov/item/usrep414563

Esposito, A. G., and Baker-Ward, L. 2013. "Dual-language education for low-income children: Preliminary evidence of benefits for executive function." *Bilingual Research Journal*, 36(3), 295–310.

Gándara, P. 1997. *Review of research on the instruction of Limited English Proficient students: A report to the California legislature*. Davis, CA: University of California Linguistic Minority Research Institute.

García, O. 2009. "Emergent bilinguals and TESOL: What's in a name?" *Tesol Quarterly*, 43(2), 322–326.

González, R. D., and Melis, I. (Eds.). 2000. *Language ideologies: Critical perspectives on the official English movement: Vol. 2*. Mahwah, NJ: Lawrence Erlbaum.

Gort, M. 2019. "Bilingualism matters: Myths and facts about early bilingual development." Ed Talks 2019. University of Colorado, Boulder, June 10, 2019. Retrieved from https://www.youtube.com/watch?v=i9L9-wtRjmo

Greene, J. P. 1997. "A meta-analysis of the Rossell and Baker review of bilingual education research." *Bilingual Research Journal*, 21, 103–122.

Haver, J. J. 2013. *English for the children: Mandated by the people, skewed by politicians and special interests*. Lanham, MD: Rowman and Littlefield.

Howard, E. R., et al. 2018. *Guiding principles for dual language education* (3rd ed.). Washington, DC: Center for Applied Linguistics.

Johnson, E. 2008. "English for the children campaign." In J. M. Gonzalez (Ed.), *Encyclopedia of Bilingual Education*. Thousand Oaks, CA: SAGE Publications, 256–259.

Lambert, W. E. 1974. "Culture and language as factors in learning and education." In F. E. Aboud and R. D. Mead (Eds.), *Cultural factors in learning and education*. Bellingham, WA: Fifth Western Washington Symposium on Learning.

Marian, V., Shook, A., and Schroeder, S. R. 2013. "Bilingual two-way immersion programs benefit academic achievement." *Bilingual Research Journal*, 36(2), 167–186.

Mitchell, C. 2019. "'English-only' laws in education on verge of extinction." *Education Week*, October 23, 2019. Retrieved from https://

www.edweek.org/ew/articles/2019/10/23/english-only-laws-in-education-on-verge-of.html

Nieto, D. 2009. "A brief history of bilingual education in the United States." *Perspectives on Urban Education*, 6, 61–72.

Ovando, C. J. 2003. "Bilingual education in the United States: Historical development and current issues." *Bilingual Education in the United States*, 27, 1–24. doi:10.1080/15235882.2003.10162589

Ovando, C. J., and McLaren, P. (Eds.). 2000. *The politics of multiculturalism and bilingual education: Students and teachers caught in the crossfire.* Boston, MA: McGraw-Hill.

Ovando, C. J., and Wiley, T. G. 2003. "Language education in the conflicted United States." In J. Bourne and E. Reid (Eds.), *World yearbook of education.* London: Kogan.

Rolstad, K., Mahoney, K., and Glass, G. V. 2005. "The big picture: A meta-analysis of program effectiveness research on English language learners." *Educational Policy*, 19(4), 572–594.

Schmidt, R., Sr. 2000. *Language policy and identity politics in the United States.* Philadelphia: Temple University Press.

Slavin, R. E., and Cheung, A. 2005. "A synthesis of research on language of reading instruction." *Review of Educational Research*, 75, 247–84.

Steele, J. L., et al. 2017. "Effects of dual-language immersion programs on student achievement: Evidence from lottery data." *American Educational Research Journal*, 54(1), 282S–306S.

Thomas, W. P., and Collier, V. P. 2002. *A national study of school effectiveness for language minority students' long-term academic achievement.* Santa Cruz, CA: Center for Research on Education, Diversity, and Excellence.

Valentino, R. A., and Reardon, S. F. 2015. "Effectiveness of four instructional programs designed to serve English learners." *Educational Evaluation and Policy Analysis*, 37(4), 612–637.

Wright, W. E. 2005. "Language policy issues reported in the U.S. press." *Proceedings from the Fourth International Symposium on Bilingualism.* Somerville, MA: Cascadilla Press.

Q26. DOES HOMEWORK INCREASE STUDENT ACHIEVEMENT?

Answer: The research findings on whether homework increases student learning are mixed, and the studies themselves have been criticized for alleged design flaws. Many education researchers contend that homework assignments are often structured in ways that lead to only superficial learning, like memorization of facts or filling out worksheets. Negative effects of homework on learning are evident when certain characteristics like amount and level of difficulty are out of balance. Homework assignments can benefit learning, however, when the instructional purposes are clear and when appropriately structured to challenge and engage students. Some evidence suggests that homework is associated with helping to develop good work habits, while other evidence indicates homework leads to stress for students. Daily homework remains a common classroom tradition despite the lack of consistent evidence of its worth.

The Facts: Homework has long been engrained in American school culture. Proponents of homework believe it can instill good work habits in children, such as time management skills, and that it can reinforce learning that occurs in school. Critics find that homework involves too much busy-work, fails to result in real learning, and takes away valuable time that youth need for their growth and development. Many also believe it causes undue stress in students. In many instances, homework constitutes tedious assignments that do not engage students' interest or critical thinking skills. At the elementary school level, students are commonly given worksheets that require simple or repetitive tasks (e.g., fill-in-the blank). At the middle and high school levels, homework assignments vary across academic subjects, but usually involve some element of "search and record" or memorization.

U.S. schools continue to follow the homework routine despite mixed evidence of its benefits. In fact, studies indicate that the amount of homework assigned to students has nearly tripled since 1981. High-stakes testing policies introduced in the early 2000s triggered a surge, as teachers issued more homework in hopes of improving student scores. Interestingly, Finland and South Korea are both consistently ranked among the highest-performing nations in education, yet Finland students rarely do homework, while South Korean students do hours of homework each evening.

A 2006 meta-analysis of 69 studies done between 1987 and 2003 reported a small positive relationship in the elementary grades, and a larger one at the secondary level, suggesting that more time spent on homework was related to higher student achievement (Cooper, Robinson, and Patall, 2006). This study is cited frequently as evidence that homework increases student achievement. However, several limitations of the analysis raise questions about its utility, beginning with the authors' recognition that "all studies, regardless of type, had design flaws" (1). Moreover, of the 69 studies reviewed, only 6 were experiments. Experimental designs provide the best opportunity to detect causal relationships, such as whether doing homework is causally related to student achievement. Of these six experimental studies, two of them examined homework at the high school level; the remaining four were done at the elementary school grades. No long-term follow-ups of achievement gains were performed, and the outcomes were either teacher-written unit tests or standardized exams. Four of the six studies showed that homework had a positive effect on student achievement. None of the six studies was published in an academic journal, which means that they were not subject to peer scrutiny. One of the studies was a master's student thesis that involved a total of 40 students in two third-grade classrooms (Townsend, 1995). Students in one classroom were given vocabulary homework over a period of three weeks while the other classroom received no homework assignments. The homework group recorded higher scores on a vocabulary test than the no-homework group. However, it is not known whether the two classrooms were composed of students of similar ability, which could have contributed to outcome differences.

The vast majority of studies reviewed in the 2006 meta-analysis relied heavily on correlational designs. In contrast to experimental designs, correlational designs can only tell how variables relate to one another; they cannot tell if one variable *caused* changes in another variable. Two-thirds of the correlational studies from the 2006 review yielded positive correlations, and the other third produced negative correlations. The strongest and most consistent correlational relationship found was between time spent on homework and performance on in-class exams. In other words, the more time that students spent on homework, the higher they tended to score on in-class tests. As noted above, a limitation of correlational designs is their inability to determine cause and effect. More time spent on homework could plausibly increase test scores. But the reverse could also be true: Students who do better on tests might also do more homework, because their parents stress both studying in school and out. Or a different variable altogether could be responsible for the correlation between homework and test scores, such as the student's level of motivation.

A 2017 meta-analysis summarized research that examined the effects of homework on math and science achievement, in particular (Fan et al., 2017). The researchers reviewed 28 studies—which yielded 41 independent samples—done in the United States and international contexts and found a small, yet positive effect of homework on math and science achievement. Relatively larger effects were found in the Unites States. In addition, the meta-analysis found a stronger relationship between homework and math proficiency at the elementary and high school grades than in middle school. It is unclear what portion of the studies were experimental. A 2008 analysis of a large, nationally representative sample of U.S. students found that while more daily homework assigned appeared to help high- and low-achieving students score higher on math tests, it was counterproductive for average learners (Eren and Henderson, 2008). Other smaller studies have suggested homework has nonacademic benefits for students of different school levels. For instance, completing homework assignments can improve student confidence in learning, planning skills, and engagement in school.

Other Considerations in Assessing Homework Assignments

The majority of studies of homework examine how the amount of *time* spent on homework relates to student achievement. A smaller set looks at the relationship between other measures of homework (e.g., homework effort, homework completion, homework grades) and student achievement. Findings are not altogether consistent depending on how homework is measured (see Trautwein, 2007; Trautwein et al., 2009). A major limitation of these studies is that all types of homework assignment are often treated the same. Homework assignments can call for repetition, review, exploration, or rote memorization of facts. Complexity of tasks differs. A vocabulary worksheet is quite different from an essay assignment. Taking these different kinds of homework into consideration is important in future reviews of literature and meta-analyses. Furthermore, most of the existing studies explored short-term achievement effects, and so less is known about long-term effects. Homework studies also tend to rely on large survey data sets and thus are correlational studies, which, as noted above, are limited in their ability to discern causal relationships.

A smaller body of research has examined the effects of homework on affective outcomes and students' well-being. For example, a 2013 study that examined a sample of 4,317 students from 10 high-performing, affluent high schools found that students did an average of more than three hours of homework per night. The students who did more hours of homework reported being engaged in school, but also experienced more academic stress, physical health issues, and an absence of balance in their lives. Other studies published in 2011, 2012, and 2015 have found that homework creates tension between parents and their children (Katz, Buzukashvili, and Feingold, 2012; Martinez, 2011; Pressman et al., 2015).

Homework Guidelines

In response to concerns about how much time children spend on homework, experts have recommended age- and grade-level appropriate guidelines. A popular textbook on classroom teaching advised that homework should be realistic in length and difficulty, and it should be commensurate with students' abilities to work independently (Good and Brophy, 2017). Thus, 5 to 10 minutes per subject might be appropriate for fourth-graders, whereas 30 to 60 minutes might be suitable for college-bound high school students. The aforementioned 2006 meta-analysis suggested that the optimum amount of homework for twelfth-graders could be between 1.5 and 2.5 hours per night, but cautioned that there is no definitive answer (Cooper, Robinson, and Patall, 2006).

A 2007 study cites the now common "10-minute rule," which dictates that all daily homework assignments combined should take about as long to complete as 10 minutes multiplied by the student's grade level (Cooper, 2007, 92). The National Education Association (NEA) and the National Parent-Teacher Association also endorse the general guidance of "10 minutes of homework per grade level." These guidelines treat homework as a daily necessity, an undefined input that, if given in the right amounts, will produce desired student outcomes. Furthermore, issuing two hours of homework for high school seniors per night (10 minutes × 12 = 2 hours) seems excessive to many educators, parents, and students; that amount of homework represents a full third of the standard six-hour school day. They assert that homework that is appropriately challenging, is worthwhile, and does not interfere with needed leisure and sleep time from adolescents seems all too elusive in today's high-pressure school culture.

Homework assignments may also exacerbate social-class inequities brought on by unequal home access to the internet. The Pew Research Center analyzed 2015 U.S. Census data and found that "some 15 percent of U.S. households with school-age children do not have a high-speed internet connection at home" (Anderson and Perrin, 2018). In its 2018 survey of 743 U.S. teenagers, the Pew Center reported that "one-quarter of black teens say they are at least sometimes unable to complete their homework due to a lack of digital access, including 13 percent who say this happens to them often. Just 4 percent of white teens and 6 percent of Hispanic teens say this often happens to them" (Anderson and Perrin, 2018).

The research base on the benefits of homework has addressed several important questions, such as its influence on student achievement, study habits, and well-being. Generally missing from the research, however, are several other areas deserving of attention, such as investigating how students experience homework across subject areas; exploring the quality and impact of teacher feedback; and examining long-term benefits of homework. Another interesting line of research may be examining how often (and why) students find homework answers from peers or the internet; in other words, what would be the point of assigning homework if some students are more concerned with completing it than learning from it? There is no shortage of websites that give students shortcuts to completing homework without actually doing the work themselves.

Questions that parents, teachers, administrators, and policy makers may have about homework have not necessarily been addressed in the research literature. Subject-area teachers may want to know what types of homework assignment are most beneficial for students at particular grades. Administrators may want to know how they can help middle and high school teachers coordinate homework assignments so as not to overburden students. Parents may want to know if the time spent on homework has long-term benefits, both academic and otherwise. Finally, U.S. policy makers may want to know if other countries are using homework more effectively than others.

FURTHER READING

Anderson, M., and Perrin, A. 2018. "Nearly one-in-five teens can't always finish their homework because of the digital divide." Fact Tank: News in the Numbers. Pew Research Center, October 28, 2018. Retrieved from https://www.pewresearch.org/fact-tank/2018/10/26/nearly-one-in-five-teens-cant-always-finish-their-homework-because-of-the-digital-divide

Buell, J. 2008. *Closing the book on homework: Enhancing public education and freeing family time*. Philadelphia, PA: Temple University Press.

Cooper, H. 2007. *The battle over homework: Common ground for administrators, teachers, and parents*. Thousand Oaks, CA: Corwin Press.

Cooper, H., Robinson, J. C., and Patall, E. A. 2006. "Does homework improve academic achievement? A synthesis of research, 1987–2003." *Review of Educational Research*, 76(1), 1–62.

Eren, O., and Henderson, D. J. 2008. "The impact of homework on student achievement." *The Econometrics Journal*, 11(2), 326–348.

Fan, H., Xu, J., Cai, Z., He, J., and Fan, X. 2017. "Homework and students' achievement in math and science: A 30-year meta-analysis, 1986–2015." *Educational Research Review*, 20, 35–54.

Galloway, M., Conner, J., and Pope, D. 2013. "Nonacademic effects of homework in privileged, high-performing high schools." *The Journal of Experimental Education*, 81(4), 490–510.

Good, T. L., and Brophy, J. E. 2017. *Looking in classrooms* (11th ed.). New York: Routledge.

Katz, I., Buzukashvili, T., and Feingold, L. 2012. "Homework stress: Construct validation of a measure." *Journal of Experimental Education*, 80, 405–21.

Kohn, A. 2006. *The homework myth: Why our kids get too much of a bad thing.* Boston, MA: Da Capo Lifelong Books.

Martinez, S. 2011. "An examination of Latino students' homework routines." *Journal of Latinos and Education, 10,* 354–368.

Pressman, R. M., et al. 2015. "Homework and family stress: With consideration of parents' self confidence, educational level, and cultural background." *The American Journal of Family Therapy, 43*(4), 297–313.

Stiglitz, J. E. 2000. "The contributions of the economics of information to twentieth century economics." *Quarterly Journal of Economics, 115,* 1441–1478.

Townsend, S. 1995. *The effects of vocabulary homework on third grade achievement* (Master's thesis). Retrieved from Educational Resources Information Center, ERIC No. ED379643.

Trautwein, U. 2007. "The homework-achievement relation reconsidered: Differentiating homework time, homework frequency, and homework effort." *Learning and Instruction, 17,* 372–388.

Trautwein, U., et al. 2009. "Chameleon effects in homework research: The homework-achievement association depends on the measures used and the level of analysis chosen." *Contemporary Educational Psychology, 34,* 77–88.

6

School Environment

Of course, schools are a place where teachers go to teach and children come to learn. But they are surely more than that as well. Schools are physical places, or at least once upon a time they almost exclusively were brick-and-mortar buildings. And a school is a mini-culture. It has members, practices, rules, values, and norms. School culture reflects the larger social culture of which it is a part. It is both shaped by that larger culture and shapes it to some lesser degree in return.

How are the nation's customs, practices, and attitudes toward races and genders played out in today's public schools? Does the culture of the home in which a student lives conflict with or correspond to the culture of the school? Are the schools a safe haven in a world of threatening possibilities? Is it time to forsake the physical presence of the school and move all of education to cyberspace, as so many school districts have been forced to do during the COVID-19 pandemic?

Q27. ARE STUDENTS DISCIPLINED DISPROPORTIONATELY BY RACE AND GENDER?

Answer: Yes. Black males, in particular, are at most risk of being sent from the classroom or expelled than any other group of students.

The Facts: Racial disproportionality in student discipline has a long history. Numerous formal assemblies, conferences, task forces, and publications reflect a national concern with this inequity and its dire long-term consequences for youth of color. School discipline can take many forms, but the most common types include referral to the principal's office, such as kicked out of the classroom, after-school detention, in-school suspension, out-of-school suspension, and expulsion. "Exclusionary discipline" comprises those practices, such as out-of-school or in-school suspensions, that exclude the student from school activities. In some cases, even in-school suspensions can be considered exclusionary to the extent that they bar students from regular school activities.

Researchers from the University of Michigan's "Monitoring the Future Study" analyzed longitudinal survey data from a national sample of eighth-, tenth-, and twelfth-grade students between 1991 and 2005. They found that Black, Hispanic, and Native American students were slightly more likely than White and Asian American students to be sent to the principal's office and two to five times more likely to be suspended or expelled (Wallace et al., 2008). Moreover, disciplinary rates among Black students increased during this 15-year period, while all other racial and ethnic group rates declined.

More recently, a 2014 analysis of three national surveys found that Black and Hispanic/Latinx students were suspended at higher rates than non-Hispanic White students, with *"differences in most cases not attributable to different levels of misbehavior"* [italics in the original] (Finn and Servoss, 2014, 2). However, overall, research specifically on Hispanic/Latinx students has produced mixed findings, with separate reports of both over- and underrepresentation in terms of exclusionary discipline. A 2014 report from The Equity Project at Indiana University indicates that more research is needed, because there may be geographic, historical, or acculturation factors that explain these differences (Skiba, Arredondo, and Rausch, 2014b).

A major synthesis of research on disciplinary disparities assembled by the University of Indiana's Discipline Disparities Research to Practice Collaborative found that:

> New research continues to find no evidence that disciplinary disparities are due to poverty. . . . Nor is there evidence that students of color engage in rates of disruptive behavior sufficiently different from others to justify higher rates of punishment. (Skiba, Arredondo, and Rausch, 2014b, 2)

Nevertheless, the report also found that males are suspended at higher rates than females, and Black males are the most at-risk for suspension or arrest (Toldson, McGee, and Lemmons, 2015). Two separate studies found that Black female secondary students were suspended out of school at rates "significantly higher than other females, and higher than White and Hispanic/Latino males" (Skiba, Arredondo, and Rausch, 2014b, 2). Hispanic/Latinx females were suspended at rates similar to White males and higher than White females.

Data analyzed by the United States Office for Civil Rights showed that Black students were 3.8 times more likely than White students to receive one or more out-of-school suspensions in 2013–2014 (U.S. Department of Education Office for Civil Rights, 2016). Overall, 6 percent of all K–12 students were suspended out of school at least once but for Black males, that figure was 18 percent and for Black females it was 10 percent (compared to 5 percent and 2 percent for White males and females, respectively). A 2018 analysis conducted by the U.S. Government Accountability Office (GAO) on nationwide school disciplinary data for the year 2013–2014—the most recent data available at that time—found that Black students, males, and students with disabilities were disciplined disproportionately, including with suspension and expulsion.

> [T]hese disparities were widespread and persisted regardless of the type of disciplinary action, level of school poverty, or type of public school attended. For example, Black students accounted for 15.5 percent of all public school students, but represented about 39 percent of students suspended from school—an overrepresentation of about 23 percentage points. (Government Accountability Office, 2018a)

The report cites a stark comparison in terms of absolute numbers of students:

> Although there were approximately 17.4 million more White students than Black students attending K-12 public schools in 2013–14, nearly 176,000 more Black students than White students were suspended from school that school year. (Government Accountability Office, 2018b, 13)

Exclusionary Discipline

Students receiving out-of-school suspensions, a form of "exclusionary discipline," are banned from formal school activities. In-school suspensions permit students to remain in the school building while serving their sentence, although these experiences vary depending on the school's capacity to offer learning opportunities outside the traditional classroom. Many schools will assign in-school suspended students to one room overseen by a non-classroom teacher; other schools offer individualized tutoring so that students do not fall behind academically. Depending on district policy and resources, and of course the nature of the student infraction, some schools will provide in-home tutors during times when students are temporarily expelled or suspended out-of-school for extended periods of time. This is done so that the student does not fall too far behind in their classes.

Research reveals that many out-of-school suspensions are not due to serious behaviors such as a violent act, carrying a weapon, or possessing illegal substances in school. Rather, a significant proportion of these suspensions are assigned either at the discretion of the school administrator or as decreed by schools with "zero-tolerance" policies. Zero-tolerance policies became common in schools following highly publicized mass school killings, increased perception of violence in schools, and earlier federal gun-free schools legislation (i.e., Gun-Free Schools Act of 1994, Pub. L. No. 103-882, 20 U.S.C. § 8921). A 2008 American Psychological Association Zero Tolerance Task Force reported that while zero-tolerance policies in schools were initially aimed at weapons and illegal substance possession and use, many schools adopted similar policies for infractions mostly unrelated to school safety, such as using profanity or being late to school (American Psychological Association Zero Tolerance Task Force, 2008). As of 2019, all 50 states plus the District of Columbia still require students to be expelled for bringing a weapon to school per the federal Gun Free Schools Act (Rafa, 2019). At least 26 states and the District of Columbia either require or permit suspensions for student drug use or possession while 40 states permit students to be suspended for defiant or disruptive behavior. At least 17 states and the District of Columbia prohibit exclusionary discipline solely for attendance or truancy issues.

During the mid-2010s, there was a noticeable shift away from zero-tolerance policies and toward less-punitive approaches. Between 2014 and 2019, only seven bills expanding suspension or expulsion were passed in state legislatures (Rafa, 2019). During that same period, at least 36 bills were enacted in various states that limited out-of-school suspensions and expulsions or promoted alternative disciplinary practices. Part of the support for these measures stemmed from research that showed the negative short- and long-term effects of exclusionary discipline.

According to a 2003 study, suspended students are more likely to be alienated from school (Stewart, 2003). Studies done in 2012 and 2016 also indicate that suspended students' learning is disrupted, an effect compounded for those with existing academic and behavioral challenges (Balfanz, 2016; Balfanz and Byrnes, 2012). Expulsions from school also often lead to a student dropping out of school altogether or attending an alternative school for at-risk youth. Based on several studies, including a 2000 report from the Harvard Civil Rights Project and studies done in 2007 and 2011, school suspension is among the strongest predictors of a student dropping out of school (Advancement Project/Civil Rights Project, 2000; Finn and Zimmer, 2011; Suh, Suh, and Houston, 2007). One major line of research has posited that suspensions and expulsions contribute to the "school to prison pipeline," whereby students come in contact with the juvenile and criminal justice systems later in life. A 2014 study found that the disparate application of exclusionary discipline by race and gender can contribute to this phenomenon (Skiba, Arredondo, and Williams, 2014c).

Many educators assert that out-of-school suspensions make little sense for students who are not a risk to others and in fact can lead students down an accelerated path to dropping out. Attention on the ineffectiveness of out-of-school suspensions has prompted some policy changes at the state and local levels that limit their use and replace them with alternative punishment, such as in-school suspensions. In-school suspensions require students to be in school but in an isolated or alternative setting. Not all in-school suspension experiences are equal, however, and some argue that their effect does not differ much from the out-of-school variety. Others contend that, at least in some cases, in-school suspension keeps students engaged with academic work and minimizes the adverse effects of out-of-school suspensions. At the same time, disruptions in the classroom have to be addressed so that nonoffending students are not adversely affected. To do so effectively may necessitate additional training for teachers and other educators in the building.

Racial Bias Awareness

Investigators continue to examine the reasons behind racial disparities in school discipline. Researchers from Princeton University set out to explore the relationship between racial bias and racial gaps in school discipline (Riddle and Sinclair, 2019). Racial bias data were gathered from Harvard University's Project Implicit (implicit.harvard.edu/implicit), a self-administered online survey that measures implicit racial bias. Project Implicit makes anonymous data available to researchers and at the time included data for 1.6 million participants nationwide (Xu, Nosek, and Greenwald, 2014). The Princeton researchers paired county-level racial bias data with student disciplinary data from the national Civil Rights Data Collection data set (the same data set used in the 2018 GAO study, but with 2015–2016 data). Student disciplinary actions were classified into five types:

in-school suspensions, out-of-school suspensions, law enforcement referrals, school-related arrests, and expulsions. The study found racial disciplinary gaps to be associated with racial bias scores at the county level and concluded that schools needed to develop policies "targeting racial disparities in education and psychological bias" (Riddle and Sinclair, 2019, 8255). Studies done in 2014 and 2015 also support the belief that race plays a role in educators' school disciplinary decisions (Haight et al., 2014; Okonofua and Eberhardt, 2015), or that race is otherwise related in some way to the observed disparities (Anyon et al., 2014).

A widely used program for addressing student behavior and school culture is Positive Behavioral Interventions and Supports (PBIS). According to studies done in 2011 and 2015, despite evidence of its implementation reducing office disciplinary referrals and school suspensions, administering PBIS without attention to race does not reduce the racial disparities in school disciplinary rates (Vincent, Sprague, and Gau, 2015; Vincent and Tobin, 2011). School discipline research published in 2016 finds that alternative interventions, such as restorative practice, are demonstrating effectiveness when executed well and supported by proper training (Skiba, Mediratta, and Rausch, 2016b). In addition, trauma-informed interventions have also been strongly recommended by educational psychologists who study childhood trauma (Chafouleas et al., 2019).

FURTHER READING

Advancement Project/Civil Rights Project. 2000. *Opportunities suspended: The devastating consequences of zero tolerance and school discipline*. A national summit on zero tolerance. Cambridge, MA: Harvard Civil Rights Project.

American Psychological Association Zero Tolerance Task Force. 2008. "Are zero tolerance policies effective in the schools? An evidentiary review and recommendations." *American Psychologist*, 63(9), 852–862. Retrieved from http://www.apa.org/pubs/info/reports/zero-tolerance.pdf

Anyon, Y., et al. 2014. "The persistent effect of race and the promise of alternatives to suspension in school discipline outcomes." *Children and Youth Services Review*, 44, 379–386.

Balfanz, R. 2016. "Missing school matters." *Phi Delta Kappan*, 98(2), 8–13.

Balfanz, R., and Byrnes, V. 2012. *Chronic absenteeism: Summarizing what we know from nationally available data*. Baltimore, MD: Johns Hopkins University, Center for Social Organization of Schools.

Carter, P. L., Skiba, R., Arredondo, M. I., and Pollock, M. 2017. "You can't fix what you don't look at: Acknowledging race in addressing racial discipline disparities." *Urban Education*, 52(2), 207–235.

Chafouleas, S. M., Koriakin, T. A., Roundfield, K. D., and Overstreet, S. 2019. "Addressing childhood trauma in school settings: A framework for evidence-based practice." *School Mental Health, 11*(1), 40–53.

Finn, J. D., and Servoss, T. J. 2014. "Misbehavior, suspensions, and security measures in high school: Racial/ethnic and gender differences." *Journal of Applied Research on Children: Informing Policy for Children at Risk, 5*(2), 11.

Finn, J. D., and Zimmer, K. S. 2011. "Student engagement: What is it? Why does it matter?" In S. L. Christenson, A. L. Reschly, and C. Wylie (Eds). *Handbook of research on student engagement.* New York: Springer Science, 97–131.

Government Accountability Office. 2018a. Highlights of GAO-18-258, a report to congressional requesters. *GAO Highlights.* Retrieved from https://www.gao.gov/assets/700/690827.pdf

Government Accountability Office. 2018b. *K-12 education: Discipline disparities for Black students, boys, and students with disabilities.* Report to Congressional Requesters. GAO-18-258. Retrieved from https://www.gao.gov/products/GAO-18-258

Haight, W., Gibson, P. A., Kayama, M., Marshall, J. M., and Wilson, R. 2014. "An ecological-systems inquiry into racial disproportionalities in out-of-school suspensions from youth, caregiver and educator perspectives." *Children and Youth Services Review, 46,* 128–138.

Kaufman, P., et al. 2000. *Indicators of school crime and safety, 2000.* Washington, DC: U.S. Department of Education, Office of Educational Research and Improvement, National Center for Education Statistics.

Okonofua, J. A., and Eberhardt, J. L. 2015. "Two strikes: Race and the disciplining of young students." *Psychological Science, 26*(5), 617–624.

Okonofua, J. A., Walton, G. M., and Eberhardt, J. L. 2016. "A vicious cycle: A social–psychological account of extreme racial disparities in school discipline." *Perspectives on Psychological Science, 11*(3), 381–398.

Rafa, A. 2019. "The status of school discipline in state policy." *Education Commission of the States.* Retrieved from https://www.ecs.org/wp-content/uploads/The-Status-of-School-Discipline-in-State-Policy.pdf

Riddle, T., and Sinclair, S. 2019. "Racial disparities in school-based disciplinary actions are associated with county-level rates of racial bias." *Proceedings of the National Academy of Sciences, 116*(17), 8255–8260.

Skiba, R. J., et al. 2014a. "Parsing disciplinary disproportionality: Contributions of infraction, student, and school characteristics to out-of-school suspension and expulsion." *American Educational Research Journal, 51*(4), 640–670.

Skiba, R. J., Arredondo, M. I., and Rausch, M. K. 2014b. *New and developing research on disparities in discipline.* Bloomington, IN: The Equity Project at Indiana University.

Skiba, R. J., Arredondo, M. I., and Williams, N. T. 2014c. More than a metaphor: The contribution of exclusionary discipline to a school-to-prison pipeline. *Equity & Excellence in Education*, 47(4), 546–564.

Skiba, R. J., Arredondo, M. I., Gray, C., and Rausch, M. K. 2016a. "What do we know about discipline disparities? New and emerging research." In R. J. Skiba, K. Mediratta, and M. K Rausch (Eds.), *Inequality in school discipline*. New York: Palgrave Macmillan.

Skiba, R. J., Mediratta, K., and Rausch, M. K. (Eds.). 2016b. *Inequality in school discipline: Research and practice to reduce disparities*. New York: Springer.

Stewart, E. A. 2003. "School social bonds, school climate, and school misbehavior: A multilevel analysis." *Justice Quarterly*, 20, 575–604.

Suh, S., Suh, J., and Houston, I. 2007. "Predictors of categorical at-risk high school dropouts." *Journal of Counseling & Development*, 85, 196–203.

Toldson, I. A., McGee, T., and Lemmons, B. P. 2015. "Reducing suspensions by improving academic engagement among school-age Black males." In D. J. Losen (Ed.), *Closing the school discipline gap: Equitable remedies for excessive exclusion*. New York: Teachers College Press, 107–117.

U.S. Department of Education Office for Civil Rights. 2016. *2013–2014 Civil Rights Data collection: A first look*. U.S. Department of Education Office for Civil Rights. Retrieved from https://www2.ed.gov/about/offices/list/ocr/docs/2013-14-first-look.pdf

Vincent, C. G., Sprague, J. R., and Gau, J. M. 2015. "Effectiveness of school-wide positive behavior support for reducing racially inequitable disciplinary exclusion." In D. J. Losen (Ed.), *Closing the school discipline gap: Equitable remedies for excessive exclusion*. New York: Teachers College Press, 207–221.

Vincent, C. G., and Tobin, T. J. 2011. "An examination of the relationship between implementation of School-wide Positive Behavior Support (SWPBS) and exclusion of students from various ethnic backgrounds with and without disabilities." *Journal of Emotional and Behavioral Disorders*, 19, 217–232.

Wallace, J. M., Goodkind, S., Wallace, C. M., and Bachman, J. G. 2008. "Racial, ethnic, and gender differences in school discipline among U.S. high school students: 1991–2005." *Negro Educational Review*, 59, 47–62.

Xu, K., Nosek, B., and Greenwald, A. 2014. "Psychology data from the race implicit association test on the project implicit demo website." *Journal of Open Psychology Data*, 2(1). http://doi.org/10.5334/jopd.ac

Q28. ARE SMALL SCHOOLS BETTER THAN LARGE SCHOOLS IN PROVIDING A QUALITY EDUCATION TO STUDENTS?

Answer: The research on small high schools, in particular, shows consistent positive influences on student engagement, attendance, and graduation rates, among other educational outcomes. Nevertheless, for small schools to yield successful student outcomes, they must be adequately supported for significant stretches of time and not treated as individual experiments to either flourish or perish in the short run.

The Facts: Research from decades ago showed how small high schools foster a different social climate than big high schools. In an extensive analysis of high schools with varying enrollments from 35 to 2,287 students, a 1964 study found that small high schools were associated with higher quality opportunities and experiences (Barker and Gump, 1964). That research indicated that once high schools became larger than around 500 students, they took on a sense of bigness. That is, they tended to lack community, made it difficult for teachers to know all students well, and left many students feeling lost among the crowd.

It certainly stands to reason that smaller schools, particularly smaller high schools, would provide a more intimate community for students, teachers, and parents. Students might not feel lost in a sea of children and classrooms. The building itself might be less daunting and more welcoming to students, and therefore more conducive to learning and fostering a sense of belonging. Teachers may also have more opportunity to get to know their students well, knowing them by more than just their names, seeing them more frequently, and developing a sense of individual student learning needs. Teachers who know their students' social, emotional, and learning needs are better equipped to provide effective instruction for those students.

Yet economies of scale dictate that schools be made ever bigger. Operating expenses such as heating and cooling, electricity, and student transportation can take a substantial portion of the school budget. District-sharing arrangements notwithstanding, every school needs custodians, building administrators, administrative assistants, teachers, and support staff. Large high schools are better positioned to offer a wide-ranging curriculum. Conversely, small high schools can struggle to offer Advanced Placement courses, specialized programming, or unique courses such as engineering and aeronautics. Nevertheless, a 2000 study of 121 New York

City public high schools provided some evidence that small schools operated more efficiently than many larger ones at that time (Stiefel et al., 2000).

The Small Schools Movement

Those studies helped drive serious reform efforts to make schools smaller over the last few decades. In the words of scholar Michelle Fine, the small schools movement

> was launched originally by educators and community activists to offer up intellectual possibility for poor and working class youth and to reclaim the public sphere, not retreat from it. Small schools were a strategy to reinvigorate public education with spaces of anti-racist possibility that would inspire, spread and support other schools—not islands seeking exit. . . . [Small schools were] [c]onceived by educators who crafted elaborate plans for curriculum, pedagogy and assessment to nurture the minds and souls of youth, the schools were designed to be widely accessible (without entrance criteria), to encourage inquiry, activism and commitments to community. (Fine, 2005, 12)

High schools, in particular, have been the target of small school reform. The National Center for Education Statistics reported that in 2005–2006, 14 states had an average public high school enrollment of 1,000 students or more; the average for all 50 states for high schools that year was 887. According to two 2005 publications on high school reform, smaller high schools, in contrast, were considered small at around 100 students per grade level for a total of 400 students or fewer enrolled (Fine, 2005; Meier, 2005).

Small school initiatives burgeoned in places like New York City, which opened more than 100 small high schools between 2002 and 2008—and closed several large chronically underperforming ones in high-poverty communities. In large districts across the nation, middle and high schools have worked within their existing physical structures to break up into smaller learning communities (sometimes referred to as "houses" or "schools within schools").

In 2006, federal funding was committed to assist hundreds of large public high schools in restructuring into Smaller Learning Communities (SLCs) or adopting key practices of SLCs. Major philanthropic foundations likewise poured money into supporting the small schools movement, including the Annenberg Foundation, the Carnegie Corporation of New York, and the Bill and Melinda Gates Foundation. The Gates Foundation invested more than $1.5 billion alone by 2006 to get some districts to break their big high schools into smaller schools. However, in November 2008, the founder of the Gates Foundation, Microsoft cofounder Bill Gates, stated that "simply breaking up existing schools into smaller units often did not generate the gains we were hoping for" (Gates, 2008).

Benefits for Students

The research points strongly to the benefits of small schools in terms of their influence on students' academic engagement, educational attainment, and sense of belonging. For instance, in a 2009 analysis of data from a nationally representative sample of high school students and schools, researchers found that students in smaller high schools are less likely to drop out than students in large high schools (Werblow and Duesbery, 2009). A 2010 review of research on the small high school movement toward SLCs up through 2010 found that, relative to large high schools, SLCs were associated with higher attendance, higher graduation rates, and positive student experiences (Levine, 2010). Although the massive investment in smaller high schools by the Gates Foundation was pulled back after less-than-notable student achievement gains were evident over the first five years, subsequent longer-term evaluations pointed to improvements in student attendance, engagement and persistence in school, graduation rates, and college enrollment.

Several studies of New York City's small school initiative demonstrated considerable benefits to students. A 2013 study explored the effects of attending one of New York City's small high schools between 2002 and 2008, and found increased student achievement in several subject areas, increased credit accrual, and higher graduation and college-going rates (Abdulkadiroğlu, Hu, and Pathak, 2013). Survey data also indicated students were significantly more engaged in small schools. A 2014 study conducted by the Manpower Demonstration Research Corporation (MDRC) reported a nearly 10 percent increase in graduation rates at small schools, with these effects occurring consistently across students from all backgrounds (Bloom and Unterman, 2014). A 2015 analysis of four New York City cohorts found that small school reform in New York City raised outcomes for all types of schools—large or small, new or existing schools (Stiefel, Schwartz, and Wiswall, 2015). Meanwhile, a 2015 study of Chicago's Small Schools Initiative reported that students attending small schools were "substantially more likely to persist in school and eventually graduate," although there was no discernible impact on test scores (Barrow, Schanzenbach, and Claessens, 2015, 100).

Cautions and Conflations

Simply making schools smaller, however, does not result in improved student outcomes. Small schools are not inherently beneficial to students and certainly not so when they operate in complete isolation. They should be sufficiently resourced and supported by a central office. Moreover, research indicates that attention to interpersonal relationships and communication, as well as the core practices of teaching and learning, are critical to any small school success (Supovitz and Christman, 2003).

In addition, some scholars contend that the small schools movement has been co-opted by neoliberal reformers interested in making schools independent, autonomous, and accountable. Others see portfolio models that use small schools as a vehicle to diverse choices in a district. In the early 2000s, for example, Oakland, California, undertook an effort to diminish the size of individual schools under a system of Results Based Budgeting, in which "each school is treated as a small business, with funding tied to average daily attendance" (Fine, 2005, 12). Chicago's Renaissance 2010 triggered construction of small schools, but this led to gentrification of affluent families re-enrolling in these new high-quality urban schools.

FURTHER READING

Abdulkadiroğlu, A., Hu, W., and Pathak, P. A. 2013. *Small high schools and student achievement: Lottery-based evidence from New York City* (No. w19576). Cambridge, MA: National Bureau of Economic Research.

Barker, R. G., and Gump, P. V. 1964. *Big school, small school: High school size and student behavior.* Stanford, CA: Stanford University Press.

Barrow, L., Schanzenbach, D., and Claessens, A. 2015. "The impact of Chicago's small high school initiative." *Journal of Urban Economics,* 87(C), 100–113.

Bloom, H. S., and Unterman, R. 2014. "Can small high schools of choice improve educational prospects for disadvantaged students?" *Journal of Policy Analysis and Management,* 33(2), 290–319.

Fine, M. 2005. "Not in our name: Reclaiming the democratic vision of small school reform." *Rethinking Schools,* 19, 11–14.

Gates, Bill. 2008. "Remarks—A Forum on Education in America." Bill and Melinda Gates Foundation, November 11, 2008. https://www.gatesfoundation.org/Media-Center/Speeches/2008/11/Bill-Gates-Forum-on-Education-in-America

Klonsky, M., and Klonsky, S. 2008. *Small schools: Public school reform meets the ownership society.* Abingdon, UK: Routledge.

Lee, V. E., and Loeb, S. 2000. "School size in Chicago elementary schools: Effects on teachers' attitudes and students' achievement." *American Educational Research Journal, 37*(1), 3–31.

Levine, T. H. 2010. "What research tells us about the impact and challenges of smaller learning communities." *Peabody Journal of Education, 85*(3), 276–89.

Meier, D. 2005. "Creating democratic schools." *Rethinking Schools, 19,* 28–29.

Meyer, P. 2015. "New York City's small-schools revolution." *Education Next,* May 12, 2015. https://www.educationnext.org/new-york-citys-small-schools-revolution

Raywid, M. A. 2002. "The policy environments of small schools and schools-within-schools." *Educational Leadership, 59*(5), 47–51.

Ready, D. D., and Lee, V. E. 2008. "Choice, equity, and the schools-within-schools Reform." *Teachers College Record, 110*(9), 1930–1958.

Ready, D. D., Lee, V. E., and Welner, K. G. 2004. "Educational equity and school structure: School size, overcrowding, and schools-within-schools." *Teachers College Record, 106*(10), 1989–2014.

Schneider, J. 2016. "Small schools: The edu-reform failure that wasn't." *Education Week, 35,* 20–21.

Schwartz, A. E., Stiefel, L., and Wiswall, M. 2013. "Do small schools improve performance in large, urban districts? Causal evidence from New York City." *Journal of Urban Economics, 77,* 27–40.

Shear, L., et al. 2008. "Contrasting paths to small school reform: Results of a 5-year evaluation of the Bill and Melinda Gates Foundation's National High Schools Initiative." *Teachers College Record, 110*(9), 1986–2039.

Stiefel, L., Berne, R., Iatarola, P., and Fruchter, N. 2000. "High school size: Effects on budgets and performance in New York City." *Educational Evaluation and Policy Analysis, 22*(1), 27–39.

Stiefel, L., Schwartz, A. E., and Wiswall, M. 2015. "Does small high school reform lift urban districts? Evidence from New York City." *Educational Researcher, 44*(3), 161–172.

Supovitz, J., and Christman, J. 2003. *Developing Communities of Instructional Practice: Lessons from Cincinnati and Philadelphia.* Philadelphia, PA: Consortium for Policy Research in Education, University of Pennsylvania, Graduate School of Education.

Werblow, J., and Duesbery, L. 2009. "The impact of high school size on math achievement and dropout rate." *The High School Journal, 92*(3), 14–23.

Q29. ARE AMERICAN SCHOOLS LESS SAFE NOW THAN IN THE PAST?

Answer: Although mass school shootings remain a fear of parents, students, teachers, and school administrators around the country, those incidents have been on the decline. Likewise, reported victimizations among students ages 12–18 have decreased since the turn of the twenty-first century. Moreover, these decreases have been consistent across race and gender. Physical bullying has also declined overall, but in its place, there has been a sharp increase in online or cyberbullying. With respect to the bullying of female students specifically, the evidence is less clear, with one major review reporting that face-to-face bullying increased between 1998 and 2017, while federal survey data showed a decline in bullying (broadly defined) between 2005 and 2017. LGBTQ students remain at the greatest risk of being bullied or harassed.

The Facts: Aggressive behaviors in schools, such as assaults between students, and even between students and teachers, seem to make headlines almost weekly. School bullying has become a national issue, and most states have responded with strong anti-bullying legislation or policies to curb such behaviors.

Social media platforms have, unfortunately, given rise to cyberbullying and other insidious forms of child intimidation and harassment. Students are far more vulnerable these days to harassment via instant messaging, group chats, and the recording or sharing of photos, videos, and memes. A federal bill proposal, the Safe Schools Improvement Act (SSIA), which focuses heavily on student bullying and harassment to help ensure student well-being and security, has stalled several times in Congress. The SSIA was first introduced in 2010 and has been reintroduced five times since. The SSIA has not yet been reintroduced in the 117th Congress. There are also many other safety issues in schools worthy of attention.

Reports of Bullying

Federal data from the 2019 National Crime Victimization Survey and the School Crime Supplement show that between 2001 and 2017, the percentage of students aged 12–18 who indicated they were victimized at school (including theft and violent victimization) during the previous six months decreased substantially from 6 percent to 2 percent. Percentages also decreased for students reporting violent victimization (down 2 percent to

1 percent), which includes rape, sexual assault, robbery, aggravated assault, and simple assault (National Center for Education Statistics, 2019b).

A 2019 research review of 91 studies reporting bullying statistics between 1998 and 2017 found no statistically significant trends over time in face-to-face bullying victimization; however, cyberbullying did increase over time (Kennedy, 2019). In terms of gender, face-to-face bullying among boys decreased over time, while it increased over time for girls. Younger adolescents were significantly more at risk for bullying than older adolescents, and this difference sustained over time. When broken down by type of bullying, face-to-face verbal bullying and physical bullying declined from 2005 to 2017 (from 23 percent to 9 percent and 29 percent to 8 percent, respectively) (Kennedy, 2019).

Similar declines in reported bullying were evident from federal statistics collected by the National Center for Education Statistics (2019b), which reported on trends from the National Crime Victimization Survey and School Crime Supplement. Between 2005 and 2017, the percentage of students aged 12–18 indicating they were bullied at school decreased from 28.5 percent to 20.2 percent. Declines were evident across all student subgroups on which data were disaggregated. A prior 2010 study showed physical bullying decreased from 22 percent in 2003 to 15 percent in 2008 (Finkelhor et al., 2010). However, a 2013 study reported that the number of students reporting being victims of cyberbullying increased from 6 percent in 2000 to 11 percent in 2010 (Jones, Mitchell, and Finkelhor, 2013). In 2017, female students aged 12–18 reported being bullied at higher rates than males (24 percent versus 17 percent). Rural students (27 percent) indicated a higher percentage of bullying than their suburban (20 percent) and urban (18 percent) counterparts (National Center for Educational Statistics, 2019b). Public school students reported more incidences of bullying (20.6 percent) than private school students (16 percent) in 2017 (National Center for Educational Statistics, 2019a).

The lesbian, gay, bisexual, transgender, and queer (LGBTQ) community is particularly vulnerable to harassment in today's schools. The Gay, Lesbian and Straight Education Network (GLSEN) administers the National School Climate Survey to a representative sample of students identifying as LGBTQ in sixth to twelfth grade. In 2009, the survey indicated that 84.6 percent of students identifying as LGBTQ experienced bullying and harassment due to their sexual orientation. Another 63.7 percent indicated they were harassed because of their gender expression. Nearly a decade later, 2017 data present a similarly disturbing picture, with 87.3 percent of LGBTQ students reporting being harassed or assaulted based on personal characteristics. In that same year, 7 of 10 LGBTQ students experienced verbal harassment at school based on their sexual orientation, and 6 of 10 based on gender expression (GLSEN, 2017).

Mass School Shootings

The tragic mass shooting events that occurred at Columbine High School in Columbine, Colorado (1999), Sandy Hook Elementary School in Newtown, Connecticut (2012), Stoneman Douglas High School in Parkland, Florida (2018), and Santa Fe High School in Santa Fe, Texas (2018), have permanently changed the landscape surrounding school safety. Over the last two decades, schools across the country have added security measures and staff, including security guards, metal detectors, and school resource officers, to instill a sense of safety and deter violence. One 2019 study reported that school security is now a $2.7 billion industry (Rowhani-Rahbar and Moe, 2019).

Criminology researchers from Northeastern University analyzed active shooter data from a range of sources, including *USA Today*, the FBI's Supplementary Homicide Report, the Congressional Research Service, and the Gun Violence Archive. Their 2018 study found that the number of students killed in schools has declined between 1992 and 2015, noting that "[f]our times the number of children were killed in schools in the early 1990s than today" (Nicodemo and Petronio, 2018).

Although much of the media attention has focused on school shootings with multiple victims occurring in majority-White schools, Livingston, Rossheim, and Hall (2019) document that about 61 percent of school shootings in their database occurred in nonmajority-White schools. A large majority of school shootings involved only one shooter who used a handgun (Rowhani-Rahbar and Moe, 2019).

Meanwhile, resources for student support services, including mental health, remain scarce in many schools. For instance, the American School Counselor Association recommends a minimum student-to-counselor ratio of 250:1, but the 2017–2018 national average was nearly twice that at 442:1 (American School Counselor Association, n.d.). Student mental health has nevertheless been a focus in policy discussions on school violence. While efforts to create data systems capable of detecting youth susceptible to violence, either self-inflicted or done to others, have been launched, their efficacy and scalability remain a challenge. In general, responses to student psychological well-being have been eclipsed by wider and ongoing political tensions over gun rights and gun control.

FURTHER READING

American School Counselor Association. N.d. "Student-to-School Counselor Ratio, 2017–2018." American School Counselor Association-ASCA. Retrieved from https://schoolcounselor.org/asca/media/asca/home/Ratios17–18.pdf

Chouhy, C., Madero-Hernande, A., and Turanovic, J. J. 2017. "The extent, nature, and consequences of school victimization: A review of surveys and recent research." *Victims and Offenders, 12*(6), 823–844.

Finkelhor, D., Turner, H., Ormrod, R., and Hamby, S. L. 2010. "Trends in childhood violence and abuse exposure: Evidence from 2 national surveys." *Archives of Pediatrics and Adolescent Medicine, 164*(3), 238–242.

Fox, J. A., and Fridel, E. E. 2018. "The menace of school shootings in America: Panic and overresponse," In H. Shapiro (Ed.), *The handbook of violence in education: Forms, factors, and preventions.* New York: Wiley/Blackwell Publishers.

GLSEN. 2017. "2017 National School Climate Survey. The experiences of lesbian, gay, bisexual, transgender, and queer youth in our nation's schools." Retrieved from https://www.glsen.org/research/2017-national-school-climate-survey-0

Greytak, E. A., Kosciw, J. G., Villenas, C., and Giga, N. M. 2016. "From teasing to torment: School climate revisited. A survey of US secondary school students and teachers. Executive summary." New York: Gay, Lesbian and Straight Education Network (GLSEN).

Hughes, M. R., Gaines, J. S., and Pryor, D. W. 2015. "Staying away from school: Adolescents who miss school due to feeling unsafe." *Youth Violence and Juvenile Justice, 13*(3), 270–290.

Hymel, S., and Swearer, S. M. 2015. "Four decades of research on school bullying: An introduction." *American Psychologist, 70*(4), 293–299.

Jones, L. M., Mitchell, K. J., and Finkelhor, D. 2013. "Online harassment in context: Trends from three youth internet safety surveys (2000, 2005, 2010)." *Psychology of Violence, 3,* 53–69.

Kennedy, R. S. 2019. "Bullying trends in the United States: A meta-regression." *Trauma, Violence, and Abuse.* https://doi.org/10.1177/1524838019888555

Lessne, D., and Cidade, M. 2015. *Student reports of bullying and cyberbullying: Results from the 2013 School Crime Supplement to the National Crime Victimization Survey* (No. NCES 2015–056). Washington, DC: National Center for Education Statistics.

Livingston, M. D., Rossheim, M. E., and Hall, K. S. 2019. "A descriptive analysis of school and school shooter characteristics and the severity of school shootings in the United States, 1999–2018." *Journal of Adolescent Health*, 64(6), 797–799.

National Center for Education Statistics. 2019a. *School Choice in the United States: 2019*. Retrieved from https://nces.ed.gov/programs/schoolchoice/index.asp

National Center for Education Statistics. (2019b, May). School Crime and Safety. *Condition of Education*. Retrieved from https://nces.ed.gov/programs/coe/indicator_cld.asp

Nicodemo, A., and Petronio, L. 2018. "Schools are safer than they were in the 90s, and school shootings are not more common than they used to be, researchers say." News@Northeastern. February 26, 2018. Retrieved from https://news.northeastern.edu/2018/02/26/schools-are-still-one-of-the-safest-places-for-children-researcher-says

Rowhani-Rahbar, A., and Moe, C. 2019. "School shootings in the US: What is the state of evidence?" *Journal of Adolescent Health*, 64(6), 683–684.

Waasdorp, T. E., and Bradshaw, C. P. 2015. "The overlap between cyberbullying and traditional bullying." *Journal of Adolescent Health*, 56(5), 483–488.

Waasdorp, T. E., Pas, E. T., Zablotsky, B., and Bradshaw, C. P. 2017. "Ten-year trends in bullying and related attitudes among 4th- to 12th-graders." *Pediatrics*, 139(6), e20162615.

Yanez, C., and Seldin, M. 2019. "Student victimization in US schools: Results from the 2017 School Crime Supplement to the National Crime Victimization Survey." Stats in brief. NCES 2019–064. Washington, DC: National Center for Education Statistics.

Q30. ARE PUBLIC AND PRIVATE SCHOOLS STILL RACIALLY AND ECONOMICALLY SEGREGATED?

Answer: Yes, private as well as public schools remain highly racially and economically stratified. Among public schools, between-school segregation improved in the 1960s and 1970s following court-ordered racial segregation. Much of the progress in school racial desegregation receded in the 1990s and 2000s in the face of court reversals. Racial and economic public school segregation today is reflective of U.S. residential segregation. Private schools remain underrepresented by low-income students and students of color, and overrepresented by White students.

The Facts: Public schools are, overall, substantially more racially diverse than private schools. According to a 2018 report by The Civil Rights Project of UCLA, the U.S. private school population was 68.6 percent White, 10.4 percent Latinx, 9.3 percent Black, and 6.9 percent Asian in 2015 (Ee, Orfield, and Teitell, 2018). By contrast, in 2016, the U.S. public school population was 48.4 percent White, 26.3 percent Latinx, 15.2 percent Black, 5.5 percent Asian, and 1.0 percent Native American. Private school enrollment among White students has remained stable over time, while non-White private school attendance has declined slightly. White students represent 51 percent of the total school-age population, but make up 69 percent of all private school enrollment. Black and Latinx students are significantly underrepresented in private schools (25 percent public schools versus 10 percent private schools). Compared to Catholic and non-Catholic religious schools, secular private schools have increased the most in terms of racial diversity, although not at the levels of public schools.

White students have remained the most concentrated group in private schools for the past two decades. In 2015, the average White student attending a private school went to a school where 81 percent of the students were also White (Ee, Orfield, and Teitell, 2018). Black and Latinx private school students attended schools with relatively more White students, on average, than their public school peers; based on a 2016 research report published by the Southern Education Foundation, this is likely due to the overwhelming majority of White students attending private schools (Suitts, 2016). Over time, Black students have witnessed a modest decrease in the degree of same-race isolation in private schools; twenty years ago, the average Black student attending private school went to a school that was more than 50 percent Black, while in 2015 those schools are on average 44 percent Black. In 2015, the average Latinx private-school student attended a school that was 40 percent Latinx, a figure that has remained unchanged.

Economic Segregation

The Civil Rights Project's 2018 report found that low-income students are underrepresented among private schools, with only 9 percent enrolled in private schools; secular private schools serve the smallest percentage of low-income students, at 5.4 percent (Ee, Orfield, and Teitell, 2018). In comparison, more than half of the total public school population are low-income students.

According to a 2014 study, since the 1980s, residential economic segregation has risen dramatically (Bischoff and Reardon, 2014), with the segregation due not so much to an expanding lower class, but to a lower-middle class separating from the wealthier middle and upper classes. Based on an analysis published in 2016, public schools and school districts became more economically stratified between 1990 and 2010, mirroring this growing income inequality in the United States (Owens, Reardon, and Jencks, 2016). In fact, economic segregation between schools in the nation's 100 largest school districts rose in both the 1990s and 2000s (Owens, Reardon, and Jencks, 2016). By 2012, segregation was about 40 percent higher than in 1990.

Racial Segregation by Region

Another 2019 report published by The Civil Rights Project found that since 1968, the public school enrollment of Latinx students has increased by 11 million while White students declined by the same amount (Frankenberg et al., 2019). White students now constitute a population minority across the nation's public school population, meaning that they no longer account for more than fifty percent of the total public school population. Regionally, Latinx students are the majority subgroup in the West (42.3 percent) and second largest in the South (28.1 percent)—higher than Black student enrollment in that region (23.6 percent). Latinx students also constitute the second-largest ethnic group in the Northeast (20.7 percent). The Northeast and Midwest remain majority White, enrolled at 55.1 percent and 64.9 percent, respectively.

Segregation for Black students is increasing significantly across the country, despite a declining proportion of total student enrollment and higher numbers living in suburban areas. In the South, schools have held steady the desegregation progress made following the seminal Supreme Court ruling in *Brown v. Board of Education* that "segregation is inherently unequal." Relative to other parts of the country, the South remains the least segregated region for Black students.

Latinx and White students are currently the most segregated subgroups, although segregation among Black students is on the rise. Latinx students, on average, attend public schools in which 55 percent of the students are Latinx. White students attend public schools in which 69 percent of students are White. Researchers from The Civil Rights Project concluded that Latinx segregation, in particular, presents "[a] troubling development":

> the enormous growth and intensifying segregation by ethnicity and poverty of the Latino students, who are now by far the largest

nonwhite community. They are now more segregated in their own group than are blacks; and often, particularly in the Southwest and the West, African American students are not only isolated from whites and from the middle class but they are, on average, attending schools where they are a minority group within a Latino school. Latino students now are typically in schools with insignificant white and middle-class populations, a particularly dramatic historic change in the West. Sometimes they are also segregated from students whose home language is English. (Frankenberg et al., 2019, 8)

The Role of Law

A 2014 analysis by The Civil Rights Project reports that legal challenges led by Presidents Ronald Reagan and George H. W. Bush, including a momentous Supreme Court decision, led to a major retraction in federal involvement in school desegregation efforts (Orfield et al., 2014). In 1991, a conservative-leaning Supreme Court ruled in *Board of Education of Oklahoma City Public Schools v. Dowell* that a school district should be released from school desegregation orders if it could demonstrate compliance and not "return to its former ways." The decision opened the door for hundreds of large districts to follow suit and discontinue racial desegregation orders. Researchers from The Civil Rights Project at UCLA found that in districts that terminated those plans, most became resegregated shortly thereafter (Orfield et al., 2014).

Another Supreme Court ruling, *Parents Involved in Community Schools v. Seattle School District No. 1* (2007) significantly curtailed school districts' legal authority to use race in voluntary integration programs. The decision has caused numerous districts with voluntary desegregation policies to either abandon them for fear of litigation or alter them to use some other social characteristic—namely, socioeconomic status—in the place of race. For instance, the 2019–2020 school choice lottery conducted by the Connecticut State Department of Education's Regional School Choice Office switched to using a measure of socioeconomic status exclusively, based on the U.S. Census block group in which students lived. In years prior, the racial and ethnic composition where students lived was used as a proxy for student race and ethnicity. The school choice programs have served as the main remedy to address racial and economic isolation of Hartford, Connecticut, students; they were prompted by the school desegregation court case, *Sheff v. O'Neill*, which began in 1996.

FURTHER READING

Bischoff, K., and Reardon, S. F. 2014. "Residential segregation by income, 1970–2009." In J. R. Logan (Ed.), *Diversity and disparities.* New York: Russell Sage Foundation, 208–233.

Ee, J., Orfield, G., and Teitell, J. 2018. *Private Schools in American education: A small sector still lagging in diversity.* Los Angeles, CA: University of California, Los Angeles, The Civil Rights Project-Proyecto Derechos Civiles.

Frankenberg, E., Ee, J., Ayscue, J. B., and Orfield, G. 2019. *Harming our common future: America's segregated schools 65 years after Brown.* Los Angeles, CA: University of California, Los Angeles, The Civil Rights Project-Proyecto Derechos Civiles.

Monarrez, T., Kisida, B., and Chingos, M. 2019. *When is a school segregated? Making sense of segregation 65 Years after* Brown v. Board of Education. Washington, DC: The Urban Institute.

Orfield, G., Frankenberg, E., Ee, J., and Kuscera, J. 2014. *Great progress, a long retreat and an uncertain future.* Los Angeles, CA: University of California, Los Angeles, The Civil Rights Project-Proyecto Derechos Civiles.

Owens, A., Reardon, S. F., and Jencks, C. 2016. "Income segregation between schools and school districts." *American Educational Research Journal, 53*(4), 1159–1197.

Reardon, S. F., Grewal, E., Kalogrides, D., and Greenberg, E. 2012. "Brown Fades: The end of court-ordered school desegregation and the resegregation of American public schools." *Journal of Policy Analysis and Management, 31*(4), 876–904.

Reardon, S. F., and Owens, A. 2014. "60 Years after *Brown*: Trends and consequences of school segregation." *Annual Review of Sociology, 40,* 199–218.

Suitts, S. 2016. *Race and ethnicity in a new era of public funding of private schools: Private school enrollment in the south and the nation.* Atlanta, GA: Southern Education Foundation, Inc.

Q31. DO TODAY'S FULL-TIME VIRTUAL SCHOOLS OFFER A HIGH-QUALITY EDUCATION FOR STUDENTS?

Answer: No. The evidence consistently shows that full-time virtual schools grossly underperform their brick-and-mortar counterparts. Most troubling, enrollment continues to grow in this sector despite its poor achievement record and despite numerous instances of misused public funds. The continued expansion of virtual schools was fueled in the 2010s by intense lobbying on behalf of profit-seeking private companies and weak state regulations. It remains to be seen what the long-term impact of the shift toward online and hybrid schooling during the COVID-19 pandemic will have, both on virtual schools and traditional in-class instruction.

The Facts: Virtual education has expanded considerably over the last two decades. As of 2017, an estimated 2.7 million (5.5 percent) K–12 students participated in some form of online learning, although exact numbers are difficult to pin down (Editorial Projects in Education Research Center, 2017). Online education can be episodic, as when students attending a brick-and-mortar school also enroll in a supplemental (e.g., Advanced Placement) or credit recovery course. There are also "blended" schools and classes, which combine face-to-face instruction in classrooms with online learning. On the other end of the spectrum are full-time virtual schools, where instruction is offered entirely online. Full-time virtual school students participate at home via the internet and by other means of electronic communication. Teachers engage remotely and usually asynchronously. Thus, there is a distinction between *full-time virtual schools* and virtual education, virtual learning, or virtual schooling more broadly. This question focuses on full-time virtual schools and what the evidence says about their effectiveness.

Full-time virtual schools have grown rapidly since 2000. According to a 2019 report by the National Education Policy Center, full-time virtual or blended schools were in operation in 39 states in the 2017–2018 school year (Molnar et al., 2019). In 2017–2018, 501 full-time virtual schools enrolled nearly 300,000 students while 300 blended schools enrolled more than 132,000. Slightly fewer than half of all virtual schools (46.5 percent) are charter schools, but they account for 79.1 percent of total enrollment (Molnar et al., 2019). The remaining virtual schools are smaller district- or state-run schools and independent schools. Historically, there were a small number of virtual schools that served homebound children who because of disabilities were not able to attend brick-and-mortar schools.

In 2017–2018, the average enrollment in virtual charter schools was 1,345 students, considerably larger than the 344- and 320-student averages among district and independent virtual schools, respectively. The larger average size is likely due to virtual charter schools targeting students statewide, incentivized by the financial benefits of enrolling more students. Private, for-profit Education Management Organizations (EMOs) operated 26.5 percent of all full-time virtual schools in 2017–2018 but accounted for 60.1 percent of all virtual school enrollment. Nonprofit EMOs operated a much smaller percentage, accounting for 7.4 percent of all virtual schools.

Virtual schools appeal to private EMOs because they are set up to be highly profitable. They also appeal to neoliberal policy makers who believe they offer choice, spark innovation, and run more efficiently. The costs to operate virtual schools are considerably less than running traditional brick-and-mortar public schools, yet in most states, virtual schools receive the same per pupil funding (Pazhouh, Lake, and Miller, 2015). The two largest EMOs, K12 Inc. and Connections, accounted for 59.5 percent of all full-time virtual schools enrollment in 2015, but their share of the total enrollment dropped to 48.4 percent in 2017.

Some virtual charter schools are exceedingly large. Ohio's first online charter school, Electric Classroom of Tomorrow (EMOT), enrolled nearly 14,000 students in 2016–2017. EMOT was run by the for-profit EMO, Altair Learning Management. In January 2018, EMOT was unceremoniously closed after grossly overreporting its student enrollment by nearly 60 percent. According to a *Columbus Dispatch* news article, at one point, the state of Ohio sought up to $80 million in repayments from EMOT (Siegel, 2017).

Poor Academic Outcomes

Although there are a limited number of empirical studies of virtual school outcomes, the overriding consensus is that virtual charter schools perform substantially worse on measures of student achievement and attainment than traditional public schools. The most comprehensive study to date was conducted by a collective of three major research organizations in 2015. The Center for Research on Educational Outcomes (CREDO), Mathematica, Inc., and the Center on Reinventing Public Education published the three-part report, *National Study of Online Charter Schools*. Mathematica, Inc. studied instructional delivery in 127 online charter schools (Gill et al., 2015), the Center on Reinventing Public Education examined the policy environments of online charter schools, and CREDO estimated the effects of online charters on student achievement (Woodworth et al., 2015).

The CREDO study has received the most attention because it focused on student achievement. The study set out to answer, among other questions, how the academic growth of online charter school students compared to a group of similar students attending traditional public schools. The researchers analyzed student achievement growth data from online charter schools in 17 states and the District of Columbia. Without the opportunity to use an experimental design, the researchers applied a sophisticated algorithm to match statistically each virtual school student to similar students in two different control groups. Students were matched on the basis of race, gender, grade level, poverty, English language learner status, special education status, and prior test score on state assessments.

The first control group included students attending a nearby or feeder traditional public school, and the second group involved students enrolled in a brick-and-mortar charter school.

One strength of the study was that it measured growth in academic achievement over multiple years rather than single-year scores. The findings were conclusive. Online charter students exhibited substantially smaller growth overall compared to traditional public school students. Comparisons between virtual and brick-and-mortar charter students also revealed major achievement differences in favor of the brick-and-mortar schools. Although no statistical matching process can ever completely remove what researchers refer to as selection bias, the strength and consistency of these results lends them credibility.

In the 2015 Mathematica examination of instructional delivery, researchers found that online charter schools provided less live contact time with teachers in a week than traditional schools provided in a day (Gill et al., 2015). Online charter schools also relied heavily on parents to assist with student instruction. One-third of online charter schools left the pacing of instruction up to the students *only*. The lead author of the report commented:

> Challenges in maintaining student engagement are inherent in online instruction, and they are exacerbated by high student-teacher ratios and minimal student-teacher contact time, which the data reveal are typical of online charter schools nationwide. These findings suggest reason for concern about whether the sector is likely to be effective in promoting student achievement. (Quoted from CREDO, 2015)

Other studies of virtual schools show similar poor academic results. A 2017 study of nearly 1.7 million students in Ohio's online charter schools showed that students in online schools performed worse on standardized exams than their counterparts in brick-and-mortar charter and traditional public schools (Ahn and McEachin, 2017). Similar conclusions were drawn from a 2009 analysis of Ohio charter schools (Zimmer et al., 2009).

In some states, virtual charter schools have performed so poorly or mismanaged money so egregiously that they have been challenged legally or shut down. According to the watchdog group *In the Public Interest*, California's largest for-profit online public charter network (California Virtual Academies) had an overall graduation rate over a four-year period of 36 percent, less than half the state average of 78 percent. Moreover, California Virtual Academies parent company, K12 Inc., took, as profit, 49 percent of the $95 million in public education funds that the virtual school received in 2012–2013. Data from other states show similar trends.

Businesses that depend on long-term subscriptions—Netflix, health clubs, and so on—speak of the "churn." Churn is the movement in and out of the service. Virtual schools also have a churn, and it is quite large. Typical rates of enrolling in—and then dropping out of—traditional public school in the elementary grades is very low (under 10 percent) and usually involves families moving residences. Dropping out midyear at the brick-and-mortar high school level is more common, and often happens for academic reasons. Nevertheless, a churn rate for a typical brick-and-mortar high school seldom reaches 20 percent.

The situation with virtual schools is quite different. Even an elementary grade for a virtual school can experience more than 50 percent churn, with many of the students choosing to leave and return to a traditional school. In a 2019 study of the Milwaukee Public Schools, among 1,174 students who started the school year enrolled in a virtual school, 25 percent returned to the Milwaukee Public Schools before the end of the year. Even more dropped out of school altogether, left for a private school, or, conceivably, enrolled in a different virtual school. In an account conducted by the *Journal Sentinel* in 2018, 38 percent of students enrolled in one of Wisconsin's 42 virtual charter schools dropped out within the school year; half of the dropouts returned to brick-and-mortar schools (Thomas and Richards, 2018).

A 2016 investigation by *Education Week*, meanwhile, uncovered dozens of cases of mismanagement and misuse of funds (Education Week, 2016). *Education Week* published the list of more than 300 news articles across 24 states on which they based this report. The investigation also revealed millions of dollars were spent on lobbying by for-profit EMOs to influence legislation favorable to virtual charter schools (Prothero, 2016).

Credit Recovery: Another Face of Virtual Education

Individual online courses for students who have flunked face-to-face coursework have appeared on the virtual education scene. The Global Student Network, a subsidiary of the International Virtual Learning Academy based in Seattle, offer online courses to schools dealing with large numbers of students failing their courses. Operating under the banner Apex, online instruction is delivered to students over the course of a semester following the term in which they received an F in their brick-and-mortar school. They take a final exam; and if they pass, they have recovered their lost credit hours. Monitoring attendance and exams are the responsibility of the contracting brick-and-mortar school. This option enjoyed growing popularity. But not all was in good order.

Denver North High School in Colorado took the students who flunked Algebra I and enrolled them in the Apex online course. Unfortunately, the course and the final exam became something of a sham, as described by a 2011 investigative report (Asmar, 2011). Students earned credit for the course even when they only logged on a few hours during the entire semester. For the final exam, all of the students were assembled in an auditorium to take the online exam proctored by a school administrator. Students had smart phones and iPads and knew the location of several websites that solve algebra problems. Denver North's graduation rate jumped from 65 percent to 75 percent in one year, but quickly drifted back to 65 percent following news of the improprieties.

Charges of Mismanagement and Malfeasance

One might wonder why the growth in full-time cyber schools continues in the face of inferior academic results, not to mention the siphoning off of public education funds to private companies that dominate this sector.

Market-based reformers argue that the pursuit of profits and high-quality products are mutually reinforcing. In other words, profit opportunities in education should incentivize EMOs to deliver high-quality schools in order to make their profits. However, this logic is challenged when EMO operators redirect money intended for instruction to boost their bottom line. The Center for American Progress cite K12 Inc.'s *Form 10-K*, which is a report required by the U.S. Securities and Exchange Commission to make public fiscal operations and management of domestic companies transparent. The form showed how K12 Inc. provides its senior executives with large bonuses if they reduced instructional costs and increased profits (Benner and Campbell, 2018).

In addition, Ronald J. Packard, the CEO of K12 Inc., received compensation of more than $19.48 million from the company from 2009 to 2013 (SourceWatch, n.d.) He then left K12 Inc. to found his new venture: Accel Schools, a for-profit EMO operating 40 charter schools in Ohio. Accel Schools have operated on slim budgets and produced poorer educational outcomes than comparable traditional public schools in Ohio.

Finally, the COVID-19 pandemic led to substantial increases in full-time virtual school enrollments. In the spring of 2020, when the pandemic shut down schools in many areas of the country, many parents were desperate for alternatives to the distance learning that was abruptly forced upon brick-and-mortar schools. Some parents reasoned that since virtual schools had already been engaged in online instruction, they must know how to do it well. As an example, a July 23, 2020, *Associated Press* article reported that Oklahoma's Epic Charter Schools has seen a surge of 1,000 new students per day (Associated Press, 2020). Epic Charter Schools has been in existence since 2011 and seen a steady rise in enrollments, up to 21,000 students in 2018. School officials predicted that number would be closer to 46,000 by October 1, 2020. However, in October 2020, Epic was ordered to repay the state of Oklahoma $11 million for falsifying the number of students enrolled in its schools—a falsification that it used to claim millions of additional dollars from the state.

FURTHER READING

Ahn, J., and McEachin, A. 2017. "Student enrollment patterns and achievement in Ohio's online charter schools." *Educational Researcher*, 46(1), 44–57.

Asmar, M. 2011. "Are high school seniors Googling their way to graduation?" *Westword*. May 25, 2011. Retrieved from https://www.westword.com/news/are-high-school-seniors-googling-their-way-to-graduation-5112854

Associated Press. 2020. *Pandemic spurs enrollment at Oklahoma virtual charter school*. Associated Press. July 23, 2020. Retrieved from https://apnews.com/2b1600ae9484757a8e70f74a560fdcd6

Benner, M., and Campbell, N. 2018. *Profit before Kids*. Washington, DC: Center for American Progress, October 10, 2018, footnote 22. Retrieved from https://www.americanprogress.org/issues/education-k-12/reports/2018/10/10/459041/profit-before-kids

Center for Research on Educational Outcomes (CREDO). 2015. *Online charter school students falling behind their peers* [Press release]. CREDO. October 2015. Retrieved from https://credo.stanford.edu/sites/g/files/sbiybj6481/f/online_press_release.pdf

Editorial Projects in Education Research Center. 2017. "Issues A-Z: Online classes for K-12 students: An overview." *Education Week*. June 23, 2017. Retrieved from http://www.edweek.org/ew/issues/online-classes

Education Week. 2016. *Rewarding failure: An Education Week investigation of the Cyber Charter Industry*. Education Week. November 3, 2016. Retrieved from https://www.edweek.org/ew/projects/rewarding-failure-cyber-charter-investigation.html

Ferrare, J. J. 2020. "Charter school outcomes." In M. Berends, Primus, A., and Springer, M. G. (Eds.), *Handbook of research on school choice*. New York: Routledge, 160–174.

Gill, B., et al. 2015. "Inside online charter schools. A report of the National Study of Online Charter Schools." Mathematica Policy Research, Inc.

In the Public Interest. 2015. "Virtual public education in California: A study of student performance, management practices and oversight mechanisms at California Virtual Academies, a K12 Inc. managed school system" [Press release]. In the Public Interest, February 26, 2015. Retrieved from https://www.inthepublicinterest.org/virtual-public-education-in-california-a-study-of-student-performance-management-practices-and-oversight-mechanisms-at-california-virtual-academies-a-k12-inc-managed-school-system

Molnar, A., et al. 2019. *Virtual schools in the U.S. 2019.* Boulder, CO: National Education Policy Center. Retrieved from http://nepc.colorado.edu/publication/virtual-schools-annual-2019

Murphy, S. 2019. "Oklahoma latest to grapple with online school problems." *Associated Press*, August 12, 2019. Retrieved from https://apnews.com/8436bb4f515346648b6b558631af59f4

Pazhouh, R., Lake, R., and Miller, L. 2015. *The Policy Framework for Online Charter Schools.* Seattle, WA: Center on Reinventing Public Education.

Prothero, A. 2016. "Outsized influence: Online charters bring lobbying 'A' game to states." *Education Week.* November 3, 2016.

Riser-Kositsky, M., Herold, B., and Prothero, A. 2017. "Map: Cyber charters have a new champion in Betsy DeVos, but struggles continue." *Education Week.* December 14, 2017. Retrieved from https://www.edweek.org/ew/section/multimedia/cyber-charters-widespread-reports-of-trouble.html

Siegel, J. 2011. "Online schools poor performers, study says." *Columbus Dispatch.* May 12, 2011. Retrieved from http://www.dispatch.com/live/content/local_news/stories/2011/05/12/online-schools-poor-performers-study-says.html

Siegel, J. 2017. "State tells ECOT it owes $19.2 million more for unverified enrollment." *The Columbus Dispatch.* September 29, 2017. Retrieved from https://www.dispatch.com/news/20170928/state-tells-ecot-it-owes-192-million-more-for-unverified-enrollment

SourceWatch. N.d. "Ron Packard." Center for Media and Democracy. Retrieved from https://www.sourcewatch.org/index.php/Ron_Packard

Thomas, P., and Richards, E. 2018. "Online schools and student mobility: When kids churn, scores drop." *Journal Sentinel.* November 5, 2018. Retrieved from https://projects.jsonline.com/news/2018/11/5/online-schools-popular-but-40-percent-students-dont-stay.html

Woodworth, J. L., et al. 2015. *Online charter school study 2015.* Center for Research on Educational Outcomes. Retrieved from https://credo.stanford.edu/sites/g/files/sbiybj6481/f/online_charter_study_final.pdf

Zimmer, R., Gill, B., Booker, K., Lavertu, S., and Sass, T. R. 2009. *Charter schools in eight states: Effects on achievement, attainment, integration, and competition.* Santa Monica, CA: RAND Corporation.

Q32. DO STUDENTS LEARN MORE IN SMALLER CLASSES?

Answer: Yes. Tested achievement rises as class size falls. But questions remain: How much does achievement increase for each reduction in class size, and what is the financial cost of making such reductions? When all of these questions are taken into account at the same time, the returns in terms of achievement for significant reductions in class size are seldom considered to be worth the cost. The cost-effectiveness of class size reductions lags behind other means of improving learning. In the end, class size reduction is more a matter of teacher workload than student achievement.

The Facts: Concern for the size of classes organized for educational instruction is as old as education itself. The trend toward smaller classes can be documented in data collected by the federal government for more than a century and a half. Elementary school classes in 1870 in the United States averaged about 35 students; by 1980, that average had dropped to approximately 20, a decline of more than 40 percent. In 2010, the ratio of K–12 public school students to the number of teachers equaled 15. This ratio strikes an average among a widely divergent collection of classes from very small—in the case of some classes serving a few students with special needs—to very large—secondary school classes in some large city schools, for example. Nevertheless, the historic trend is clear. Teachers, their students, parents, and even some taxpayers prefer smaller class sizes.

Research into the question of whether student students learn more in smaller classes is more than one hundred years old. In 1909, O. P. Corman studied records of promotion from grade-to-grade in Philadelphia public schools to address the class size question. He divided third-grade classes into three sized groups: fewer than 40 students; 40–49 students; and 50 or more students. Corman observed the following promotion rates: class size of fewer than 40 students, 88 percent promotion rate; 40–49 students, 85 percent promotion rate; and 50 or more students, 81 percent promotion rate.

Remarkably, Corman's early day calculations presaged decades of empirical research on the class size question. However, for several decades to come, the results of class size and achievement research produced mainly confusion. In the third edition of the *Encyclopedia of Educational Research* published in 1960, the author of the entry on class size stopped short of trying to make any sense of an inconsistent corpus of research studies:

> There is nothing in the evidence to suggest that large classes materially affect attainment in subject matter . . . studies of the relation of class size to student attention, discipline, self-reliance, attitudes, and work habits failed to establish a research basis for decisions on class size. (Goodlad, 1960, 224)

That the studies of class size that had accumulated by 1960 were not easily integrated into a comprehensible conclusion is not surprising. While one researcher was studying the effects of reducing class size from 30 to 25 students in twelfth-grade chemistry, a second researcher was publishing the results of a study of fourth-grade reading scores in classes of size 24 versus 20. It was not until several dozen studies had been published by the late 1970s and new methods of research integration had been developed that conclusions about class size and achievement could be drawn with any confidence.

Education researcher Gene Glass and his collaborators developed what came to be known as methods of meta-analysis—the statistical coalescing of multiple studies on a single topic—in the mid-1970s. After the initial illustration of meta-analysis using the voluminous literature on psychotherapy outcomes was published in 1978, they published the results of the meta-analysis of the class size and achievement literature (Glass and Smith, 1979).

The studies of class size and achievement that were available in 1979 to Glass and Smith numbered 77 and stretched from 1905 to mere months before the publication of their meta-analysis. To qualify for inclusion in the meta-analysis, a study had to involve the comparison of two or more classes of different sizes evaluated on one or more objective tests of achievement and have statistical measures of central tendency and spread sufficient to allow the calculation of what are called "effect sizes."

A 1971 study performed by researchers James P. Shaver and Dee Nuhn is illustrative of the type of study involved in the meta-analysis. Shaver and Nuhn (1971) performed their research in the rural schools of Cache County, Utah. Students from the fourth, seventh, and tenth grades served as the subjects of the experiment. More than 40 students were taught in an individual tutoring arrangement; 45 students were taught in 15 groups of 3; and 60 students were taught in 3 groups of 20 each. The different size groups were taught reading and writing for one hour each day for an entire school year. The average achievement test scores for students taught in the classes of size 1 and 3 were more than one standard deviation above the average for the classes of size 20. Furthermore, the individually tutored students scored approximately one-quarter standard deviation above those students taught in classes of size 3.

When Smith and Glass (1980) subjected the same body of research to a meta-analysis of the effects of class size on students' attitudes and feelings of satisfaction, the relationship was even more pronounced. There can be little doubt that, all other things equal, smaller classes learn more than larger classes, and the smaller the better.

In 1984, the Tennessee legislature allocated $9 million for the most ambitious and comprehensive experiment on the class size effect that has ever been performed. Researchers in the Tennessee Department of Education designed what has come to be known as Project STAR for Student/Teacher Achievement Ratio. As described in a 1999 article, the experiment was textbook perfect (Boyd-Zaharias, 1999):

1. All Tennessee schools with K–3 classes were invited to participate.
2. Each school included in the study had to have a large enough student body to form at least one of each of the three class types—Small (13–17 students), Regular (22–26 students), and Regular with a full-time Teacher Aide (22–26 students + teacher aide). 6,000 students participated.
3. Schools from inner-city, rural, urban, and suburban locations were included in the experiment.
4. Students and teachers were **randomly assigned** to their class type.
5. Student achievement was to be tracked by standardized tests, which were carefully monitored. During testing, monitors ensured that test instructions were followed.
6. An outside consultant was contracted to perform all primary statistical analyses.

The Tennessee STAR experiment served as a large field trial that could support or disconfirm the Glass–Smith meta-analysis. The results for Small versus Regular class sizes fell almost precisely on the curve representing the diminishing returns relationship between class size and student achievement generated by Glass and Smith (1979) (Figure 32.1). At the lower end of the curve, e.g., class size 1 versus 10, the benefits of smaller classes—individual tutoring in this case—are indisputable. But at the other end of the curve, e.g., class size 30 versus 40, indisputable evidence also exists: classes of 30 will learn no more than classes of 40. There appear to be no learning benefits in reducing very large classes to "not so large" classes. Teachers generally agree. The difference between a class of 30 and a class of 40 is simply not enough to allow big changes in how instruction is

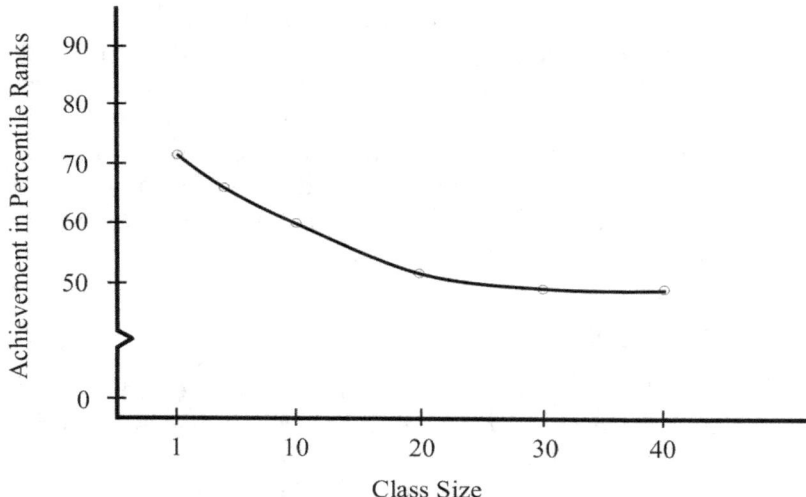

Figure 32.1 Curve representing the diminishing returns relationship between class size and student achievement (based on Glass and Smith (1979) meta-analysis of 77 studies).

conducted or in opportunities to address students individually. However, teachers, who are generally loathe to ask for any support that does not pay off in better performance for their students, are reluctant to point out that class size changes at any point along the continuum are certainly related to their workload. The difference in workload between a class of 30 students versus 20 students for a high school English composition teacher is considerable. The student in the class of 30 might not learn much more, but the teacher may be at greater risk of "burning out"—becoming frustrated and exhausted with the demands of the job.

A 2009 meta-analysis examined the effect of class size on student achievement across 17 studies conducted in the United States between 1989 and 2008 (Shin and Chung, 2009). The results indicate that small classes exhibited higher student achievement than large classes by .20 standard deviations, on average. This is roughly the equivalent of saying that the average student in a small class performed at the 58th percentile of the average student in a large class. Digging deeper, the researchers learned that the effect of class size reduction was more pronounced in elementary schools compared to high schools. The meta-analysis was unable to project the ideal class size, however, due to a lack of information in the studies reviewed.

Arguments over the existence of a positive class-size benefit for achievement have largely disappeared from education policy discourse as a result of the meta-analysis and the Tennessee STAR experiment. But one question remains. Is the achievement gain from smaller classes worth the cost? Dean Jamison (1982), an economist with the World Bank, working off of the Glass–Smith class size curves concluded that class size reduction is generally less cost-effective than other interventions to improve achievement, e.g., computer-assisted instruction (CAI) and televised instruction. Jamison's conclusions were supported by other research providing cost-effectiveness analyses of class size reduction, extended school year, and CAI (Levin, Glass, and Meister, 1985; 1986).

FURTHER READING

Boyd-Zaharias, J. 1999. "Project STAR: The story of the Tennessee class-size study." *American Educator*, 23(2), 30–36. https://www.aft.org/sites/default/files/periodicals/STARSummer99.pdf

Corman, O. P. 1909. "Size of classes and school progress." *The Psychological Clinic*, 3, 206–12.

Glass, G. V, Cahen, L. S., Smith, M. L., and Filby, N. N. 1982. *School class size: Research and policy*. Thousand Oaks, CA: SAGE Publications.

Glass, G. V, McGaw, B., and Smith, M. L. 1981. *Meta-analysis in social research*. Thousand Oaks, CA: SAGE Publications.

Glass, G. V, and Smith, M. L. 1979. Meta-analysis of research on the relationship of class-size and achievement. *Educational Evaluation and Policy Analysis*, 1, 2–16.

Goodlad, J. I. 1960. "Classroom organization." In C. W. Harris (Ed.), *Encyclopedia of Educational Research* (3rd ed.). New York: Macmillan, 220–226.

Jamison, D. T. 1982. "Reduced class size and other alternatives for improving schools: An economist's view." In Glass, G. V., et al. *School Class Size: Research and Policy*. Thousand Oaks, CA: SAGE Publications, 116–129.

Levin, H. M., Glass, G. V, and Meister, G. R. 1985. "Eficiencia de costes de cuatro intervenciones educativas." *Revista de Educacion*, No. 276, 61–102.

Levin, H. M., Glass, G. V, and Meister, G. R. 1986. "The political arithmetic of cost-effectiveness analysis." *Kappan*, 68(1), 69–72.

Shaver, J. P., and Nuhn, D. 1971. "The effectiveness of tutoring underachievers in reading and writing." *Journal of Educational Research*, 65, 107–112.

Smith, M. L., and Glass, G. V. 1980. "Meta-analysis of research on class-size and its relationship to attitudes and instruction." *American Educational Research Journal*, 17, 419–434.

Index

Accountability, 10, 61, 111–116, 122–124, 129–134, 145
  charter schools, 62–63, 71, 95, 105
  high-stakes testing, 129–134
  teacher evaluation, 139
  value-added measurement (VAM), 145–150
ALEC, 158, 160–162
American Federation of Teachers (AFT), 60, 80, 163
American Legislative Exchange Council (ALEC), 158, 160–162

Bilingual education, 171–178
  bilingualism benefits, 173, 175
  dual language programs, 177–178
  emergent bilinguals, 172
  English-immersion, 174
  English-only instruction, 173–175
  sheltered English instruction, 174
Bill and Melinda Gates Foundation, 148
Board of Education of Oklahoma City Public Schools v. Dowell, 207
Boulding, Kenneth, 25

Brown v. Board of Education, 30, 206
Bullying, 200–202
  cyberbullying, 201
  LGBTQ students, 201–202
  Safe Schools Improvement Act (SSIA), 200
Bush, George W. H., 10, 21, 113, 146, 207
Bush, George W., 8, 114, 146–147

Cause and effect, xiii, 40, 41, 85, 167, 182
Charter management organizations (CMOs), 69–70, 80, 102–107
Charter schools, xii, xiii, 7–8, 9–10, 15, 17, 24, 26, 29, 33–34, 40, 56, 59–107, 161, 209–214
  accountability, 62–63, 64, 69, 72, 95–101, 105
  authorizers/sponsors, 62, 63, 64–65, 69, 73, 95, 96–97, 98
  charter contract, 61, 62, 63, 95
  cyber or virtual charters, 65, 80, 82, 92, 209–211

effectiveness, 85–93
funding, 68–69, 71
innovation, 59, 60, 61, 79–83
management organizations (CMOs), 69–70, 80, 102–107 (*see also* Education management organizations)
"no excuses" charters, 74, 79, 80, 81, 82–83, 85, 91, 92–93
vs. private schools, 66–67, 69–70, 75, 85–93
segregation, 33–34, 72–73
students with disabilities, 72–73, 92
vs. traditional public schools, 70–71
types, 64–65, 80, 81
Class size research, 216–220. *See also* Smaller classes
Clinton, Bill, 61, 114
Common Core State Standards (common core), 112–113, 115, 117–120, 125, 126
Competition, measuring school, 25–27
Condition of Education report, 18
Controlled school choice, 32–35
Corman, O. P., 216–217
Correlational designs/research, 26, 182, 183

DeVos, Betsy, 8, 10, 13, 14, 32, 100, 101, 215
Discipline. *See* Student discipline

Education management organizations, 59, 65, 80, 102–107, 209–210, 212, 213–214. *See also* Charter management organizations (CMOs)
vs. charter management organizations, 69–70, 103
Education savings accounts. *See* Vouchers
Education tax credits. *See* Tuition tax credits; Vouchers

Effect size, 173, 217
Elementary and Secondary Education Act (ESEA), 111, 114, 122, 159. *See also* No Child Left Behind Act (NCLB)
English as a Second Language (ESL), 174
English language learners, 92. *See also* Bilingual education, emergent bilinguals
Establishment clause, 55
Exclusionary discipline, 189–191
Experimental design, 181–182. *See also* Random assignment, randomized experiments
Every Student Succeeds Act (ESSA), 124, 127, 150

High-stakes testing, 129–134, 181. *See also* Standardized testing
Campbell's law, 133–134
Homeschooling, 38–45
Homework, 180–185
Hurricane Katrina, 62, 81
New Orleans, 62, 72, 81–82

Improving America's School Act, 61–62
Individualized Education Plan (IEP), 15
Individuals with Disabilities Education Act (IDEA), 14–16, 73
charter schools, 72–73
due process, 15
private schools, 14–17
International test comparisons, 152–156
Ivy League feeder schools, 16

KIPP charter schools, 69, 74, 79, 82–83, 92–93, 107

Lau v. Nichols, 172, 173, 174
Longitudinal data/study, 49

Magnet schools, 33, 70–71, 74, 75
Mann, Horace, 1
Market competition, 2, 8, 11, 22–30, 67, 103–106
  competition definition and measures, 27
  school closures, 23–24
  school improvement, 24–25
Market-based reform, 22–30, 67, 71, 100, 102, 103–106, 213
Meta-analysis, 26, 89, 166, 217

National Assessment of Educational Progress (NAEP), 4, 127, 131–132
National Education Association (NEA), 158, 162, 184
Neoliberal reform, 61, 67
Network for Public Education (NPE), 163
No Child Left Behind Act (NCLB), 114, 122–124, 161, 176

Obama, Barack, 8, 68, 119, 127, 146–147
Online schools. See Virtual schools
Open enrollment, 28–29, 34, 82

Parents Involved in Community Schools v. Seattle School District, 33, 34
Politics of education, 158–163
Private schools
  vs. public, 2–6
  quasi-private school, 16–17
  religious schools, 1, 45–46
  segregation, 204–207
  students with disabilities, 14–17
Private vs. public school research, 4–6
Privatization, 23
  and charter schools, 67–68, 69–70
Public schools
  vs. private, 2–6
  segregation, 204–207

Race to the Top (RTTT), 68, 118, 125, 147
Racial disparities, in school discipline, 191–192
Random assignment, xiii, 3, 41, 42, 87–88, 218
  experimental studies, xiii, 2, 41, 48–49, 51
  lottery designs, 47, 87–88, 91
  randomized experiments, xiii, 3, 48–49, 87–88, 167
Ravitch, Diane, 7, 10–11, 118, 119
Reagan, Ronald, 21, 61, 207
RespectAbility, 16
Rudner, Lawrence, 40–41, 42

School start times, 165–169
School vouchers. See Vouchers
Segregation, 30, 204–207
  economic segregation, 205–206
  racial segregation, 204–207
  resegregation, 32–35
  school choice, 32–35
Self-selection bias, 87, 92, 103, 211
Shanker, Albert, 60–61
Sheff v. O'Neill, 207
Shootings, school, 202
Small schools movement, 196–198
Smaller classes, 216–220
  study by O. P. Corman, 216–217
Smith, Adam, 22, 25
Standardized testing, 121–128
  high-stakes testing, 129–134
  opt out movement, 126–127
  in private schools, 127–128
Standards-based reform/education, 112–116
  Common Core State Standards, 112
Student discipline, 187–192
Students with disabilities, 14–17, 18
  charter schools, 72, 92
  private schools, 14–17
  vouchers, 35, 45–47
Suspensions, 189–191

Teacher evaluation, 139–142
Tenure, 140–141
　due process, 141
Trump, Donald, 8, 9
Tuition tax credits, 35, 46, 54–57

Unregulated school choice, 3, 32–35.
　　See also Controlled school choice

Value-added measurement (VAM),
　144–150
　and American Psychological
　　Association, 148–149
　and Bill and Melinda Gates
　　Foundation, 148
　criticism for, 149
Virtual schools, 208–214
　academic outcomes, 209–210
　charter schools, 209–211, 213–214
　churn, 212
　credit recovery, 212–213
　mismanagement and malfeasance,
　　210, 211, 212, 213–214
　vs. virtual education, online
　　learning, 209
Vouchers, 7–9, 21, 35, 45–53, 54–58, 61
　education tax credits, 35, 46, 53–58
　　(see also Tuition tax credits)
　education savings accounts, 35, 46,
　　53–58
　federal voucher plan, 61
　neovouchers, 35, 46, 54, 57
　school tuition organization, 54–55
　voucher-like policies, 7–9

Welner, Kevin, 46, 54, 72

About the Authors

Casey D. Cobb is the Raymond Neag Professor of Educational Policy at the University of Connecticut. A National Education Policy Fellow and former elected member of the Executive Committee for the University Council for Educational Administration (UCEA), his current research interests include policies on school choice, accountability, and school reform. Cobb is former Editor of *Educational Administration Quarterly*, serves on the editorial boards for *Education Policy Analysis Archives* and *Education Sciences*, and is coauthor of *Fundamentals of Statistical Reasoning in Education* and *Leading Dynamic Schools*. He holds an AB from Harvard University, an MS from the University of Maine, and a PhD from Arizona State University.

Gene V Glass is an American statistician and researcher working in educational psychology and the social sciences. According to the science writer Morton Hunt, he coined the term "meta-analysis" and illustrated its first use in his presidential address to the American Educational Research Association 1976. He is an Emeritus Regents' Professor at Arizona State University. Currently, he is a senior researcher at the National Education Policy Center and a Lecturer in the Connie L. Lurie College of Education at San Jose State University. In 2003, he was elected to membership in the National Academy of Education.

www.ingramcontent.com/pod-product-compliance
Lightning Source LLC
Chambersburg PA
CBHW070337240426
43665CB00045B/2138